Care-therapy for Children

Related titles:

Beta Copley and Barbara Forryan: *Therapeutic Work with Children and Young People*

Steve Decker, Sandy Kirby, Angela Greenwood and Dudley Moore (eds): *Taking Children Seriously*

Ann Farrant: *Sibling Bereavement: Helping Children Cope with Loss*

Valerie Jackson: *Racism and Child Protection: The Black Experience of Child Sexual Abuse*

Janet Key: *Protecting Children*

Carole Sharman, Wendy Cross and Diana Vennis: *Observing Children* (Second edition)

John Triseliotis, Joan Shireman and Marion Hundleby: *Adoption: Theory, Policy and Practice*

Ved Varma (ed.): *Coping with Unhappy Children*

CARE-THERAPY FOR CHILDREN

Direct Work in Counselling and Psychotherapy

Ken Redgrave

CONTINUUM
London and New York

Continuum
Wellington House
125 Strand
London WC2R 0BB

370 Lexington Avenue
New York
NY 10017-6503

First published 2000

British Library Cataloguing-in-Publication Data
A catalogue record for this book is available from the British Library.

ISBN 0 8264 4811 9

Designed and typeset by Ben Cracknell Studios
Printed and bound in Great Britain by Cromwell Press, Trowbridge, Wilts

Contents

Foreword by John Triseliotis — vi
Preface — viii
Acknowledgements — x

CHAPTER **1** General introduction — 1

CHAPTER **2** The use of insight and sensory materials when counselling or treating a child — 21

CHAPTER **3** Insight work — 52

CHAPTER **4** More insight work — 95

CHAPTER **5** Sensory experience — 137

CHAPTER **6** The assessment process — 172

CHAPTER **7** The attachment process — 198

Appendices — 223
Glossary — 230
References — 234
Further reading — 239
Index — 241

Foreword

At a time when a significant part of social work intervention with looked-after children stops at the assessment stage, it is most refreshing to read a book that carries direct work much further, to the actual interactions taking place between the children and those who try to help them. Ken Redgrave's book about the actual process of 'therapy' for children who have been traumatized as a result of their past, and often continuing, painful experiences, goes to the heart of the restorative and healing process. It is in the tradition of the work of such figures as Bettelheim, Dockar-Drysdale, Winnicot and Fahlberg.

In this book Ken Redgrave draws heavily from his long experience in therapeutic work with looked-after children to share, not just his personal insights, but to demonstrate practical ways of engaging and communicating with vulnerable and often traumatized children in what he calls 'care-therapy'. What is different about this book from previous ones is that the theoretical concepts, and sometimes research and practice issues raised in each chapter, are illustrated with examples, children's paintings, games and exercises. What are described as 'ice-breakers', flowcharts, life-story books and symbolism are all there, displaying a step-by-step approach. Whilst some of the exercises will be known to some practitioners, many others are new, some developed by Ken Regrave himself.

The obvious aim of all these exercises is to demonstrate how they can be used to reach children and how, through these, children can be helped to reach feelings that they had either shut out or of which they were unaware. I doubt that any reader will remain unmoved by Donna's drawings illustrating her gradual awareness and understanding, first of 'dirty feeling' and then of 'clean feeling', the latter depicted with washing hanging on the line and the sun shining behind it; or Samantha's 'scribble' of her dad and her 'first mummy'.

A large part of the book is devoted to demonstrating how the concept of the 'third object' (initially developed by Winnicott) and of 'art therapy', can be used in almost all work with children using, again, flowcharts, exercises, activities and drawings. One example in the use of the third object is what is called the 'people tree', and another the family nest. Depending on the case, children can be encouraged to put themselves on the tree, and in the nest, or outside it, in relation to their birth families and other people in their lives. Other key topics that are developed, and their application demonstrated in the same way, are those of assessment and attachment.

Words such as 'therapy', 'counselling and psychotherapy' may sound far removed from the busy and emergency-oriented world of the social services departments, and possibly of child and family psychiatric clinics, but nothing could be further from the truth. It is unlikely that any professional whose job it is to help children reflect on past painful experiences and to consider where they go from there, will not find the approaches informative and, more important, usable. The strength of the book lies in the way that concepts and practice are brought together in the interests of the children who need more than simply administrative arrangements.

John Triseliotis, Emeritus Professor
at the University of Edinburgh
and Visiting Professor
at the University of Strathclyde

Preface

I had a number of objectives in mind when writing this book. I wished to produce something which would be of value to anyone interested in the welfare and the psychology of children, especially those children and adolescents who suffer as a result of emotional deprivation or privation. I also wished to produce something which could become a guide to people who work with or look after such vulnerable children. These people will include foster or adoptive parents, residential or 'field' social workers, psychotherapists and natural parents. People in all these groups, and students and college lecturers, have from time to time asked me to write about my practice and to 'put in print' the substance of many seminars and supervisory sessions.

So, while I hope the book will emphasize the use of art and other media as part of the counselling process, I also hope that it will point to how much carers and professional childcare workers need to know if they are to function in ways most helpful to children.

Then again, I was concerned that people should look critically at what I call 'corporate parenting', where children are looked after by the state or by charitable organizations. There is evidence enough across the whole western world to cause governments to be concerned about the quality of corporate parenting.

Throughout the book I have used both masculine and feminine personal pronouns, sometimes referring to 'she' or 'her' and at other times to 'he' or 'him', rather than the tedious him\her repetition.

Descriptions of children and adults in this book, although drawn from similar situations and people I have known, do not describe actual individuals – children or adults. I have used oft-repeated situations and circumstances, and where I have described case-histories these have been based upon many that were similar. Where I have had particular children in mind, I have disguised circumstances (such as age, sex, place and time) in order not to cause psychological damage to the child or the family described.

Ken Redgrave
April 2000

Acknowledgements

I wish to express my thanks to the editorial staff of the Continuum International Publishing Group, in particular to Anthony Haynes and Alan Worth for their guidance and scrutiny, and to Emma Cook, editorial assistant.

I am grateful to certain publishers and other organizations for allowing me to reproduce material for which they hold the copyright. These include: The Boys and Girls Welfare Society of Cheadle and the American Psychiatric Press, Inc. for permission to reproduce from *Diagnostic and Statistical Manual of Mental Disorders* (Fourth Edition) (© 1994 American Psychiatric Association).

My gratitude also to Sheila Redgrave for typing and retyping my manuscript, and for her patience.

CHAPTER 1

General introduction

'Symbolization is the only way in which these deprived youngsters can communicate their desperate feeling.'
Dockar-Drysdale, B., 1990

The therapeutic approach outlined in this book is practised and taught by some professional childcare workers, for example social workers, psychotherapists, childcare consultants and professional foster-parents. These people are working with children and adolescents who may be in residential care, for example children's homes or in foster-homes or in blood-tie family units.

Many of the children involved behave in a manner which tends to attract the label of 'conduct disorder'. A high percentage has been sexually abused, and many will be described as 'emotionally disturbed'.

For some years now, people have been periodically scandalized by media reports and official inquiry reports highlighting not only poor quality childcare by local authorities and voluntary organizations but also instances of neglect and abuse in the very settings which warrant a high standard of professional care and skill. Governments have issued various guidelines concerning the care of children and adolescents, and in Britain there has been a spate of training guidelines issued by training bodies such as the Central Council for Education and Training in Social Work. (See Further Reading: Reports and guideline documents.)

Yet, although the public seldom hear about it, some very excellent practice in childcare and child therapy is to be found in many places in Britain and the USA. Much of this excellent work embraces the approach set forth in this book. One reason for this good work failing to be recognized may lie with the fact that various segments of care-therapy are taught and applied in isolation. Sometimes this is done half-heartedly because the people actually working with the children and attempting to use the approach are not wholly supported or encouraged by their managers, who may not have been trained along these lines themselves.

Where the total approach – a **holistic approach** – is practised, some encouraging results emerge. Some of the blame for this failure to work in a holistic way may lie with the current teachers and practitioners who have not seen fit to present their findings in writing or describe their practice so as to show its holistic, systematic approach. Again, some childcare workers are into sensory stimulation treatment, **third objects** and creative stimulation. What are these? And how do they relate to each other to provide what we have called a systematic psychosocial approach?

The care-therapy approach, although applied in its fullness by some practitioners and used partially by others, awaits a broad presentation of method and aims. The present volume is an attempt to do that. Care-therapy, however, is not a new psychology or a new form of treatment. Practitioners have made use of particular methods such as art therapy, and they have emphasized the importance of certain aspects of child psychology, such as the attachment process. Our Chapter 7 gives an introduction to this process.

An important aspect of this holistic approach concerns the treatment and experience that the child gains in the various settings which modern life imposes upon people. This means that the approach must embrace not only the therapist's work centre, where the child may be 'treated', but the school, the classroom, the family setting and any residential establishment caring for the child. Moreover, as well as focusing on the emotional and historical, e.g. social, experiences of the child, the various care-givers will work with sensory and other physical aspects, and with cultural mores and ethical aspects of life. Usually these areas of living will be the special concern of one or other adult involved in helping the child; so that, for instance, the 'key' worker in a residential establishment, i.e. a member of staff who carries certain specified responsibilities for a particular child, may take a special interest in helping a girl to socialize, while the therapist is especially concerned with helping her to make sense of early traumatic events in her life (or as some would say 'come to terms with' those events). But the lines of demarcation do not need to be rigid. It becomes a matter of organization and how best to help this (particular) child in this set of circumstances. An example care-therapy approach case is given in Chapter 2. But an important element in the approach is the co-ordinating of these various aspects of treatment and care.

So what else is special about this psycho-social, this care-therapy approach? These days one is susceptible to criticism from various 'schools' as well as 'anti-schools' as soon as particular words are used. There is also the danger of speaking in such broad terms that one merely makes a statement or claim which could be applied to many approaches. If, for example, I describe the approach, as I might, as a healing–mending approach, I may immediately be in trouble with some existentialist groups for alluding to 'healing', which carries a medical connotation not acceptable to them. Then again, many counsellors and other workers would make the same therapeutic claims for very different approaches.

Yet there is a distinction to be made between forms of childcare, especially residential care, where at the end of the period of care the child or adolescent is seen merely to have been held, fed, clothed, controlled, maintained and finally returned to her previous environment (or to a lonely alternative) just as unhappy, destructive, depressed or otherwise disturbed as when she entered care. There is a distinction between that sort of purely *minding* care, and a form which helps the child or adolescent to grow emotionally and socially, and to lose the inner tensions which were carrying so much actual misery despite, often, a facade of steely bravado.

Bearing in mind, therefore, the possibility of semantic criticism from the 'schools', we shall list three attributes of this approach by way of clarification. They are:

1 An approach which is aimed an enabling **affective** (feeling) changes to take place, which result in a decrease of tension and stress and which help the child to deal with **narcissistic** problems so that an increase in self-value (self-esteem) results and progress is made in the development of the self.

2 An approach, in psychodynamic terms, which is concerned with the **psyche** and the healing of the inner child.

3 An approach, so far as 'control' is an interest, which tends to establish inner control in the child (not quite the same thing as self-control, which even an unhealed child may attain to). The approach tends to encourage the child to gain a greater control over his or her own impulses in a maturing way.

Although we have described our work as an approach, it is important that we emphasize how available to most childcare practitioners are the treatment methods offered in this book.

It is common practice these days to speak of 'talk' (or 'talking') therapies, by which we mean the various forms of counselling or psychotherapy. However, it becomes increasingly clear that treating a child without reference to changes which may also be required within a family group may be quite futile. But we need to broaden the care-giving horizon beyond child and family. The child is developing within a whole network of interactive factors: parents, siblings, school, relations, peer group, church, clubs, friends and 'enemies' – and much more.

Anyone working to help a child becomes part of such a network and must be in touch with at least several other parts of the network. In this book we concentrate very much on methods, using various media (drawing, painting, music, etc.) aimed at increasing communication between child and worker and helping the child to make the best use of talk therapy, but not *only* talk therapy. We want also to help the child to so relate to those various interactive factors in the network that he or she grows up, possessing 'an inner life which is rich and rewarding' (Bettelheim, 1987).

Important Incorporated Theory

Before introducing the theory and practice that have influenced our approach it is important to say something concerning would-be practitioners and their attitude and skills, as there is an important element of personal interaction (as in any therapy counselling) between child and practitioner which is essential so far as this work is concerned.

One reason for emphasizing this interaction is that although it is possible to give examples of various 'games' and equipment used in **direct work** (see, for example, Redgrave, 1987), the really effective therapist must be frequently adapting these to the needs of individual children. Moreover, the therapist needs to be aware of his or her skills and gifts and not simply to use an illustration, a game or a technique, as demonstrated by us or any other therapists, in an unaltered state. Some of the examples quoted in this book might be ineffective so far as some therapists or some children are concerned. Not every therapist or counsellor, nor every child, is comfortable, for example, with **role-play**.

It is often apparent, because of the personality, the unique experience and the particular interests of the child, that an entirely new game or piece of equipment (third object) is required. This will become clearer in following chapters when it should be evident that the therapist will need to be inventive, full of imagination, prepared to experiment with direct-work equipment, and endowed with empathy and intuition so far as children and young persons are concerned.

Although we shall use the terms 'therapist' and 'counsellor' as well as 'worker', it will be understood that other people, such as foster-parents, may (under supervision) use some or all of the materials and methods described in this book.

Attachment

The importance of the process known by psychologists as attachment is central to the approach that we are outlining and we shall, therefore, return to the subject in later chapters. Its importance, however, permeates our subject. We shall refer frequently to the works of John Bowlby, whose main titles will also be found in Further Reading. The quality of the attachment (of child to parents, siblings and others) is postulated to relate to the quality of child nurture.

The quality of the nurturing experience is therefore also a vital variable in this psychosocial approach. I have used the term child nurture as almost synonymous with the term parenting. The reader is directed to the inclusive description (and definition) of child nurture provided in Appendix 1. The quality of the attachment process depends upon both the child nurture and the particular innate temperamental and organistic qualities of the child's endowment.

It is further postulated (and various references will be provided to substantiate the postulate) that as a result of variations on the themes of poor nurturing, poor attachment experience, and in many cases traumatic emotional–physical experiences, four important developmental modes are negatively affected. These are the **behavioural**, **affective**, **cognitive** and **somatic** modes.

'Stuck' Children

Developmental retardation is an important concept associated with the psychosocial approach outlined here. Occasionally, in the literature, one comes across the use of the commonplace term 'stuck'. The child is described as being stuck. Of course the terms retardation and cognitive developmental delay, etc. sound more acceptable and more scientifically respectable but, especially in connection with emotional and personality development, we are often dealing with conduct (or behaviour) which, in one or more respects, may represent the actual stuck, infantile stage. Quite often this retarded element is not to be seen or measured in terms of intelligence. It is often not a cognitive retardation in that sense, nor a physical retardation or under-development, but it is seen in the behaviour of the child or adolescent although often described as violence, aggressiveness, irrational guilt, **frozen awareness** or anger – and indeed a child who is emotionally stuck may exhibit any of these behaviours. Here are some short quotations from writers who actually used the word stuck. First, Ryce-Menuhin, writing about the use of sandplay:

> The analyst's job, according to Jung, is to mediate the symbolic function for the patient particularly through dream analysis and through the 'waking dreams' of sandplay analysis. The term 'transcendent function' (used previously by the writer) here only means that this function helps a person 'transcend' or move through and across existing attitudes or a state in which they may be *stuck*. (Ryce-Menuhin, 1992, p. 22, my emphasis)

And here Barrett and Trevitt link learning disablement with emotional or feeling experiences:

> The links between learning and feelings are more difficult to examine and assess. Although there is a danger in classifying learning-disabled children, particularly since there is so much overlap between the groups, we believe that the process helps us to identify the emotional stage where they (and their families) became '*stuck*'. It is against this background that we address the feelings related to the lost capacity for learning. (Barrett and Trevitt, 1991, p. 146, my emphasis)

The care-therapy approach acknowledges that much of the emotionally tied reactive behaviour witnessed in older children and in adults is in fact infantile behaviour. The infant often has little or no control over his or her gross impulses, but in a good-enough nurturing setting this is accepted, despite the fact that when 'old enough' the child is encouraged to behave differently and is gradually able to get along in the peer group. It is easy to overlook the fact that, often the 11-year-old who consistently smashes up a toy because he hasn't won the game, or performs some other antisocial behaviour, is being the $2\frac{1}{2}$-year-old or the 3-year-old in a temper tantrum. Again, the 6-year-old who constantly disrupts the school class because he demands all the attention from the teacher and will only settle down when sitting beside the teacher, may still be screaming in his cot for some unfulfilled emotional demand.

The everyday word, stuck, is not used very often by authors, but the concept appears in many contexts and part of our thesis is that as a result of poor attachment experiences and poor-quality infant nurture, much of the infantile behaviour (often dysfunctional even in infancy, but not always) remains fixated, although it is perceived as something else by many adults. We must also remember that in the case of children submitted to abuse, or to neglect, what may be construed as 'dysfunctional' behaviour may actually be (in childhood and infancy) extremely functional in an ago-preserving (sanity-preserving) way.

This phenomenon may be included in the **gestalt therapists**' concept of 'unfinished **Gestalten**'.

Unresolved childhood situations are often experienced as 'unfinished situations' or 'incompletely formed Gestalten'. These unfinished situations continue to disturb the person in adult life. They tend to interfere with behaviours, perceptions and thinking related to effective functioning in the here-and-now ... Pathology may be caused when an unfinished or incomplete Gestalt is inappropriately or prematurely 'closed' under stress. This Closure may take physiological, affective, cognitive or behavioural form. (Clarkson, 1989, p. 7)

The idea of the stuck child (and stuck adult) is prevalent in the thinking of Winnicott and Miller. Adam Phillips, writing about the work of Winnicott, states:

To make sense of psychopathology it was as if Winnicott was asking a simple question: given the infant's dependence on the mother, what resources were available to the infant and child that could make up for the deficits in the mothering he needed to sustain the continuity of his development? He (Winnicott) found that the paradox of these childhood solutions was that they enabled the child to survive, but with the unconscious project and hope of finding an environment in which development could start up again. A life could be lived, that is to say, in suspended animation. (Phillips, 1988)

Finally, a reference (one of many possible) to Alice Miller's thinking. Here she describes the discovery by the patient of the child within himself:

But another, weightier mortification is added to the first when this analysand discovers the introjects within himself, and that he has been their prisoner. For his anger, demands and avarice do not at first appear in a tamed adult form, but in the childish–archaic one in which they were repressed. The patient is horrified when he realizes that he is capable of screaming with rage in the same way that he so hated in his father or that, only yesterday, he has checked and controlled his child, 'practically', he says, 'in my mother's clothes'. (Miller, 1986)

In each of these contexts the idea of retardation, fixation (often emotional), standing still, or just plain stuck is understood.

Symbolism

Another incorporate in so far as theory is concerned relates to the importance, in human psychology, of symbolism. This phenomenon, present not only in dreams but, albeit often unconsciously, in much of our behaviour and thinking, is recognized in care-therapy and utilized in the treatment approach. Children make use of symbolism in a lot of their daily activity, especially in their play.

Readers will discover that in the course of helping the unhappy child, perhaps a traumatized child, to become more at peace with herself, facilities will be provided which lend themselves to the use of symbolism. These include the sand-world technique (see Chapter 4), the use of guided imagery (during which the child imagines places and events) and of course drawing and painting. In the final section of a book edited by Carl Jung, Von Franz said:

> The powerful forces of the unconscious most certainly appear not only in clinical material but also in the mythological, religious, artistic, and all other cultural activities by which man expresses himself. Obviously, if all men have common inherited patterns of emotional and mental behaviour (which Jung called the archetypes), it is only to be expected that we shall find their products (*symbolic* fantasies, thoughts and actions) in practically *every* field of human activity. (Von Franz, 1964, my emphasis)

The Eclectic Approach

Before concluding this brief résumé of the main theory incorporates, it will be appropriate to say something about the psychotherapeutic approaches (or schools of psychology) not so far mentioned. Their lack of mention does not imply that they are rejected. Indeed, as this book reveals more of the care-therapy approach, readers will spot the incorporation of methods and ideas which are used primarily by cognitive, behaviourist, or Gestalt schools. While this might be anathema to the purist, it has been argued that few, if any, practitioners avoid these approaches completely either in everyday life or in their work with children, but we would add (and we trust this work will bear us out) that an eclectic or synthesis approach is actually more effective. In fact, the importance of drawing upon a number of techniques correlates well with the avoidance of rigidity demanded when working with and reacting to individual children. We must forever keep before us the question 'How can we help this particular (unique) child in this particular (never to be repeated) moment of time?' Sad indeed if the only viewpoint or technique which could have helped is eschewed because of the pride of the therapist.

This danger of rigidity due to what can amount to doctrine (an almost religious approach to a particular school or theorist) and the sad effect of doctrinaire attitudes are exemplified even in the work of two wonderful women who each must have helped very many children. I am referring to the disagreement which existed in the 1920s between Anna Freud and Melanie Klein, both of whom were Freudians (or at least post-Freudians).

Whereas Anna Freud used to take what Melanie Klein called 'elaborate and troublesome' means to ensure that the child felt comfortable and welcomed, especially on his first treatment session, Klein argued that to cultivate a positive **transference** only colluded with the child's denial of his most unacceptable, hostile feelings. However, for Freud the child analyst was less an interpreter of unconscious conflict than an exemplary adult with whom the child could identify as part of his education in self-control.

So, between these two analysts, whether or not the child was put at ease and felt a sense of confidence at the start of his treatment depended on which analyst he landed up with. But could it be that children require different introductions, in fact different milieux, depending upon a multitude of idiosyncratic and experiential factors?

Certainly, care-therapy considered in a holistic way may require of some therapeutic relationships a deeply satisfying involvement, even (as in the case of the residential worker) an attachment. While it may be therapeutically appropriate for one member of the care team to face the child with social reality factors, and to use 'reward' systems in a so-called behaviourist pattern, it may also be necessary for the same child to begin (perhaps for the first time in his life) to form an attachment as a result of being allowed, in the appropriate milieu, to regress.

Certainly, also, there are records of some of the most emotionally damaged children being healed (or regenerated) by a treatment approach surpassing even Anna Freud's accommodation.

For instance, Barbara Dockar-Drysdale, who founded the Mulberry Bush School for children needing residential psycho-therapeutic care, describes her work with Susan, a $3^1/_2$-year-old child who needed to regress to babyhood in order then to develop satisfactorily. She says 'During her first three months with us she called all night and I came to her every time she called' (Dockar-Drysdale, 1990). This does not mean, however, that in another situation she would acquiesce in a child's demands. She distinguishes between demands and needs.

In this volume the reader will come across the expression Infant Nurture Programme. It is part of the total therapy approach and is applied where necessary. Dockar-Drysdale was in fact providing an extreme form of infant nurture programme. But it may also be helpful in upgrading an older child's self-esteem if he can be helped, speedily, to stop bed-wetting. And sometimes, in fact, the most appropriate methods may be those of behavioural therapy. But this would only be part of the total care-therapy approach – part of the treatment plan for the child.

So much for the eclectic approach! It is worth noting that Stephen Palmer points out that some specialists in transcultural therapy assert that with clients of South Asian origin 'the therapist variables are probably more important in the process and outcome of therapy than particular schools of therapy' (Palmer, 1999). We shall return to this point later.

Important Incorporated Treatment Concepts and Methods

Although the overall picture of the care-therapy approach is presented in this work, the bulk of the book will deal with methods of helping children in which the individual therapist is concerned in a one-to-one work relationship. We shall concentrate on the foci and methods being used in the clinical setting but will aim to help the reader see how these fit into the broader context of the work with the child, and often with the child's parents, work which will depend, as we have stated, upon a team of people.

This team concept is important. A recent British government publication which could well have carried the title 'care-therapy' but is called *Working Together to Safeguard Children* (Department of Health, 1999) emphasizes the team work and states that childcare is an interdisciplinary, inter-agency concern.

Two very important treatment concepts are concerned with, on the one hand, what is often referred to as **insight**, and on the other with what practitioners have called sensory stimulus (or more poetically, the reawakening of the senses). For these concepts we have used the expressions 'awareness experience', and 'sensory experience' respectively.

Awareness experience

We would remind the reader that many of the children requiring the help of the therapist will have undergone the most shattering life experiences. Although we can list 'common' experiences and events in the lives of these children, it must be remembered that a high percentage of them will have experienced several items from the list. The list includes:

1 Emotional rejection by parents, often by the mother.
2 Emotional ill-treatment (being locked in dark cupboards, jeered at, stigmatized, etc.).
3 Physical cruelty.
4 Sexual abuse.
5 Constant 'let-downs' by care-givers. Some children have experienced fifteen, or even twenty changes in 'parents' by the time they are 10 years old by changing foster homes.
6 Mental conflict.
7 Psychological confusion (concerning their identity and why they are rejected or abused).

Many people who experience this sort of childhood carry psychological problems into adulthood, and much of the work undertaken by psychotherapists is concerned with helping them to understand how things really were. For example, they often cling to ideas or beliefs that their parents were 'good' to them. Yet they carry the anger about their parents, and maybe they carry (irrational) guilt because of their anger. Much of this generates from the unconscious. They need to understand, to become aware (awareness-experience) of how things really were. This usually means accepting in their conscious mind what they have harboured for years in the unconscious. It may involve losing the need to rationalize around damaging experiences or their own conduct disorder.

Feelings (emotional states) are involved. We have already referred to anger and guilt. We could add self-hate, fear and a host of others. Because these people may often project their feelings onto others, and may blame current events rather than childhood experiences, therapists often talk of the need for them to be helped to 'get in touch with' their feelings. Therefore the term 'insight' has been used. Awareness experience involves insight.

Various theorists and most schools of psychotherapy, as the literature will show, pay tribute to this insight or getting in touch process, although some use very different terminology to express themselves or to distinguish their particular outlook. For example, Diana Whitmore, a **psychosynthesis** counsellor, writes concerning her work:

One client who approached life primarily through her mind rather than through her feelings, sought counselling because of psychosomatic stomach problems. She was out of touch with her emotional life which obviously, for her own well-being, needed to become a *conscious* experience. (Whitmore, 1991, p. 63, my emphasis)

But the **Jungians (analytic psychology)** also emphasize the essential quality of insight in so far as their therapy is concerned:

Jungian analysis takes place within a dialectical relationship between two persons, analyst and analysand, and has for its goal the analysand's *coming to terms with* the unconscious: the analysand is meant to gain *insight* into the specific unconscious and dynamics that emerge during analysis, and the structures underlying ego-consciousness are meant to change in their dynamic relation to other, more unconscious structures and dynamics. (Stein, 1995, my emphasis)

And the Gestalt therapist includes the 'aha' experience:

The *process* of figure/ground shift may occur slowly over years of training, as for example the need to qualify as a medical doctor. It may also occur in a matter of seconds as in the sudden 'aha' experience when a client suddenly integrates a new *insight*, such as a fundamental similarity between what he needed from his mother and what he continues to need from his wife. Such an insight may completely alter the relationship between past and future, expectation and understanding, figure and ground. (Clarkson, 1989, my emphasis)

Awareness experience, however, includes far more than repressed experiences, important though they are. It includes more than the processes of **denial** and **rationalization**. There is a cognitive element in awareness experience, and there is a clarification element. Many children referred for treatment have lost their past history: this may sound dramatic but it is true. Children 10 and 12 years old, who have moved about within the care system, may not be in possession of actual facts about their birth, place of birth for example, or who looked after them between the ages of new-born and 6 years old. Perhaps they do remember (and have happy memories of) the foster-parents they had when they were 6 but they have a quite erroneous idea of why they were suddenly removed from the foster-family.

We recall one 8-year-old boy (Jamie) who told us that he had been removed from his foster-home (and in his mind rejected by the foster-parents) because he 'wet the bed' when he was 5 years old; so that was his picture of why he had moved, why he had been rejected. But this left him with a conflict, 'People love you, but can turn you out, because you wet the bed', and he carried another conflict-producing thought, 'I am nasty, dirty, because I wet the bed'. But the facts were different: he had been moved when the foster-mother had died (no one had told him) and the foster-father had suffered a breakdown. Apart from all else, the early rejection by his natural mother, the physical abuse by his natural father and the anger generated within the child, he needed to know what the facts were. He needed the insight, the awareness, associated with facts.

Awareness experience, or insight treatment, is concerned with history, with relationships (past and present), with feelings (past and present) and with possible future experiences. The reader will discover that in order to help the child, the team of workers involved in the case will be as interested in encouraging her to share her ideas about the future as they are in sharing the child's current anxieties and helping her to handle ('come to terms with') necessary truths about people in her life.

We have emphasized awareness experience and shall be discussing sensory experience because, in the following chapters, readers will become aware that the main emphasis of this book is on the practice of using materials and activities when working with children in a counselling, care-giving or therapy role. For descriptive purposes we have divided these materials and activities, i.e. third objects, as we call them, into those which will be used mainly to help the child to obtain insight and those used mainly to help the child to explore the senses (sight, sound, touch, etc.) and to compensate her to some extent for what she has missed as an infant.

Feelings are important. Feelings may not be measurable. They may be assumed from the child's behaviour or guessed at! – and if you are 'close' to the child she may tell you about her feelings, but this is hard even for adults to do. Apart from the emotional restraint it is hard to find the right words. Because of this, various methods, using games and many other techniques, have been developed by people practising care-therapy. Some of these are described in later chapters of this book. But remember, feelings are real, and they are important. 'Feelings' here include emotional states, affective states, attitudes and prejudices, anger, fear, anxiety and guilt. And, of course, the existential experience differs for different children, even the same shared experience is different for individuals in the sibling group.

There is accumulating evidence concerning the links between feelings (or emotional and affective states) and cognitive (and even physical) states. Lask and Bryant-Waugh in their review of anorexia nervosa write:

> Hsu (1990) has helpfully proposed a coherent theory of aetiology in which he suggests that 'adolescent dieting provides the entree into an eating disorder if such dieting is intensified by adolescent turmoil, low self and body concept, and poor identity formation . . . whilst other risk factors may include such personality traits as long-standing feelings of emptiness and ineffectiveness, overcontrol of emotionality and conformity'. (Lask and Bryant-Waugh, 1992)

Elsewhere we shall be emphasizing the link between the affective and cognitive aspects of child development. As we are discussing the importance of feelings in this section it is useful to consider this link between feelings and understanding in children and, in the following excerpt, between siblings. The message of Judy Dunn's research is, as she says:

> That we should recognise how important emotion may be in the development of understanding and vice versa. There is a far more general lesson here than simply the message that children understand their siblings well: what is important is the issue of why they understand them so well. We return here to the link between the emotional depth of the sibling relationship and the children's understanding of the sibling. (Dunn, 1984)

In the work with the child, in so far as awareness experience is concerned, a lot of time will be spent on past and present feelings. Use will be made of 'feeling drawings' (and of paintings), role-play in which the child expresses feelings about people and events, and such techniques as psycho-imagery which help the child to practice (in a safe setting) how he may handle feelings of fear, anger, etc. The child will be helped to accept, understand, clarify and otherwise get in touch with his feelings.

Sensory Experience

It would be more realistic, but far more difficult, to write about awareness and sensory experience all mixed up in one section instead of separating them as we have done. We are back to the holistic theme, of course, but it cannot be overemphasized that in nature, in the development of the human person, body sensation, emotions, and cognition are all in process together. The last thing we want is for readers to separate completely physical and psychological aspects, putting them neatly into their own 'boxes'.

Having said that, we may also say that it is easier to focus on these aspects by artificially splitting them in this way. But in the literature on child development, and in many accounts of the development of human behaviour, the psychological and social aspects are usually emphasized and the importance of sensory experience minimized or overlooked. Yet the study of the disturbed or 'conduct disorder' child frequently reveals a background experience of sensory deprivation if not sensory abuse. True, the 'sensory deprivation' in many of these examples results from a primary **aetiological** source, such as rejecting or depressed parents who are unable to satisfy the child's needs for physical holding, patting, touching and so forth (Wolff, 1989; Politano et al., 1992; Barnett, 1991).

Important though it is, and we shall have much more to say about it later in the book, touch is only one of the so-called five senses. The practitioner of care-therapy is just as interested in the other four: vision, audition, olfaction and gustation (or in plain English, sight, hearing, smell, and taste).

In the clinical setting the therapist will provide the obvious 'touch' materials such as good quality (soft) potter's clay and other manipu- lative art materials (see Chapters 3 and 4), but he or she may also provide 'taste experiences' for the child, and 'sound experiences', as well as 'sight experiences' involving colour and objects in movement, and then there will be 'smell experiences'. Often smell, taste and colour experiences, and even touch experience are obtained from one simple object.

The theoretical background to care-therapy holds that, quite apart from sensory exploration invoking memories (which the therapist does not ignore) there can be a healing process involved in the re-run of focusing on sensory experience in a pleasurable context. Indeed, the author has noticed that in the day nurseries or family centres where mothers are encouraged to come and play alongside their children, what often happens when touch and manipulative materials are provided is that a mother (possible deprived of early enjoyment with such materials) will become the 'child', so to speak, and will become engrossed in the play activity – even getting a little irritated when a child 'spoils' her enjoyment of the play, be it with sand, water or clay, etc.

We shall not expand on the various materials or techniques here as this is done in other places in the book. Suffice it to say that some of the objects in use, such as a feeding bottle, may provide not only taste but also touch in the form of the bottle teat touching the lips (more on this later).

The good therapist will not limit sensory experience to clinical settings. Depending upon circumstances, there may be advantages to be got from special sensory experiences in everyday settings and in the open air. So many of the children referred have never walked in a wood through dry leaves, kicking them as they go. And imagine the fun and the feel, on a warm day, of running barefoot on wet grass. And how about standing still (exhausted?!) in a wood and listening to sounds? In later chapters we shall have something to say about the use of imagination concerning the senses; 'Imagine you can see . . .' and 'Imagine you can hear . . .'

in so far as this approach appears to be emphasizing the importance of sensory experience it will be worthwhile to consider what certain other writers have had to say. We think that one very important aspect of the holistic emphasis is the juxtaposition of psychological and physical events. We are wishing to emphasize the juxtaposition here rather than the linear idea of cause followed by effect. Take, for example, the affective experience which we call joy. In a good-enough environmental situation an infant may experience joy in juxtaposition with his own manipulation of the environment – with the development of a skill, or with some achievement. Here the sensory, the cognitive and the emotional become one. And it is developmentally valuable to have such an experience. Margaret Donaldson writes about joy:

> In the life of a child, joy in the immediate involvement of the body in skilled activity comes early and spontaneously. As we have seen already, this is by no means an unthinking joy, but it is not reflective. The later exercise of the reflective capacities can bring joy too – but this is a joy that does not come unaided. (Donaldson, 1978)

Ashley Montagu wrote the classic *Touching: The Human Significance of the Skin* (1978) and focused on the developmental necessity of touch in animals and humans. He showed that even the licking (cleaning?) process carried out by the mother in many animal species was in fact far more than just cleaning. The process is essential for stimulating growth and development. We are now aware that many heavily institutionalized babies which Montagu records as having failed to thrive, infants who were placed in orphanages in the nineteenth and early twentieth centuries, but who were hardly ever picked up and held, probably died as a result of touch neglect.

In an article entitled 'Prevention of Psychiatric Disorders in Early Childhood' McGuire and Earls state:

> Since it is unclear what strategies will improve parenting skills and which parents will benefit most from an intervention, it may be more useful to intervene directly with children, particularly if there are sensitive periods in brain behaviour development relative to social skills. While this approach is common with pre-schoolers, some recent work has been developed by Field and colleagues (1982) with high risk infants. These investigators provided an experimental group of neonates with pacifiers during intravenous tube feeding and compared them with a matched group who received only the feeding condition. Weight gain was more rapid in the experimental group. They were also discharged an average of 8 days earlier than controls . . . In a subsequent study, neonates were given tactile stimulation in the form of body stroking and passive limb movement for three 15-minute sessions over 10 days (Field *et al.*, 1986). These infants were found to be more alert and active than a control group, obtained better scores on the Brazelton scale, demonstrated more mature habituation, evidenced greater weight gain, and were discharged an average of 6 days earlier than the controls. Schanberg and Field (1987) have identified a biochemical basis for the enhanced growth and suggest that this simple intervention has a profound influence on the growth of body and brain. (McGuire and Earls, 1991)

The Gestaltists too, subscribe to the importance of sensory experience even though the grounds for their doing so may rest on less researched but nevertheless valuable hypotheses. Readers will note that Oaklander, from whom we have taken several quotations, involves her child patients in specific sensory experiences.

Although we subscribed to the belief that infant and childhood experiences partly lay the foundations of later behaviour, it is important that we should acknowledge both the strong influence of genetic factors and the ability of many children and adults in overcoming early influences. We also feel that treatment itself should not get stuck on the past, but make use of the child's strengths in dealing with the 'now' and the future.

Having briefly described the central themes of this book, themes which link counselling aims with various working materials (paints, clay, sand, water, etc.), let us say that we find it encouraging to note that Ranju Roy (1999), in proposing three essential tools for 'culturally sensitive therapy', names three which form part of our more extensive list. They are:

1 Art work externalization, which enables the child to 'externalize' problems during the time he is actually inwardly dealing with them.
2 The **genogram**, which is one way of drawing a diagram of a family.
3 Curiosity.

We shall add Imagination as a fourth 'essential'.

Ethnic Minority, Racial and Cross-cultural Factors

The reader will become increasingly aware (especially on reading Chapters 3 and 4) of the importance to us of meaningful communication. The reason for our focusing here on racial and cross-cultural factors is that carers and counsellors are sometimes in as much danger as anyone else of carrying bias and prejudice resulting from ethnic and cultural differences. Much of this prejudice will be 'unconscious' in that the prejudiced person will not be aware of it, or will not be aware of how different is his or her experience of society from that of a client or a foster-child from a different cultural background.

It was said, above, that the therapist variables (approaches, attitudes, etc.) are as important as his or her school of therapy, or even more important. Clearly the attitudes and beliefs of foster-parents and adopters are just as important. But attitudes and beliefs may be linked to prejudice and bias. We may be failing utterly to communicate meaningfully, not because we are rejecting another person but because we and the other person, a child we are working with or a child's parents for example, hold totally different assumptions about a single event.

The eminent professor of psychology, Dr Pittu Laungani, who is not, in ethnic terms, English, gives a luminous account of an experience he had with Bernie, his English helper or major-domo. Bernie used to clean, iron the shirts, paint the flat – anything. One day he paid Dr Laungani 'what he thought was the supreme compliment'. He said: 'You know, Dr Laungani, you are almost a true Brit.' 'But not quite?' said Laungani. 'You're getting there,' said Bernie. (Laungani, 1999)

As Dr Laungani points out, there were several anglocentric cultural assumptions in Bernie's thinking: one of them was that the desire to be British was the standard, the goal to which all non-Britishers automatically aspired.

Many of our own assumptions may not, to us, seem as barefaced, and they will often not be recognized by us as simply part of our own special cultural or even micro-cultural baggage: we may simply assume certain forms of emotional or cognitive response as 'normal' or 'natural'.

All the processes of personality development and parenting as well as the processes of counselling and therapy may be adversely affected as a result of ignorance, assumption, or prejudice. This includes the process of attachment and all the examples of direct work provided in later chapters. We shall provide vignettes which highlight the way in which the various media (painting, music, art therapy, etc.) have been used in counselling situations involving cross-cultural differences.

Of course, it is not only between different ethnic groups that we find cultural and sub-cultural clashes and faulty assumptions. These factors may emerge as a result of ideas and beliefs which relate to class, status, religion, and age difference. They may be present even where regional accents are a factor.

If a child of one culture, who is also of the minority ethnic group in a country or a region, is placed with care-givers of a different cultural background and of the majority ethnic group, it is possible that some wrong assumptions will be held by child and care-givers. The child may even experience the style of parenting as strange or 'funny', or even 'nasty'. Similar dangers exist in the counselling, social work, or therapy roles. This is not, however, intended as an argument for rigid rejection of such placements. In Chapter 6 there is some discussion on the importance of assessing children's individual needs resulting from their individual and unique life experiences and individual personality factors. This is important because it is easy to fall into the trap of stereotyping. Take, for example, a child of cross-cultural parenting. A child, say, who has one parent who is white Anglo-American and one who is Indian, i.e. brought up in India. There is a need here in a counselling situation for the therapist to be someone who clearly understands the possible areas of conflict which may emerge between the cultural practices and beliefs, and prejudices.

In later chapters we shall return to this aspect of racial and cross-cultural factors as one aspect, albeit an important one, in working with children and young people and in helping them to feel comfortable concerning their own background, history, ethnicity and beliefs.

This chapter has introduced the reader to care-therapy. We have mentioned certain aspects of child development and child psychology which we feel it is important to remember when caring for children (nurturing and parenting them). These include the theory of attachment, and we later provide a separate chapter (Chapter 7) on this subject.

However, we have also pointed out that because this book is mainly concerned with the use of materials (third objects) in counselling and therapy, we shall not (except in Chapter 2) be providing detailed and full descriptions of case examples, nor shall we be using space to 'teach' psychology or counselling as such. We shall, however, provide vignettes and brief case outlines.

This chapter has also described the two main categories, awareness experience and sensory experience, into which the materials and activities fall. In the following chapter we shall present a case study which will, again, concentrate on the use of these third objects. The study will, it is felt, clarify for readers the way in which these materials become an essential part of the counselling and the 'healing'.

CHAPTER 2

The use of insight and sensory materials when counselling or treating a child

'If the child is defined as a failure, he will almost certainly fail, at any rate in the things which the definers value.'
Donaldson, M., 1978

This chapter will be devoted to practical illustrations intended to assist the reader by linking the theoretical approach to actual examples of work undertaken with a particular child, Donna.

We shall outline the case in full and take the reader, albeit swiftly, through the main events of this child's life, the treatment from the point at which we became involved, and the outcome. At the same time we shall view the treatment approaches in broad terms. In later chapters we shall look in greater detail at the interventions, techniques and tools (instruments or third objects) which are used at particular points in the treatment of children. Their use will be related in finer detail to the theory of care-therapy.

CASE STUDY – Donna

When Donna was born, her mother, an intelligent young woman, was only 17 years old. She herself had suffered a disruptive childhood. From shortly after the time of Donna's birth her parents lived together. The father (we shall call him Jay) took a great interest in his daughter, despite the fact that he himself was involved in drug-pushing.

Jay and Heather, Donna's mother, were soon rowing with each other. Jay accused Heather of mis-spending housekeeping money on 'drink', which she did – often ending up drunk. Heather would often be in a depressive state, and she actually left home, leaving Donna to be cared for by Jay, when the child was about 3 years old. She was absent for a period of about six months on one occasion.

Although Jay was very fond of Donna and had given her some feeling of having at least one parent representing security, and although she was clearly attached to him emotionally, he served her badly by ending up with a three-year prison sentence for drug-running. Donna was 5 years old when this happened. He never went back into the family.

Donna's mother, partly for her cash needs, began to take in lodgers. It transpired later that Donna was used sexually by at least two of these lodgers between her sixth and seventh birthdays. The mother used to leave Donna in the care of the lodgers, who would 'baby-sit' for her when she went out. Another lodger eventually became mum's 'boyfriend' and unofficial 'stepfather' to Donna, whom he not only despised and objected to, but also sexually abused. He was called Dave.

A half-brother to Donna arrived when she was about $7\frac{1}{2}$ years old. Another person to arrive on the scene was 'Uncle Mike', the brother of Dave, Donna's 'stepdad'.

The various social care agencies had not been unconcerned, nor had the education authorities, over Donna's welfare, although of course nothing was known with any certainty about the sexual abuse. There had, however, been certain worrying signs. By the time she was 9 years old, Donna appeared 'secretive', 'aloof' and at the same time 'demanding and hostile' in school. Twice she had 'gone missing' from school and, after several months of the school putting up with it, she was referred to the medical services on account of heavy soiling and wetting herself, which other children found objectionable.

Because it was known that 'Uncle Mike' had a conviction for sexually abusing a child, Donna's mother had also been warned by health visitors and on one occasion by a local authority social worker, not to leave the child exposed to the attentions of Mike – in fact not to leave her on her own with him. It transpired later that after being so warned, Heather had on one occasion caught Mike sexually interfering with her daughter, but had merely told him not to do it again and promptly left her in his 'baby-sitting' care!

Following the medical referral for her incontinence, she was removed to what was known in law as a Place of Safety (in fact a children's home). The sexual abuse had come to light. She was $10^{1}/_{2}$ years old when a Care Order was made putting her into the care of the local authority. There followed three unsuccessful and disrupted fostering placements in which Donna became progressively more withdrawn, uncommunicative, destructive in a subtle way, over-selective so far as relationships were concerned, and also (selectivity's polar opposite) rejecting.

The treatment programme we are outlining started when Donna was again residing in a children's home. She was 12 years old. She presented with the personality features listed above plus the fact that she would flirt with males, particularly older teenaged lads. She had developed a strong rebuffing pattern towards adults who attempted to get emotionally close to her. This was what might be referred to as a 'protective mechanism', helpful in the sort of childhood she had experienced, but likely to cause her problems as she grew into adulthood. But, typical of the abused and rejected (and 'used') children I am writing about, she was functioning in many ways at an infantile level, especially on the emotional plane. Examples of this infantile (or stuck) behaviour were seen in various reactions to ordinary domestic events. For example, although outwardly she was a pubescent pre-teenager, interested in pop music, boys and clothes, she would be devastated if some cheap little toy which she had her eye on was given to another child – even if that child were a baby. On one occasion a cuddly toy – a teddy-bear type of soft toy – arrived at the centre, given by a friend of a member of the staff. Donna showed her appreciation of it but reacted in a devastated way when it was given to the 3-year-old in the centre. Not only did she sulk for three whole days and nights, but she found a way of hurting members of the staff by destroying articles which belonged to them.

Another example of her infantile behaviour was to be seen in her rocking, which she would do if upset. She would sit in her bed and rock to and fro while sucking her thumb. Many disturbed infants obtain comfort by this means, and for Donna it had remained one of her chief comforters. Then again, it seemed likely that some of the soiling was infantile, although one needed to be circumspect in making a judgement because anal penetration had been part of the sexual abuse and that often leads to soiling.

In the outline of the treatment provided for Donna, the reader may discern the following aspects or foci of the approach:

1 Help given to the child to enable her to reflect on, or become more aware of, certain feelings, emotions, ideas, and beliefs (awareness experience).
2 Sensory work, clinical (sensory experience).
3 Clarification of life events, personal history and motivation (awareness experience).
4 Infant nurture programme (involving the care-giving staff of the children's centre). Involves sensory experience, non-clinical.
5 'Befrienders Scheme' (social visiting).
6 Team-work. The involvement of various professionals, family, and foster-family, including the therapist, residential and field social workers, school staff, and 'befrienders'.
7 'Bridging'. Preparing the child to move into a new family or other placement and helping her during the 'settling-in' phase.

We shall draw the attention of the reader to these foci as the treatment scheme unfolds.

Becoming Aware of Feelings
We shall start, then, by discussing some of the methods used to help Donna get in touch with her feelings (see 1, above). The therapist introduced psycho-imagery quite early on in the programme, as it was found that Donna liked to do these imagination exercises. In this work we ask the children, having experienced beforehand the method, to relax back in the comfortable chair or settee and then to think back to any really happy occasion, or a happy day. If they wish they may close their eyes, and most of them do, but one needs to be careful because some children would become worried if they were *instructed* to close them. Violet Oaklander tells them to 'go into their own secret space'. With a little help they may recall a birthday or a family holiday or even something very unromantic so far as other people are

concerned. One 14-year-old youth recalled happy occasions when, seated outside a pub, his father would allow him to drink the froth from 'dad's pint!'. Actually, that memory was very comforting to the lad, whose father had died a year or so before.

Donna recalled several happy days quite clearly, even though they mostly related to the time when she was something between 3 and 5 years of age, and there was one special holiday she enjoyed when just she and her mother went away alone and Donna was about 7 years old.

Let us state here, quite categorically, that we are not involving the child in so-called **recovered memories**. We are dealing with what the child remembers but is never given the opportunity to talk about. Of course his or her memories may be inaccurate as far as facts are concerned at this stage.

When the child recalls something worth discussing, child and therapist may decide to spend half or even the whole of the next session recapping that matter. Unless the child wants to talk about an unhappy event first, it is best, and easier, to recap on happy occasions. Allow the unhappy ones to emerge if and when the child raises these herself. This is not **disclosure work**.

We ask the children to see if they can recall what they were wearing, what the weather was like, how they felt. Can they recall any special tastes or smells associated with that happy day? Can they remember any music or any other sounds that went along with their experience? We get them to describe sounds, smells, colours, voices, and sometimes to draw pictures of the event. It is important to share not only the events but also the feelings which accompanied those events, and may still accompany the remembering and the visualizing of the events.

The sharing of events and feelings may not be the main objective of the exercise nor the chief therapeutic effect, but with many children, when they are ready for sharing, it is valuable. We can so easily overlook the fact that in a family (or in a communal setting) people who have been brought up together, or have spent long periods of their lives together, enjoy remembering, recapitulating, going over incidents (often seen as amusing) which they shared together in some way. 'D'you remember the time when . . .' And parents will often tell their children what was done 'when you were only a toddler . . .' This sort of sharing has a binding ('I belong') effect on relationships.

Sharing important, and often emotionally loaded memories, when you have more or less become isolated from family and friends, can become the next best thing to sharing memories of those events with others who were around at the time. Especially when you felt, at the time, that you could share them with nobody safely. We will repeat the injunction, which applies to so much in this book, that in all the work we must go at the child's pace, and wait until the child is ready to share.

Usually Donna came up with recalls of incidents and times, and the therapist would invite her to say how she felt then, and how she felt 'now', i.e. at the time of the therapy, so that gradually a number of feelings emerged which included anger, guilt, and feeling 'dirty'. There were also the nice or happy feelings such as 'cosy', and one described as 'a long-time-ago feeling'.

The way in which the therapist can help a child (or an adult) by recapitulating on feelings, or dealing with present emotional experiences, will be discussed in later chapters. Clearly this is an area which is very central to counselling and psychotherapy. What we are attempting to do in this presentation is to show the reader the range of foci and techniques involved in care-therapy, even with one child.

Because she enjoyed it, and made such a valuable use of it, Donna was invited to turn some of her feelings into 'feeling paintings'. We shall be discussing the use of feeling paintings elsewhere in this book, but here in the following illustrations are four of Donna's paintings which seemed to help her enormously. It should be noted that although the primary function here was to help this child to come to terms with and understand more about her feelings, i.e. awareness experience, the actual use of the paint was also a sensory activity, with both hand-manipulation (touch when she used finger paints) and visual, colour sensation (sensory experience).

Feeling paintings are done only if the child wants to do one, and only when she is actually feeling what she is about to paint, or such feelings have been part of a past experience we have just been sharing with the child.

Figure 2.1 shows Donna's 'happy' feeling painting. She had also selected a piece of pop-music which she played as background to this happy feeling. She stood (and moved her body rhythmically) while she painted her feeling. Donna used bright, primary colours, and there is a general liveliness to the painting: it has a lot of movement in it. It gives the impression of a coloured fountain or even a firework display. One of the special times she remembered while doing this was her first school party. Notice the seven little whirls. The therapist asked her about these. 'They are surprises', said Donna. Then there followed a discussion about surprises Donna had experienced, and others she would like to experience.

The next feeling painting, shown in Figure 2.2, was meant to show Donna's 'scary' feelings – her fear. She seems to have blended two

Figure 2.1 *Donna's 'happy' feeling*

colours, red and blue. She was able to work through quite a lot of fear feelings (sometimes associated with past events) with this painting. It was never used by the therapist to 'interpret' what was going on in Donna's mind, but it was reviewed several times and was looked at when Donna had brought up some scary feeling. On those occasions she might be invited to see if she could find something in the painting that reminded her of what she was now feeling. In the middle of the picture there is a gap (we often find such gaps) but notice how jagged and tooth-like the edges of the gap are.

Even interpretation or 'understanding' by the child is not, in care-therapy, so important as the actual doing of the painting and the unconscious expression and release which the experience brings. And of course the recall (of which more later) and sharing of feelings are invaluable when used by the child in a therapeutic relationship with a skilled worker or with any other care-giving adult such as a foster- or adoptive parent.

The third feeling drawing shown here (Figure 2.3) is perhaps the most dramatic. This is not to be wondered at as while producing this Donna must have been recalling, if not re-experiencing, some of the terrible things done to her. And the feeling she selected was a 'dirty' feeling. In fact, she at first said she would do her 'horrid' feeling, and a few moments later, having started the painting, she described it as 'dirty'.

Figure 2.2 *Donna's 'scary' feeling*

Figure 2.3 *Donna's 'dirty' feeling*

It would be easy to ascribe many of the features, including the colours, to what we see as appropriate parts of Donna's life experience. But we could be far from the truth in our conclusions. There is a general messiness in the picture. The brown colour may or may not represent faeces. In fact the 'dirty' feeling was more symbolic than that, and reflected a feeling of having been contaminated. Not only that but, it emerged, this contamination was associated with feelings of guilt, of self-blame for her having been sexually abused. This is a fairly common reaction in cases of persistent sexual abuse. The child, having been taught to trust adults, begins to assume that there must be something in herself which is either nasty and needs punishing or is the cause for the attacks having taken place.

There were other self-condemnatory factors in Donna's case. Remember that her natural father had left home at about the time that she was 5 years old. Self-blame can develop in the emotionally abandoned child. It is a form of defence in fact, defending the ego from the fact that here is an unworthy parent. Children sometimes disown the unworthiness in the parent – not the parent. By being 'at fault' herself, by having something 'nasty', 'dirty', about her, her 'righteous', 'clean', daddy couldn't stand it – she drove him away. That was how Donna saw it! She would need eventually to come to understand that it was not her fault – insight!

One special feature was added to this painting with the aid of a felt pen. It is the eye. The eye, said Donna, is looking 'inside me'. But the eye, it transpired, was not, as one might have guessed, a part of herself, an inward-looking aspect of the self. The eye here is not symbolic in itself of the awareness experience. It is an aspect of her environment, particularly her past environment, an aspect which started as dangerous and external but has become internalized and dangerous. The picture as a whole is contributory towards her awareness experience.

The fourth example (see Figure 2.4) was described by Donna as her 'clean' feeling. This is the only feeling painting which makes a complete use of actual articles to symbolize a psychological state she is expressing. Perhaps it carries a heavier cognitive (thought-out) element. Perhaps it was more difficult to express otherwise. This line of washing is, nevertheless, elegant in its simplicity and directness. It would be easy to relate it directly to the soiling problem, and perhaps that element is there, but Donna had also been making use of psycho-imagery in order to lose her feelings of self-disgust and self-unworthiness. She described the 'clean' feeling as 'something nice and clean inside me'. As well as using bright colours, Donna has, probably unconsciously, introduced a feeling of warmth by her inclusion of the bright yellow sun with its rays.

clean feeling Donna

Figure 2.4 *Donna's 'clean' feeling*

Before describing a few more of the methods (and equipment) used in helping Donna to get in touch with and express her feelings as part of awareness experience, we want to point out that the basic theories relating to counselling and psychotherapy are assumed so far as professional readership is concerned. Therefore we are not discussing aspects of treatment such as **catharsis** and the purpose of expressing anger as a cathartic exercise, nor are we spending time on the basic psychodynamic concepts, such as ego, the unconscious and the preconscious, or explaining the phenomenon of transference. The assumption is that readers have this knowledge. Our aim is to show the way that the various elements and techniques, as well as caring and good-enough parenting, have been used to help children and adolescents.

Remember, this child, Donna, had not only experienced the traumatic upbringing described above, but had also experienced the traumatizing effect of what is termed disclosure, i.e. explaining events to the police, solicitors, etc., with all the court proceedings involved. She carried many conflicts, self-doubts, anger, as well as beliefs which were incongruent with reality. Several rapid-feedback instruments were used by the therapist, and some, by agreement, by other workers to encourage quick interchange of ideas. For example, there was the 'feelings thermometer'. This little toy was used often at the beginning and the end of a session. The feelings thermometer (Figure 2.5) consists

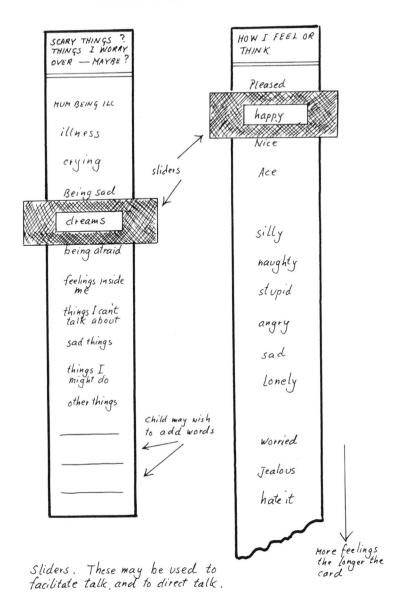

Figure 2.5 'Feelings thermometers'

of a slider, which can be moved up or down a card on which are written various 'how I feel now' words. Usually the negative feelings are at the bottom of the card and the positive feelings at the top, but they may be placed the other way round or in a haphazard way up and down the slide. If possible, the therapist and child decide together what words to use. This means they start with a blank card, or maybe a card with a few words on but spaces for many more.

So the card could have such words as 'miserable', 'lonely', 'sad', 'not bad', 'just OK', 'pleased' or 'happy', or it may contain a richer group such as 'shitty', 'sick', 'mad', 'cool', 'great' or 'brilliant' – obviously worked out according to the child's age and vocabulary. So Donna would be invited to put the slider on the word she felt was appropriate to 'how I feel now'. Because of the need to alert Donna, to not only her feelings but how she was coming across to others, the therapist would, if the occasion was appropriate, take the opportunity of remarking 'You look a bit down today' or 'You seem full of beans'. Of course, the feelings thermometer would sometimes be the start of some important disclosure, or an agreement to spend time on the particular feeling expressed.

Another feelings tool was the 'feelings pots'. This is a device which seems to be readily accepted by most children and young persons. It helps them to make statements not only about fixed attitudes but also fleeting and changing feelings about people. Donna used the feelings pots to reflect current (changeable) attitudes towards members of staff and other children, as well as her mother, her social worker, and her therapist.

All you need for feelings pots is a row of little pots or jars (even the plastic or cardboard picnic cups will do) which are labelled from 'negative' to 'positive' showing how the child feels (at this moment) about various people in his life. So the most negative pot is labelled 'I hate' then we go up the line with something like: 'do not like', 'not bad', 'I quite like', 'like them a lot', 'I love'. The therapist also provides a number of small pieces of paper just large enough to write names on. Either certain names may already be on the pieces of paper, with a few pieces left blank, or the therapist and child can decide together what names to write down. You have to be intuitive about this, and 'tuned in' to the child. The child is invited to put the names in the 'appropriate' pots thus saying how he feels about these people at this moment.

Don't be rigid about the use of this or any other direct-work equipment. If the situation calls for it you can hint that people who are no longer in the child's life may be included – feelings remain. Pets and other animals may be included. We can think of one child who had only pets in the 'I love' pot. Parents and others came further down the line. The amount of discussion depends on many factors, including the readiness of the child. Do not force the pace. After use the pots can be left until the next session, or one several sessions away, and the child then invited to see if he wants to keep the names in the same pots. They will often be moved about.

These changeable attitudes and feelings are important. For the child whose feelings have been entangled with conflict, guilt and anger, the use of equipment like feelings pots and feeling paintings is in line with regular practice by various schools of psychotherapy. If we take only two quotations, this will be evident:

> The existential counsellor will generally have to initiate the client into the practice of self-observation. By paying attention to all the fleeting feelings and opinions without attempting to make them fit into a causal explanation the client will gradually discover herself as the source of this complex inner world. (Deurzen-Smith, 1988)

Violet Oaklander, a Gestalt therapist, writes:

> Some children are not familiar with what feelings are. This seems like a strange statement, for children certainly feel. But I find that children have limited ability to communicate their feelings. They also tend to see things as black-and-white. I find that it is very helpful to give children experience with the vast variety of feelings and their nuances. There are games and exercises, too, that help children contact their own feelings. (Oaklander, 1978)

Donna was helped by the daily routine of the establishment. Much of this routine, however, was planned though it may have appeared as casual. It is therapeutically important, for example, for children to be able to contribute as well as being cared for. No-one really feels happy just sitting in a corner and 'being loved'. So doing something for someone, making a cake for example, and helping – are important functions. But it was equally important to find out how Donna felt about helping, and how she thought other people felt when she had made a contribution.

Donna's anger feelings were helped by physical outlets as well as by discussion. She used the 'anger pillow'. She also responded to the use of 'anger ping-pong (table-tennis) balls'. After a talk session in which anger feelings had emerged, one of the workers would play the game of hurling ping-pong balls at Donna, who of course expended a lot of energy hurling them back at the worker!

Most of what we have outlined so far in connection with the direct work with Donna has been directed at focus number 1 in the list given above, i.e. helping her to become more aware of certain basic feelings or emotions. We shall now describe some of the sensory work undertaken with this child, as in focus number 2 of our list.

Sensory Work with Donna

Very often the sensory material in the clinical setting is what we might call 'pure', in that it has been designed just for the purpose of stimulating body sensations, but there are other activities such as foot-painting (yes, painting with your feet!) which also have an end-product, in this case the painting or picture that can be put up on the wall. And then there's something else which may go along with foot-painting, and that is foot washing. You see it is a gloriously messy game, trying to paint with your feet, and so, at the end of slithering about on the large board or thick (4×4 ft or 122×122 cm) paper pinned to insulation board, Donna was invited to sit down on a chair placed nearby and the worker (therapist or residential staff member) washed, dried and powdered her feet – more body sensations together with a nurturing effect!

We shall not labour this example by providing details of how to do foot-painting and what to use. Clearly the ready-mixed, squeezy-bottle paints are best, and you need flat, open dishes for the child to dip her feet into. In passing, here is a quote from Petruska Clarkson:

> The Gestalt approach to counselling can embrace a wide variety of diverse but specific techniques within an holistic frame of reference which integrates mind and body, action and intro-spection. Techniques are not prescribed but Gestalt practitioners are encouraged to invent appropriate 'experiments' which invite people into heightened experience of the body–mind self, authentic encounters with meaningful others, and an impact relationship with the environment. The richness of technique in Gestalt is constrained only by the personal limitations of imagination, intellect or responsiveness of individual counsellors or clients. (Clarkson, 1989)

Donna also experienced a 'taste tray', a useful sensory third object which is discussed in greater detail elsewhere in this book. Essentially the child and therapist, when using the taste tray, partake of small tastes of various edible materials. Some of these may be exotic and some are common foods but tasted in an unusual condition (such as small pieces of raw potato or hot root ginger). We even use raw fresh peas. Children these days seldom open pea-pods and taste the sweet taste of raw peas. We wouldn't be surprised if some readers were already getting a mental picture of some place, sometime when, as children, they did just that!

Then of course there are the touchy feely things such as pottery clay. We are not talking of modelling materials like Plasticine, which we do also use – but that beautiful, soft, clean potter's clay – the sort of stuff readers will have seen, or used, on the potter's wheel. Donna often decided to use the clay once she had been introduced to it. But as well as her experiencing something in her fingers, something else happened while she was engaged in this, to her, enjoyable occupation. What happened was what we have witnessed many times. While in a sort of trance involvement with the clay, Donna would talk! Children find it is much easier to talk when they are engaged in some absorbing activity of this sort (not during the absorbing activity of computer games). This release of conversation may be experienced while a child is painting, cutting out, crayoning, and so forth. It is a sort of indirect conversation which goes on while another part of the mind is engaged in the sensory experience.

Donna was able to benefit from many other sensory experiences, including music (using various percussion instruments), dance and massage, involving the use of aromatic oils as part of the sensory experiences of touch and smell.

It is important not to lose sight of the fact that this use of concentrated sensory experience relates to the basic theses of care-therapy, attachment and nurture, and although not yet fully understood we can hypothesize and work on the assumption that sensory experiences play a vital role in the early days, weeks and months of a child's life, both physical and psychological. Winnicott has written on this point:

> The mother allows the baby's face to touch the breast. At the beginning babies do not know about breasts being part of mother. If the face touches the breast they do not know at the beginning whether the nice feeling comes in the breast or in the face. In fact babies play with their cheeks, and scratch them, just as if they were breasts, and there is plenty of reason why mothers allow for all the contact that a baby wants. No doubt a baby's sensations in these respects are very acute, and if they are acute we can be sure they are important. (Winnicott, 1964, p. 46)

Although we have not provided details here, Donna's early mothering nurture left a lot to be desired. She may have missed out on the pleasurable aspects of sensory development. This is why she was provided with what in many ways represents a regressive experience, but only in the sense that the therapist and residential social workers were providing the missed-out nurturing sensory experiences.

Clarification, Awareness Experience

We shall now deal briefly with some of the methods and techniques provided in order to help Donna clarify events, and the feelings which went along with those events or developed out of them. This is all part of what we have termed awareness experience and would fall under focus number 3 of our list.

We must remember that Donna was a confused child in terms of psychological and social conflict. Most children who have had similar childhood experiences (of long duration) and particularly those who land up 'in care' suffer in this way. There was confusion concerning affection. Donna had experienced affection from a particular male figure, her natural father, but her trust in him had been betrayed when he 'disappeared'. He had of course been sent to prison. She had responded to what looked and felt like affection from some of her abusers. So, in her mind, affection could be something connected with behaving sexually? Then again, she both wanted male affection (the missing, lost, fatherly love) and yet was now rejecting anyone, male or female, who seemed to be getting emotionally close. She had already been hurt, as she expressed it, by affection. Her reactions were of course not thought out but were driven by unconscious as well as conscious factors, and sometimes by unexplainable repulsion.

Like many children in care, Donna had unverbalized questions which we, though not she, could précis thus:

Who am I?

Who do I belong with?

What is to happen to me?

Her feelings towards her mother were ambivalent, yet she clung to the precept that mum must be right in all respects. One aspect of awareness experience which had to develop was Donna's need to reach her own understanding of her mother's weaknesses. Often, the development of this insight is only gradual and the child has to be helped to understand reality without at the same time experiencing purely destructive processes in relation to parents.

Many months passed before we began to feel that Donna was really making psychological improvement which was reflected in her general demeanour and moods, as well as in what she was able to report.

'Loving Water'

We shall discuss the use of water-play and the use of water in a symbolic way in later chapters. However, for some years now those concerned with children who have experienced emotionally disrupted childhoods have used water in a special manner to symbolize the flow of love from one individual to another. Furthermore, they have sometimes coloured (tainted) the water so that it became symbolic of a damaging form of 'love' which perhaps was not real love at all. At one stage in the long healing process, Donna found that she could use the 'loving-water' symbolism.

None of these third objects should be used lightly, carelessly, or without careful thought before introducing it to the child as a medium which he may be able to use. Children and older people will use whatever media they find helpful and comfortable (as well as comforting) at an appropriate time.

In Donna's case a very sensitive worker made the loving water available when it became clear that the child wanted to share some of her feelings concerning the series of sexual (and emotional) abuse experiences in her life. Quite often, we have found, abused children are only 'ready' to talk, i.e. it has become a need, when they have really become attached to care-givers (adopters or long-term foster-parents) and they then tentatively open a conversation by some comment. Usually, sometimes under guidance, care-givers are then the best people to help the child in resolving the emotional conflicts which emerge.

In our work with adults, however, we have met people who found it 'impossible' to tell anyone about their feelings and even more so about their beliefs. (One young woman explained how she had spent her later childhood and adolescence with the terrifying belief that her own thoughts had caused her mother to die.) Because of these possibilities it is sometimes advisable to provide openings for the child to share thoughts, fears, etc. It is of course essential that the skilled help we are talking about should then be available. It is availability at the right time which is important, not that, to use modern jargon, we have a product so we must give it to the child.

This use of loving water in Donna's case was spread across many months and it would take a whole chapter to give the counselling and therapeutic details involving the insight which the child gained and the conflicts which were resolved. What we shall do here is to describe a few ways in which water may be used in counselling.

Clear water passed from one container to another may be likened to love passing from one person to another. In fact the water can be made to flow back and forth from the two containers to show how love does 'flow' from parent to child, child to parent.

One container, the one representing 'dad' in Donna's case, may be moved away – 'dad went'. One, or more in some cases, may have coloured or even discoloured water in them to represent what may have been felt to be love, but which was in fact contaminated. When this impure water is poured bit by bit into the container representing the child, it discolours the water in his or her container.

Many children, not only the sexually abused but also those who feel they have been abandoned or rejected by people when foster-home after foster-home has broken down ('disrupted') start to reject affection. To demonstrate this in a symbolic way, the worker using the loving water method will cover the appropriate container opening with a Cellophane type of paper such as clingfilm. Then, even when pure water – real love – is poured onto the container, it bounces off! When a child has become aware of such a rejecting state, we often talk about him having put on the 'suffering skin', which can be taken off again.

All these methods were shown to Donna and used by her from time to time. Nothing was ever done in a rush. It became part of the healing process. Then the time was reached when Donna began to accept affection from staff and school-friends. That was the time when she was told that perhaps it would show what she was feeling if she cut a small hole in the clingfilm, which of course let the love in. It also let the 'dirty water' out. (The feelings of general anger were dissipating.)

Who Holds the Power?

With an older child, who might be emotionally and intellectually much younger than Donna, and who has left home, there is the additional confusion and anxiety about actual distribution of power in terms of the care-givers. It is important for the child to be able to understand where the power resides and why it resides where it does, and why certain people outside the family are exercising power. (They may of course see their function much more in terms of caring and helping.) We shall give an example of another instrument which helped Donna from time to time. It was used at various points because it could help her to understand not only how things were, and had been, but how they might be in the future.

This device is shown at Figure 2.6, and came to us through a similar one first described by Vera Fahlberg. It consists of a board divided into three columns with appropriate headings above each column such as Natural Parents (or Mum and Dad), Local Authority (or Social Workers) and Foster Parents. Along with the board go a collection of card discs which will be used to name aspects of the child's personal characteristics, e.g. boy or girl, and the various responsibilities and functions of the care-givers, legal guardians, etc.

The worker begins by showing the child that natural characteristics, such as eye colour, were given by his parents, so the disc for 'blue eyes' would go under that heading, and of course would be one of the things which could never be shifted to another column. It can be helpful for the child to know that he has certain likeable characteristics which were 'given' by his parents for all time.

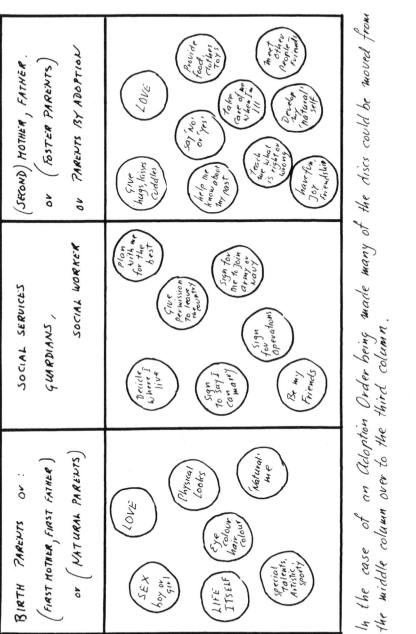

Figure 2.6 A moveable-assets board used by Donna. © Regrave 1994

The reader will see that certain factors can move about as situations change. The child may be helped to see that some factors which at one time were under one column are now under another because responsibility (or availability) or power has shifted. Some factors may appear under more than one column. Because a foster-parent gives love, for example, it does not mean that a natural parent has stopped loving, but of course this is where the actual talking, sharing, counselling therapy comes in. It is not so much the device, but the thoughts, questions, memories, protests, etc. that it produces, and the way these are handled by child and therapist which really produce results. Remember that Donna was gradually reaching her own understanding about her mother, about her mother's 'good' parenting bits and her 'poor' parenting bits – clarification and awareness experience.

Infant Nurture Programmes

In our list on page 24 of the different foci of treatment the reader will note that number 4 refers to the Infant Nurture Programme. A brief explanation is required here with further expansion later. Very often, and certainly in Donna's case, the quality of the parenting, including early parenting, has been poor and in varying degrees damaging to the child's psychosocial development. Appendix 1 gives the extent of our definition of nurture. It has already been mentioned in Chapter 1 that there appears to be a causative correlation between the quality of infant nurture and the quality and degree of parent–child attachment.

While it is possible and permissible in the more clinical one-to-one setting of child and therapist for actual regressive behaviour to occur, it is not always so practical a form of treatment in a residential setting. Nevertheless, many of the excluded care-giving 'luxuries', i.e. excluded in infancy and in the child's experience of care so far, can be included in a deliberate way in children's home, foster-home or the child's own home, provided that staff or parents are co-operative, and have the time. In any centre calling itself a therapeutic centre, time, of course, should be available. This affects the staff/child ratio.

The term infant nurture programme refers not only to the treatment of infants. We have been involved with Infant Nurture Programmes for 16- and 17-year-olds. The use of the word 'infant' implies that in subtle ways it is possible to allow the child or young person to experience to some extent some of the missed-out sensory experiences he should have enjoyed during his infancy. For example, the creation of 'cosy' and 'safe' situations and experiences, such as providing a hot-water bottle to go to bed with, even when the weather is not all that cold, or, depending on age and personality, having either a cosy chat or a story while in bed and getting ready to lie down, or having an extra long time in a warm bath with either perfumed water, bubble-bath, soap or even bath 'toys'.

With older children it is just as possible to provide Infant Nurture Programmes where they reside, or even to take them out to some eating-place for favourite foods. And with younger children it is easy to forget that many of them have missed out on *appropriate* touch. They have never been carried up to bed on dad's or anyone else's shoulders, nor have they sat on laps.

Fortunately, in Donna's case, there was an excellent, interested and keen staff in the children's centre. Her programme included:

(a) Bedtime story, at 13-plus years old, at her request.
(b) A furry animal to cuddle in bed.
(c) Having bath-towels and pyjamas warmed.
(d) Occasionally having her shoulders massaged while watching TV with several other children.
(e) Having her hair styled.
(f) Once a week having her 'favourite' meal.
(g) Monitoring her soiling and being helped to get cleaned-up when accidents occur.

Clearly, if children and young persons are to be helped by their environment and care, the main effect must be felt within the milieu of their daily living. The reader will note that the Infant Nurture Programmes become part of the child's sensory-work experience and part of her or his secure-environment experience.

Infant Nurture Programmes stand out as part of an overall programme, part of a systematic approach, which we have called care-therapy and which involves, therefore, a team approach.

The Team Involvement
This brings me to number 6 on the list of foci, namely team-work, and here the finest ideals of team-work are essential for care and therapy, including co-operative working to a planned programme of help, good communication between the principal members involved, and monitoring of the effect the treatment is having. I would go so far as to say that most clinical work, including direct work, will be ineffective if the child is receiving contrary and even contradictory messages and experiences outside the clinical setting. We are not likely to see much progress in the child if, at the same time as a therapist is attempting to provide opportunities for the child to deal with past rejection, another

form of rejection is being practised by the principal care-givers. We have had children of 6 or 8 years old who were clearly indicating a need for close affection and some regressive experience, such as an Infant Nurture Programme. We have then discovered that they had been placed for fostering or adoption with a substitute parent who felt that he or she could not tolerate an emotional or even physical closeness to the child. There have been other instances where a residential worker was being encouraged to undertake a care-therapy programme, including direct work, with a child but where the person in charge of the establishment felt such programmes to be a waste of time and contrary to the discipline or routine of the place. Often, sad to say, care-therapy is purported to be an aim, but in fact the staff have little time available. This results in failure and in a bad name for the therapeutic approach.

Fortunately, in Donna's case, the woman in charge of the centre was enthusiastic and committed to a team approach. One of her own agreed roles was to deal with what we called the establishing of age-appropriate sexual behaviour. Whereas others may have to allow a very uninhibited behaviour in Donna and may be using comparatively exotic techniques such as sand therapy (see Chapter 4), it was also necessary to give Donna the ordinary training and advice a good-enough parent would give to an adolescent. As Donna began to change in terms of self-esteem, she also began to flirt with young men, and older ones, whom she met outside, on the bus for example. There was also a bit of open masturbation that had to be dealt with. A good care-therapy programme includes a down-to-earth, social development aspect as well as techniques which some people might like to term trendy. The head of the residential centre was empathetic, had a strong sense of humour, but also knew just how to help this young woman to grow up.

Donna's school was also involved as part of the team approach. What goes on in the school setting is not something extraneous. The relationships developed between the child and her peers, and between child and teachers, is of fundamental importance. It is also vital that the child's teacher and the headteacher should be involved in case conferences and other decision-making meetings. Of course it is much harder and more time-consuming to enlist the help of a team of professionals and the child's parents and relatives (where appropriate), and one may be faced, as in the case of field or residential workers, with teachers who maintain that their only purpose is to teach a class of children, and who have no time for 'cranky' ideas concerning individual psychology. (Some Ministers of Education may hold similar views.) Many teachers, however, including those who worked with Donna, take a broader view, as do education therapists Muriel Barrett and Jane Trevitt:

We are left with the impression that many of the children referred to us feel lost. Is this because they do not truly understand who they are, or what their role in the family or surrogate family should be? This seems to apply particularly to children who are members of more than one family. When they become members of a much larger and even more complex system, a school, are their feelings of being lost, unattached as it were to any one person, likely to be even more painful to manage? (Barrett and Trevitt, 1991)

'Befrienders' (focus no. 5 on our list)

Another part of the team in Donna's case was a middle-aged couple, Don and Mary Hughes, who acted as 'befrienders'. Befrienders are people, usually but not exclusively married couples, who, as the term implies, befriend a child who is in residential care. They will visit the child at the centre, have the child out on occasions, and have overnight stays. They will give the child an opportunity to experience a different family life than he or she has experienced in the so-called natural family. But from the start the child and the befrienders understand that this is a friendship. There is no intention of befrienders becoming foster- or adoptive parents. We cannot pretend this never happens, and we shall not go into the deeper pros and cons here, except to say that in Donna's case it worked well.

Bridging

We now come to number 7 in the list of foci, namely 'bridging'. Bridging, in summary, is preparing the child to move into a new family or other placement, and helping him during the settling-in phase. Clearly team-work is required here in a big way. The care-givers in the prospective placement, the field and residential social workers, the schools involved – often a transfer to a new school cannot be avoided except at some greater cost, for example the loss of the 'only' foster-home likely to meet the requirements – the child's parents, the therapist, and the child himself all have to participate. And we have not yet mentioned foster-family selection panels and the like.

However, at this point we shall deal in detail only with the kind of work that was undertaken by Donna, her therapist and others involved in the direct-work programme, e.g. one of the residential workers.

Bridging is very important. It must not be seen as a tail-end optional extra in care-therapy. Bridging starts from the time the team feel that the child is ready to start actual planning for the kind of placement believed to be best. Discussions about the various forms of care and placements may have begun informally much earlier. Perhaps the true bridging exercise should be seen to start once the placement has been found. It must be remembered that at this stage both parties, child and, for example, foster-parents, are open to change their minds after the initial introductions, so there is an early 'introductory' period. During bridging the people involved in the direct-work programme will use various techniques aimed at helping the child to gain a clearer idea of what is happening and the consequences, expectations, gains and losses, time span, changes, and many other details of such a move. Remember, a child could make a move like this 'blind', having all sorts of fantasy notions in her head. Remember also that any move is likely to be accompanied by polarized feelings of relief and anxiety. Below are described a few of the instruments and techniques used to help Donna's move, but her planned move into a foster-home took into account many aspects, including the fact that her mother was again residing with a known sex offender.

Even before a firm idea of fostering had generated itself within the team, the therapist began to use 'wall building'. This 'game' has been around for some years now (Redgrave, 1987) and many people have used it. It is basically a way of building up an ongoing discussion concerning many aspects of life which we know from experience either need to be developed or handled well in the process of attachment formation and social adaptation involved in the placement of children and young persons. Figure 2.7 will give the reader an idea. It will be seen that various subjects for discussion, i.e. for thinking about, reflecting upon, etc., are named in the bricks. At first the 'wall' can start with dotted-in rectangles to show where the wall will be. The child and worker can make suggestions regarding subjects. As subjects are dealt with, a portion of the rectangle is shaded or coloured in, never more than a quarter at a session. Wall building and other instruments to help in bridging will be discussed again in later chapters:

Figure 2.8 introduces the reader to another of Donna's aids. This is called the 'loving steps'. We first came across the idea in a short article by Pat Curtis. (Curtis, 1983). The loving steps should be started before a child moves into her placement but will then go on being used, as should many bridging materials, during the first six months to a year of the child's placement. The message the child receives through the use of the loving steps is that the way she feels about her home or substitute home will change from time to time, especially during those months of settling in.

Sensitive carers are able to use this third object with the child, but one needs to be careful and to allow the child to say how she really

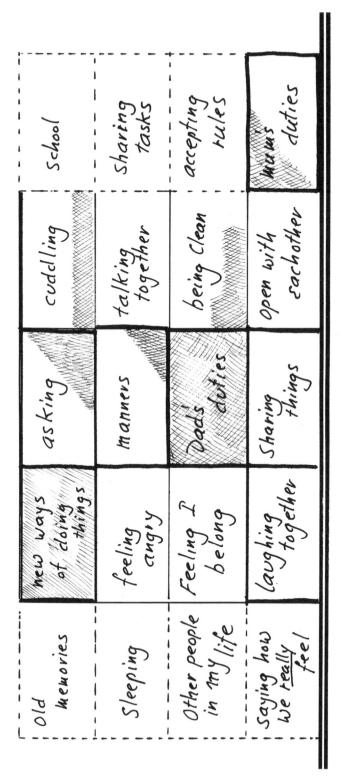

Figure 2.7 *An example of 'wall building'.* © Redgrave 1994

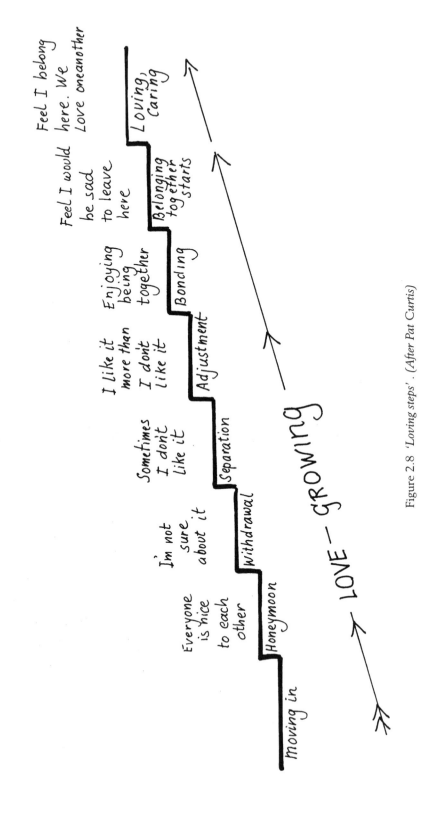

Figure 2.8 'Loving steps' . (After Pat Curtis)

does feel. Some sensitive carers have used it to give the child 'permission' to be lower down the steps.

We shall discuss the use of loving steps again later in this book, but it will help to point out that the child should be made aware that she may, probably will, feel that she is sometimes moving upwards and sometimes downwards on the steps. One week she may feel that she is on the 'adjustment' step (or this may be the agreed step as a result of discussion) but then a week later feel that she is on the 'separation' step. Gradually, however, as was the case with Donna, if all goes well she will move towards the top step 'Feel I belong here. We love one another.'

Clearly, as far as the child is concerned, there may be a high degree of anxiety associated with any move. After all, with the experiences they have often had, trust may be understandably difficult to place. 'How do I know that they will let me see my mother?' 'I shan't be able to see Aunty Julie if I leave this centre!' 'I shall feel isolated', and so forth. Because of this we used a 'contact indicator' to help Donna. This is shown in Figure 2.9. (See Appendix 2: Checklist on Preparation for Placement.)

There are many ways of designing contact indicators and others will be mentioned later. Often, as with Donna and most older children, the child constructs the actual details of the indicator, or at least expresses wishes which are then discussed and either included or dealt with in some way. Donna's indicator, made to help her cope with all those anxieties spelt out above, was simply a set of large discs indicating places of residence, some smaller discs to indicate people and animals, etc., and some contact bars (made out of cardboard) which could join up the various people and placed with which Donna wished to keep in contact. The pattern shown was not the only one devised by Donna using this simple equipment – others had gone before. Remember that we are not taking readers through all the detailed discussion with the child, and these instruments are to be used mainly with discussion, when pros and cons, possibilities and impossibilities, good ideas and bad all go into the 'melting-pot' between child and worker.

We have now, in giving this outline of work with Donna, touched upon bridging, team-work, Infant Nurture Programmes, awareness experience and sensory experience, and we have shown how all these approaches are part of the systematic approach called care-therapy. Donna moved into her long-term foster-home a month after her fourteenth birthday. From there the work went on with her. She was able to keep the same field social worker and therapist and to maintain contact with the children's centre and the staff and other children

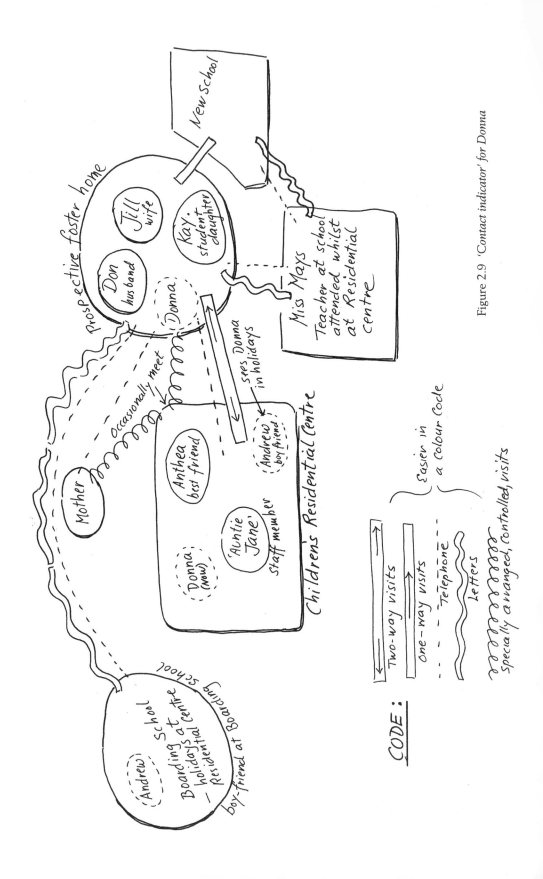

New School

Prospective foster home

Jill wife

Don husband

Kay. student daughter

Donna

Miss Mays
Teacher at school attended whilst at Residential centre

Occasionally meet

sees Donna in holidays

Mother

Anthea best friend

Andrew boy friend

'Auntie Jane' staff member

Donna (now)

Childrens Residential Centre

'Andrew' School
Boarding at holidays at centre — Residential centre

boy-friend at Boarding School

CODE :

Two-way visits

one-way visits

Telephone

Letters

Easier in a colour code

Specially arranged, controlled, visits

Figure 2.9 'Contact indicator' for Donna

there. Two years on she is doing well at school and has settled in well with the family. She sees her mother periodically. We do not pretend that each and every child given similar help will respond as well as Donna did. To begin with, so much will depend upon the calibre of the foster-parents, but we do maintain that the systematic approach outlined so far in this book does help children and young persons to overcome past shortcomings in their environment, and to develop social and psychological stability.

Further Observations on the System

It will be helpful to close this chapter with some comments by theorists whose 'schools' range from the psychoanalytic, through psychosynthesis to the behavioural therapists. Again, in this book we are focusing on the clinical setting and the direct-work aspects of the system outlined above. It is interesting to note, therefore, an observation by Karl Abraham, who as early as 1924 said 'The future of child psychoanalysis lies in play techniques'.

Juliet Mitchell, writing about Melanie Klein says:

Melanie Klein claimed that the play technique, as a technique for gaining access to the unconscious, was the complete equivalent of free association. She writes ' . . . the brick, the little figure, the car, not only represents things which interest the child in themselves, but in his play with them they always have a variety of symbolical meanings as well which are bound up with his phantasies, wishes, and experiences . . . But we have to consider each child's use of symbols in connection with his particular emotions and anxieties and in relation to the whole situation which is presented in the analysis . . .' (Mitchell, 1986)

The elaboration given so far in these chapters, which has emphasized the systematic nature of care-therapy, is echoed in psychosynthesis counselling, and, in different language, supports what has been said above concerning sensory and awareness experience as well as other principles and techniques that we have discussed. Diana Whitmore writes:

The psychosynthesis counsellor's strategy for working through tenacious and dysfunctional patterns involved addressing them on three complementary levels: experience, understanding and transformation. The *somatic* and *affective* aspects of a problem must be experienced; mental understanding is essential as well as healing in a positive direction, which includes a developmental step forward being taken by the client . . . In addition to active

> dialogue, the counsellor will encourage the client to enter into the *physical* and *emotional* experience of her difficulties. (Whitmore, 1991, p. 75, my emphasis)

As the general theme of this book is developed, various references will be given which are supportive of it. We shall provide, at this point, one example of many which relate to the effect of environment and nurture upon the development of the child. This refers to an experiment undertaken in an 'orphanage' which was understaffed and in which babies did not therefore receive good-enough nurturing. As part of the experiment, however, some of the children were provided with an enriched nurturing experience over a period of 6 weeks, and a comparison was made between these and their peers, who did not get the enriched nurturing. Interested readers will be able to check on the methodology, etc., but we give below a quotation from the summary of a paper by Yahya Hakimi-Manesh *et al.*:

> The purpose of the present investigation was (a) to examine the effects of extra interaction on the psychomotor and mental development of Iranian orphanage children, and (b) to discover the effects of the interaction following a six-month interval. . . . A group of orphanage-reared children received extra interaction in 5-minute daily sessions for 6 weeks. Their mental and psychomotor development (Bayley Scales) were compared to a matched group of infants who were subject to routines at the institution during the same period. Between-group comparisons revealed improved scores for the experimental group. Within-group comparisons indicated that the experimental group had a greater rate of improvement from pre- to post-test than the control group. The differences were present to some extent after a six-month follow up. (Hakimi-Manesh *et al.*, 1984)

Finally, a quotation reflecting the value of secure and supportive personal relationships. Dr Mark Katz, from whom we quote, is a supervising psychologist at the San Diego Center for Children. He writes:

> Intimate relationships can go a long way in bolstering how we view ourselves and the way we are viewed by others. For individuals who have been exposed to traumatizing conditions, the nature of their social ties and their social network can be critical to recovery . . . One overcomes trauma when current attachments with safety figures outweigh the terror of the past. (Katz, 1997)

As of course they finally did for Donna.

The following chapter takes the study of direct work, i.e. the use of materials, objects and activities in a counselling or care situation, further, and concentrates on those third objects which are used mainly to help children and young people to gain insight (awareness experience) into their own lives, feelings, and reasons for change, if such becomes necessary. This is perhaps, with Chapters 4 and 5, the heart of the book. These third objects may be used by persons of different background/training and from a variety of groups which have to do with childcare in many settings.

CHAPTER 3

Insight work: 'ice-breakers', flowcharts, life-story books and symbolism

'Many times, quite unconsciously, we cut off a child's feelings because they are so painful to us.'
Fraiberg, S., 1959

Figures 3.1 and 3.2 are expressive pieces of art work, one by an artistically gifted 17-year-old young woman (Dionne) and the other by a 6-year-old child (Naomi). Both these pieces of work helped the young clients to deal with certain emotional experiences and to clarify some existential position. Both examples were used psychologically in a way which we perhaps do not yet know enough about, as part of a healing process and part of an awareness process.

Dionne, who drew the dangerous-looking jaws about to crush the tender flower, was helped enormously by what amounted to a form of art-therapy. The flower, she explained, is herself; the jaws stand for her life events and show how desperately vulnerable she is feeling. Talking about the drawing and the feeling helped towards an awareness of some deeper, previously only half-conscious, impulses and longings.

Naomi, who painted the love-hearts and other symbols concerning her feelings towards her recently deceased mother, perhaps had no special gift as an artist. Our illustration, as you see, shows her work half-obliterated by thick black paint. In fact we had to construct our illustration from two of Naomi's paintings because, several times after doing the lovely symbolic work, she had demanded 'black paint' and proceeded to cover the whole of her work. This is not the place to enlarge on the symbolism and meaning in Naomi's actions, but it was something she needed to do on several occasions. Again, we are concerned with a process of healing and a process involving an

A wild feeling

By Dionne

Figure 3.1 *Dionne's 'wild' feeling*

Figure 3.2 *Naomi's painting*

awareness, but 'awareness' here may not mean quite the same thing as conscious understanding.

I have introduced these illustrations as further examples of the use of third objects in work concerned with awareness experience. Readers will recall the use of these third objects in connection with the therapy offered to Donna in Chapter 2 and the outline of awareness and sensory experience given in Chapter 1.

Before discussing further the various examples given in this chapter, it may be helpful for readers to look again at the various foci that we mentioned in Chapter 2 (p. 24). In this chapter we are concerned with foci numbers 1 and 3. Focus 1 emphasizes feelings, ideas and beliefs held by the child. Focus 3 is concerned with clarifying the child's life events, personal history and motivational aspects.

Although we shall be discussing some of the symbolism as we describe the various third objects, it will be as well to remind readers of the importance of symbolism. In some third objects the child will be the agent of the symbolism, that is to say, he will select and use objects which are symbolic for himself. This will be emphasized in sand-tray work (see Chapter 4). In other third objects the therapist may devise a road or roads symbolizing the child's journey through life so far. What cannot be overemphasized is the need for the therapist to be able and willing to use imagination in order to construct new third objects which will suit particular children and will apply in particular circumstances.

There are some activities, for example some self-invented games which certain children indulge in, often using imagination, which appear to fulfil a self-healing role. Sand-tray work is an example. But apart from the deeper self-healing or insight-promoting characteristics, apart even from their use as structured means of communicating, there appears to be a very basic function served by third objects. When children are engaged in an activity, be it walking or painting, or even making mud pies, conversation comes more easily. The sit-behind-the-desk, eye-ball to eye-ball question and answer technique often produces only 'yes', 'no', or perhaps whatever the child feels you want to hear. When children are engaged in an activity they will often pop a question to the therapist, or make some surprising comment. They will also meditate more.

Starting Treatment with a Child You Have Never Met

Residential workers and foster-parents may often be in an advantageous situation in that children and young persons will be sharing their day-to-day life events and may find it easier to talk, i.e. they are not so shy on the first treatment session. On the other hand the very fact of being part of a 'family' may inhibit some forms of therapy. Readers will therefore find that some of the third objects discussed below will be less suitable in their particular situation. But be careful here, because even some of the 'ice-breakers' mentioned below have been found useful by residential workers as they appear to signal the start of something special.

As 'outside' therapists we do use certain ice-breakers in our work. For example, we always write a letter to a child who is going to attend his first session. We do this even for quite young children who cannot read: we ask the parent or other carer to read our letter to those children. These letters are handwritten (in our best handwriting, sometimes not 'joined up' letters) and written with care so that literate children can read the letter. Such letters may be quite personal, for example they may say that 'Mrs Redgrave and I are looking forward to meeting you'.

Sometimes we described ourselves, our looks, and drew a 'funny' picture of ourselves. Obviously this depends on the age, etc. of the child; we have always had positive responses from this procedure. Some children we work with have *never* had a personal letter arrive by post – and of course you can now use e-mail or send a fax!

Another Ice-breaker
Figure 3.3 shows a few moves of a very straightforward little game which can stop after a few minutes and therefore not take up much time. We are crediting readers with the skill and sensitivity to judge which children will find this relaxing, i.e. anxiety-reducing, and quickly enter into the game. Playing a game when the child has been thinking of some previous experience, having been 'asked a lot of questions', is quite relaxing.

The little game contains a pack of stiff cards with coloured squares. The cards vary in their colours and in the 'paths' which the coloured squares make up. By placing cards alongside each other a player is able to make some very long paths. So we soon find that most children happily start to join up their cards. Some children start to tell us of a better move which could be made.

However, we have now added an extra little pack of four or five 'message cards', which we bring out after we have made several moves with the 'real' cards. We want the child who has never met us before to know just a few facts, and we find this a helpful way of impressing him. Before his next move we point out the special cards and tell him that each one contains a message, and will he take one before taking the next proper card.

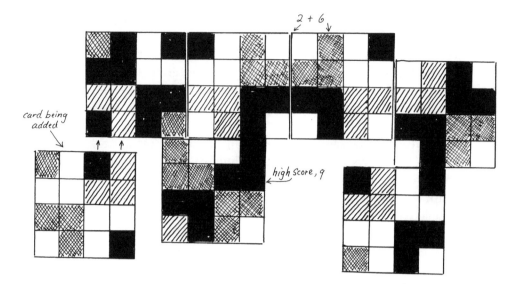

Figure 3.3 *The game of 'Continuo' (Hiron Games Ltd, London)*

He picks up one of the special cards and may find the message, 'I shall always be truthful with you'. We then briefly explain that we won't hide things just to make him happy; we shall be honest in saying what we really feel. And of course we hope he will feel able to say what he really feels. The next special card may say, 'What we talk about will be confidential . . . I will explain this word'. We then discuss briefly what this implies. The other cards may read, 'This is what I know about you so far', and 'Don't forget, you can ask me questions too'.

By the way, we have found it had to acquire further sets of the game (Continuo). It is, however, possible to find similar simple games or even play some rounds of 'noughts and crosses' or 'boxes' – they all break the ice!

Reaching Out to the Reluctant Child

We have often heard from parents and from clinics, accounts concerning older children who have never received any help because they flatly refused to visit a clinic or to meet a therapist, and that was the end of help offered to the child.

Of course, a busy clinic or hospital service would find it difficult if not out of place to run a service which in many ways began to take on the functions of a welfare service. Our contention, however, is that with highly trained and positively child-orientated social workers (field and residential) the team approach is appropriate, and the kind of skilled outreach therapy described below is possible as part of the care-therapy approach provided by a heterogeneous group of workers.

Robin was a 12-year-old boy who was 'causing havoc' in the family and was referred by social services for therapy. However, he failed to turn up, or even get out of bed, on the occasion of his first appointment. As a result of a domiciliary visit, the worker was able to report:

CASE STUDY – **ROBIN**

I had already obtained a lot of general information about Robin including the fact that he was 'football mad'. Elsewhere I have said that it is helpful, in all therapy, if the interests of the client (sports, hobbies, artistic gifts, etc.) can be utilised within the treatment plan. On this occasion, with Robin, I obtained a little board game – a football game. It had a set of rules, including something called the 'offside rule'. I called at Robin's house by appointment armed with my game plus some football journals, and was not surprised to learn that he was still in bed at 11 a.m. So I asked his dad to see if the lad would let me see him in bed as I needed his help in sorting out this football game and the 'offside rule' which, quite genuinely, I could not understand. I also explained that I would like dad or another adult to accompany me.

Having been given the O.K. I sat on the side of Robin's bed and conducted a one-sided conversation whilst he remained under the covers, completely under the covers including his head! As I described my inability to understand football rules, and as I described the board game, his head slowly emerged. Gradually he began talking, explaining, telling me what the rules meant. I left the game and the 'mags' with Robin and he said he'd come the following week to see me – and to beat me at the game!

This was the start of a successful programme of treatment. Later on the same lad conducted me and my wife on a walk round his favourite country park.

We would like readers to see something more in this approach than just a persuasive method. It is easy to forget that children (and adults) usually want to *contribute* something whether in therapy or in ordinary social life. We emphasize the need a child has for love and care, but children also need to feel that they can give, they can contribute. Robin clearly felt good about being able to 'give'. He began his experience of therapy, not with having something *done* to him, which he feared, but by being able to offer something.

A cautionary word is appropriate here. We have arrived at a stage in social work and counselling when workers need to be careful about possible allegations of abuse. In the example given above, care was taken on that point.

Nibblers and Squeezers

Sometimes, if we want to sit and chat with a child, we will have a small bowl of nibbly foods – popcorn for example – set between us as we sit looking out of a window or into a fire. This nibbling helps to relax the conversation and to make the setting less formal. Another idea is to hand out a piece of squeezy material, such as Plasticine (just a small piece about the size of a golf ball, but already softened by mild heat). Child and worker have a piece each so that each can squeeze and make shapes while talking. I see that some firms have 'cashed in' on this idea and are making squeezy, rubbery, plastic articles for de-stressing managers!

Emphasis on Insight (Awareness Experience)

In Chapter 6 we shall consider the use of particular third objects as they relate to the overall plan of treatment considered necessary for a specific child. For example, the child who has lacked a good-enough infant nurturing experience may at first be helped more by being given a lot of opportunities to explore sensory enjoyment in clay, water, painting, music and even taste. Another child may have had excellent early care, but will have experienced recent traumatic loss. In his case, even though sensory materials are always made available, the therapist may help the child to focus on feelings.

In this chapter we are aiming to give the reader as many examples as possible of the third objects available, and to develop in the reader an enthusiasm for inventing new third objects aimed at helping specific children.

'People Tree'

Trees feature a lot in therapy work and of course have always been rich in symbolism. The 'people tree' is a third object that we often use at the beginning of a course of care-therapy. We usually start this with a tree which has already been drawn or painted on a piece of board of at least 65×50 cm (see Figures 3.4 and 3.5).

We can begin by telling the child that it will help us to know more about his family and friends, and in fact anyone in his life, if he uses the little cards supplied to write the names of family members and anyone else he wishes to include and then 'sticks' the cards (using Blu-Tack) anywhere he wishes on the tree. It is important to make out one card with his own name (or just 'me') on it. The cards are about 7×4 cm. You may make some special heart-shaped cards!

Notice that our trees include the roots and the underground area with a few creepy-crawlies thrown in. We can let children know that that area is not such a nice area – or we can just leave it to them. Rejected people can be 'hidden' in the roots.

The therapist will find that children may say quite a lot in a non-verbal way simply by the positioning of the people on the tree. Often a child who is separated from natural parents will put himself next to his parents, or next to one of them. He may put daddy (or sometimes mummy) down in the roots. He is not using the tree to indicate geographical positioning but a feeling (or a wishful) positioning. In Figure 3.5 note the love-hearts used only for the child's distant dad and her cat.

Children may be invited to put people they don't like (including non-family) on the tree as well as 'best friends', school-teachers and others. Although we never suggest that a child puts the worker (as therapist) on the tree, we find that later in the course he may decide to do this. We do not interfere with this choice as the positioning of the names on the tree is entirely a matter for the child. We usually, however, ask some questions or make some observations such as 'I notice you have put yourself close to your mummy' or 'I see you have placed yourself down in the roots – all by yourself'. We may ask why he did that. I have had children tell me that they did that because they hated themselves.

A word of caution; children use the tree in different ways. It is important to leave a child's tree untouched. Keep it at the treatment centre. Note the placement of the names, but leave them where the child has stuck them. And remember to bring the tree out on later sessions, even if it just remains in sight and is not brought into the conversation. We do sometimes ask a child if he wants to move any of the names or add some new names, and the children frequently do wish to change things.

However, be very careful about what you read into the pattern a child has set. Although children often reveal their feelings and wishes or hopes by the positions they give the names, some children use a quite different principle in placing the cards. For example, one child put the younger people, including babies and infants in her family, down low, in the roots, because they were the youngest, not because

Figure 3.4 *'People Tree'*

they were disliked. She put the oldest people, the grandparents, right at the top of the tree! So be cautious in your interpretations.

One child, a girl of 11, put herself in among the roots on her first session. Her tree used to be present from time to time in later sessions. Nothing was said to her about the tree but she would declare, now and again, that she had a change to make. So saying, she would move herself up the tree several inches. As she developed confidence and

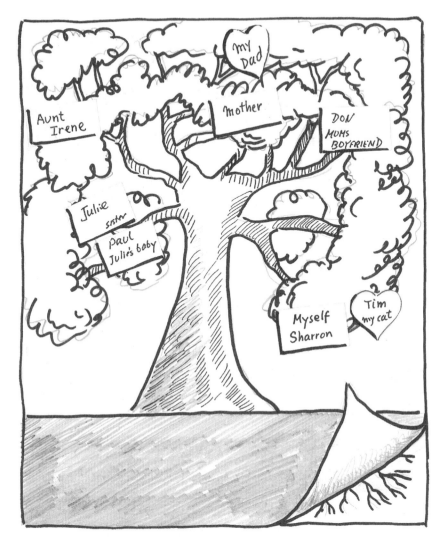

Figure 3.5 *'People Tree' with hidden roots*

more self-esteem, so she moved herself up until finally she 'sat' beside her parents, high up on the tree.

Further 'Asides' before More Insight Examples

It would be wrong to leave the impression that the therapy advocated in care-therapy consists of placing before the child a series of games or instruments and leaving no room for the child to explore and to use materials in whatever way he wishes. The third objects may be used frequently or infrequently. It will probably be true to say that a **cognitive–behavioural** therapist would use them more frequently than a psychoanalytically focused therapist. In our practice, we would usually leave three-quarters of the session for free-choice experiences and talk therapy. On occasions, because of the way the session went, we might never suggest the use of any third object. On the other hand, having offered a 'sand-tray world' experience to a child, expecting that to be a fifteen-minute engagement, the child might wish to use the material for most of the session. These instruments must only be used in a delicate and sensitive manner, and all the work should be governed by the speed of the child in terms of her readiness to explore and to gain insight.

Some children of course come bursting with an actual social problem to be solved, like 'Should I meet my natural mother whom I've not seen for six years, when I was only 4? I'm scared!' Others are truly 'disturbed' by experiences and circumstances which impinge on the ego but which they can neither understand nor explain.

Dora Lush *et al.* (1998) in describing a child in a single-case follow-up study concerning adopted and fostered children observes:

> Paul lived in a constant state of confusion about many things . . . what went on in his mind and what occurred in the outside world. He lived in a world he found incomprehensible and puzzling. (p. 60)

Then again:

> Paul's behaviour in therapy threw much light on the reasons for his restlessness and referral problems. *With all his inner turmoil* he could hardly be expected to concentrate on school work. His superficial and impulsive way of relating, together with his insecurity and confusion about family relations and his own identity, would be bound to make it difficult for his adoptive parents to get through to him and to feel their care was adequate. (p. 61, my emphasis)

As a result of the **psychodynamic** work:

> *Confusions were clarified*, and as a result of this work, Paul became able to identify with more caring, attentive and also limit-setting adult figures. (p. 61, my emphasis)

We use the above quotes simply to highlight the state of mind some children experience, not for the purpose of discussing third objects. The team helping Paul was psychodynamically orientated and so far as we know practised traditional psychodynamic psychotherapy. But the work also included another aspect that the researchers were interested in – concurrent help offered to the parents when children are offered therapy. In this case help was given to the (adoptive) parents and the researches comment 'It is likely that the help the parents received contributed substantially to the (successful) outcome'. A care-therapy programme would emphasize the implied requisite of offering support not to the child alone, but to the main care-givers as well.

But the case referred to above, Paul, also highlights typical factors to be seen in the many referrals by social services likely to be needing therapy. I have previously given some 'pen-pictures' of such children (Redgrave, 1991). So, what kind of third objects might be especially helpful to such confused and perhaps emotionally 'hurting' children? We make a special use of the sand-tray world technique, and I shall describe this third object in a little more detail in Chapter 4.

'People Houses'

This is an alternative to people trees. In this case we still make out the tabs for the different names (family, friends, relatives, animals, etc.) and the child is invited to put them wherever she wishes. Again, we use a method of fastening the tabs so that they may be moved on another occasion to suit the child's changing ideas and feelings.

It is important that the worker should help the child to use this tool (for that is what it should become) in the most useful and satisfying way possible. The child may separate siblings intentionally, or she may do it without a conscious desire to separate them, but with an unconscious wish actually ruling her room or house allocations. The same will be true of where parents are placed, and where the child herself is placed relative to parents or others.

Remember that in all these games we are concerned to help the child to understand something about her own feelings. Children also need to understand other people's feelings towards them. They often misinterpret on this point. Then again, in the counselling situation, it may be important for the child to be helped in conveying to the counsellor how she is experiencing these interactions. We shall expect to meet with **transference** (see glossary) behaviour as part of the process.

Figure 3.6 is an example of 'people houses' done by Andrew, aged 11. This, like the people tree, is an instrument which can be used fairly early on when working with a child. It is also, like the tree, a game which is suitable for almost any age of child. However, you will see that Andrew has added some 'spoken words' after placing the people, and his cat 'Smog'. This happened because I asked him what he would

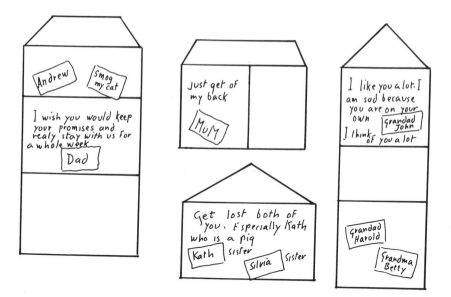

Figure 3.6 *Andrew's 'people houses'*

like to say to the different members of the family. I made it clear that he did not *have* to say anything, and of course we could put down what he would 'like' to say even though in real life he was not going to say it. Many children tell you that they have nothing to say, or that they don't want to say anything. That's fine, there is no pressure.

Andrew's placing of people and 'Smog' is interesting. Emotionally and physically he would isolate himself from the family. He would find 'secret places' to go to. He liked going fishing on his own. Notice that he puts himself in the attic, or perhaps it is an attic-room. He's away from people, but he has 'Smog' the cat with him. In real life he invested affection (libidinal energy) mostly in the cat.

The other placements reflect his relationships with the rest of his family. He and his mother experienced strong ambivalent love–hate feelings, while he utterly rejected his sisters. He desperately wanted his father but felt let down on account of the little time the globe-trotting dad was able to have at home. A warmth comes through concerning Grandad John, a widower. This is significant, and it is the kind of useful clue a trained worker should look for. It meant that the spark of empathy was alive in this child. It meant that Andrew was capable of feeling for others. This is important in the work we do with **affect-lame** children (see Chapter 7).

Later in this book readers will see an example of where the people-houses method is used when helping to get a specific message across to the child. It needs to be understood that when we are engaged in care-therapy the range to be covered in terms of dimensions of life may be very wide. Beyond dealing with specific psychological aspects such as phobias, the care agents will be concerned with the child's future and her understanding about the future: possible developments as a result of 'going home' or 'being adopted'; the meaning of adoption; the meaning of court orders of various kinds, and many other dimensions of life. This means that the games, the instruments such as people houses, may be used in different ways for different purposes.

Symbolism of Bridges

Did you ever play the game, as a child, in which you have to 'get all round the living room' (or maybe the bedroom) without letting your feet touch the floor – which in these days includes touching the carpet? There is something exciting and challenging in getting from 'A' to 'B' in an unusual way (not a horrible challenge like school exams, but a natural exuberant, fun-challenge).

So bridges have often come into our work with children. We are conscious that we sometimes use bridges in a way which is clearly behavioural in psychological terms, i.e. the bridge becomes something which the child wants to cross, or he wants to see it completed so that from then on there is a passage from 'A' to 'B'. The crossing of the bridge, or the building of the bridge in order to cross it, becomes a **reinforcer**.

CASE STUDY – NEIL

Neil was helped by a bridge. He arrived as a 12-year-old, burdened down with anxiety and neurotic thinking. He had experienced enormous loss in his life, as well as abuse. His thoughts were often imprisoned in phobias. Neil was very intelligent, but he could not rid himself of fears concerning his physical well-being. He awoke and stayed awake fearing he would otherwise stop breathing; he felt he may have cancer; he sometimes soiled himself. He had few friends at school and said he was bullied. I could go on! Mostly he was depressed and felt fear about the future. Depressives often concentrate on the past and on past failures. They often project onto the future a similar picture of events; they lack hope.

So we made a bridge into the future, or at least we made a feint outline of a drawing of a bridge (see Figure 3.7). The left

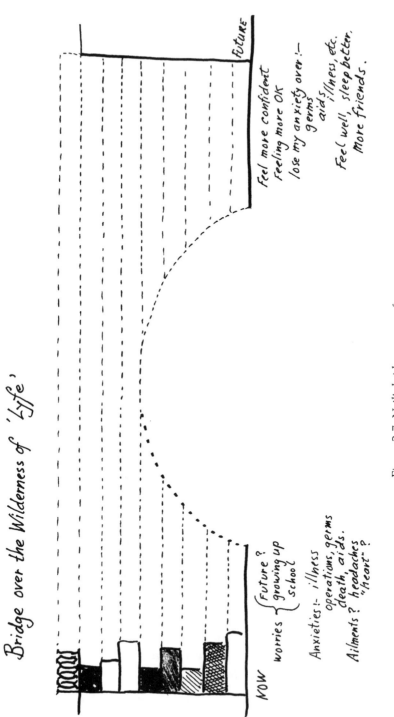

Figure 3.7 Neil's bridge at start of treatment

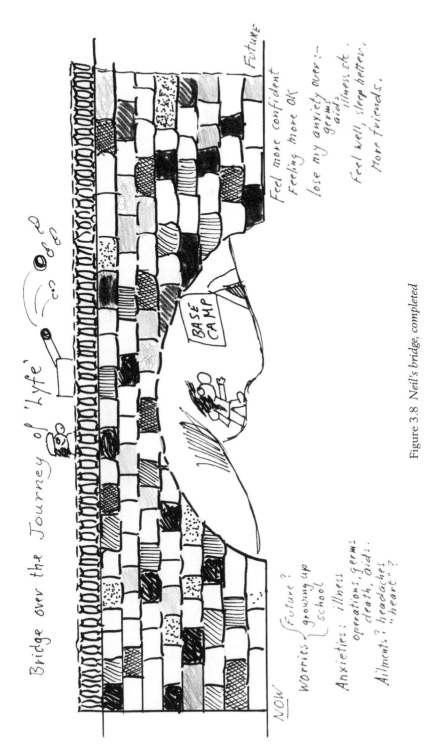

Figure 3.8 Neil's bridge, completed

bank of the river, or whatever the bridge crossed, represented Neil's experience of the present and the past. The right-hand bank represented the future we were aiming for and he would reach.

Notice that the left-hand bank has the feelings and anxieties which Neil decided to write in. The right-hand bank also has a set of statements, the result of a discussion or a series of discussions I had with him. These became our aims.

The rest of the bridge, which at the start of the therapy was called 'Bridge over the Wilderness of "Lyfe"', was outlined in dots, with the exception of a few bricks on the left-hand side. Figure 3.8 shows the completed bridge some 2½ years later, although treatment continued beyond that time for about one more year.

As the child was able to review his progress and the changes he was making, so he gradually coloured in the rest of the bricks, the railings, and any other features he freely added. The reader will see that Neil has added some figures, and a 'base camp'. Neil did reach the right-hand bank in terms of self-confidence and social poise. Of course, the bridge was only one approach, and one third object that we used. A full outline of Neil's treatment would amount to a small book in its own right, but readers will appreciate both the symbolism of the bridge and its image of hope and encouragement.

Later in this book we shall pick up again the bridge symbolism used in a process which we actually call 'bridging', which refers to preparing the child to go into a 'new' family or to be rehabilitated to his natural family, or elsewhere.

Before we leave bridges, however, let me remind readers that actual little model bridges can be built, brick by brick, using self-hardening clay. Some children love adding the bricks, and of course all these constructive and 'doing' processes allow (and encourage) a very relaxed discussion between worker and child.

Shields

The idea of using shields for helping children to become more self-aware has been around in the childcare profession for many years. Like the life-story book described below, shields have suffered as a result of being taken out of the context of a thought-through care-therapy plan and used ineffectively.

For the social worker, foster-parent or therapist working with children and young persons who may have experienced early rejection, followed by several short-term fosterings ending in breakdowns, and perhaps periods of residential care, those three unanswered questions haunt the conscious and unconscious mind:

Who am I?

Where do I belong?

What will happen to me?

Many third objects, and certainly the shield, were designed with the aim of helping the child to find some answers to these questions. The shield of course, like other third objects, is an instrument meant to help the counselling or therapy process. Without the counselling or psychotherapy, none of the third objects is going to help the child very much. Because of this the reader must constantly be asking him or herself how the various third objects might be used in a counselling or therapy situation.

The shield can be a way of helping the child to answer, or to give a particle of the total answer to, the question 'Who am I?' The idea of the shield when it first came into use was for the child on its completion to feel 'This is me': not just what emerges in the shield but what insights emerge during therapy.

The shield could be quartered or otherwise divided into sections, rather like a coat of arms, and the sections could be used to display various attributes of the child's personality. For example one section could have physical characteristics with actual small locks of hair fixed to it, while another could be used to symbolize or directly advertise the child's interests and skills, so that a pencil glued on stands for her clever drawing skills or a small screwdriver for her mechanical skills and interests. Depending upon the age of the child and upon the psychosocial factors inherent in the case and of course the child's wishes (for remember that the skilled worker may put the idea of the shield forward but the development must be something the child either leads in or happily goes along with) some sections may be used for more feeling aspects or behavioural aspects, so that under 'feelings' we may find 'I feel happy when . . .' and 'I feel sad when . . .'. (The reader will of course be aware that children often use the word 'sad' when they mean 'unhappy' or even 'angry', so you need to study such points.)

Figure 3.9 shows the shield of a psychologically disturbed 13-year-old girl, Judy. Although this shield would not be described as typical it is not unusual or extraordinary. Remember that this shield was Judy at the time she did it. Later in the therapy Judy would be able to make another shield which may reflect the changes that have taken place.

Figure 3.9 *Judy's shield*

It is clear, however, that Judy at the time of making the shield was a very unhappy child and at the same time she seems to be saying quite a lot about her sexual self. But is the sexual self shown in the top right-hand quarter of the shield her overt self or is this how she wants to be seen? These questions of course can only be answered as a result of the ongoing counselling. So the shield may be used to help answer such questions. Judy shows a piece of her hair, her 'kissable' lips and a mini-skirt, but this does not add up to happiness, for in the same quarter she draws the pills she (twice) overdosed on.

When it comes to loving and being loved – by other human beings – there's not much to show. Top priority in the 'I love' section goes to her little dog 'Pip'. Very often rejected children invest animals with love and receive 'love' from their pets, as of course Andrew did with 'Smog' his cat. She puts her dad in the 'I love' section but then says she hates him too. All this of course echoes what is being dealt with in the counselling or therapy work. (I have often undertaken therapy with adults who would have benefited had they been able, as children, to handle, work through, examine and share their feelings concerning other people in their lives.) Judy puts in 'Liam Jameson', a local pop musician (hardly a 'star' but worshipped by the local teenaged girls), but this is a kind of fantasy 'love'. Her 'love' section looks bleak at this stage.

Both the lower quarters of the shield deal with Judy's feelings, although, and this is very reasonable, she keeps some 'private' in a sealed envelope. We can see what unhappy nights Judy has, 'I'm afraid when I go to bed', and then the painting of her nightmares. She picks up the misery of the overdosing (really, in her case, used partly as a means of controlling people) and makes a crude drawing of a stomach pump.

Our shields are on average some 70 cm in length and 50 cm wide at the broadest part (28 × 20 in). Usually we have cut out the shape of the shield ready for the child to use. We use cast-off sample books of wallpaper. The child chooses the wallpapers she wants to use on the various quarters and we paste them in, using heavy-duty wallpaper paste and clipping them round the back with the paste, or sometimes using a heavier adhesive for the bits that go round the back. The base-boards are often 'throw-outs' from shops – the large cardboard display cards that they use. Figure 3.10 shows the reverse side of a partly pasted shield. There are many other ways of making shields. Shields, like people trees and people houses, are not objects which belong to only one session. Shields may be worked on for several weeks and may then appear now and again for discussion and revision. Before we begin to use a shield we discuss the idea with the child and show her examples either of mock-ups or (with the permission of the children concerned) shields made, or in the making, by other children.

Shields, however, may be used in other ways than the original 'This is me' format. The following is an account of the way a shield was used

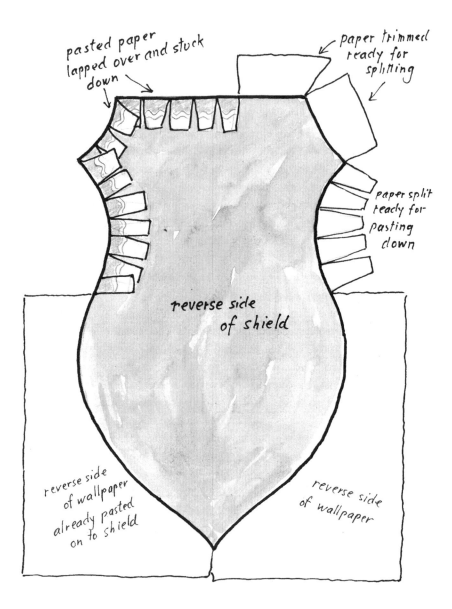

Figure 3.10 *Reverse side of partly-pasted shield*

in a care-therapy situation involving more than one agency and to bring about social as well as individual psychological and behavioural changes.

The important details of the case concerning Christopher, aged 13, were: (*a*), the death of his long-term foster-mother about a year before we saw him; (*b*), the effect this had on his foster-father; and (*c*), the arrival in the home of the foster-father's married son with his wife 'Auntie May' and their 2-year-old child, Anna.

Christopher's behaviour had deteriorated. He was described as a 'lout' who would sprawl in front of the TV set when Anna was watching a kiddy video; he aggravated Auntie May, the child's mother, by eating any 'special' tasties bought for Anna, such as crisps or chocolate wafers. He even 'stole' the child's medicine. Eventually the son and daughter-in-law declared they would have to leave if Christopher remained there. They had gone to live with Christopher and his foster-father on the death of the foster-mother, and were doing their best to care for the family.

As a sort of 'respite' move Christopher was admitted to 'The Pines', a children's reception centre. While he was in 'The Pines' he was referred to us, and this was when we used the shield in a special way. But before describing Christopher's shield I should explain that an excellent piece of social work was done in the true care-therapy style once the child was in the children's centre.

The staff at the centre were well qualified and experienced. They were able to relate to Christopher in a way which remained professional, but which helped him to feel valued. Furthermore, they arranged for **family therapy** to take place once a week at the centre, when Christopher, his foster-father, the son and daughter-in-law came together for therapy led by an experienced family therapy practitioner. Arrangements were made for Christopher to attend the school that he attended before he went to the centre. Meanwhile, we were seeing him for individual counselling.

As the work proceeded, the results were showing up on Christopher's shield, so we shall let the shield tell readers more about the case from this point on. Notice first the contrast between the milieux reflected in the two upper quarters of the shield in Figure 3.11. In the section 'At home, as it was' Christopher says he felt 'left out'. He says he was 'bored' and that he 'went out' on his own. In the 'children's centre', by contrast, we find 'Fun', and he says that there were 'things to do'. He also found friends.

I can add to this because we got to know Christopher's family. We would describe the family during the period leading up to Christopher's referral as a depressed family. Some of its members were depressed, perhaps not clinically, but certainly in terms of interests, enthusiasm and 'fun'. It was as if they existed just to eat their meals – on separate occasions from each other – and to watch TV. Nothing else seemed to happen apart from the squabbles caused by Christopher.

But there are some other clues revealed by the shield-work, clues

Figure 3.11 *Christopher's shield*

which were vital when helping Christopher and, as it turned out, other family members as well. As a result of doing other pieces of work, and helping Christopher to express his feelings, he was able to state on his shield, in the top right-hand quarter, 'Everyone had forgotten about our Mum'.

Christopher had lived with his foster-family since he was about

3 years old. His foster-mother had become mother (mum!) but the family had colluded in a subconscious sort of way not to talk about its loss. The members had not shared their grief. In fact they had avoided any memories which might trigger grief. Perhaps the foster-father was mainly 'responsible' for this unintentional family hurt. Christopher had not been able to grieve the loss of his mum, and then he began to have an experience of mingled sadness and anger because 'everyone had forgotten' about her.

As a result of the family therapy, backed by the one-to-one therapy with Christopher, various important changes in behaviour and attitudes took place. Both the attitudinal and behavioural changes affected several members of the family including the foster-father. The lower right-hand corner of the shield reflects the changes which actually emerged as a result of all the work, and the changes included behavioural changes which sprang from feelings of relief and lowering of tension. It did help the father himself to be able, eventually, to talk about his wife's death and to share his grief and his joyful memories with the family, including Christopher.

Other things were 'put right' as well. The reader will notice Christopher's comment about 'proper pocket money'. The shield, in this case, reflected the broad span of the care-therapy and the changes that were needed and which took place, on a family interactive level.

Life Flow Charts

As with the people tree, the people houses and the shield, life flow charts emphasize what we have previously called focus number 3 in our list of aspects of therapy and counselling (see page 24); clarifying the child's life events, personal history and the motives or intentions involved. We are still concerned with third objects designed mainly to help with the gaining of insight, or as we say, awareness.

I have previously (Redgrave, 1987) outlined the purpose and shown the technique that might be available when using flow charts and I am indebted to the Boys' and Girls' Welfare Society for permission to use here some of the material published in that book.

In the following section we shall be discussing the use of life-story books. However, because some of the children have such complex life histories, often having as many as ten placements with different families by their twelfth birthday (and some children many more placements) it becomes difficult for them to establish a clear picture in their minds even of the placements that they have had. Because of this it is often helpful to set out the history of their placements, so to speak, in the form of a flow chart, thus:

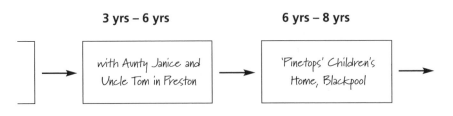

However, although I have referred here to the 'history of their placements', that function, if the flow chart is properly used as a counselling/therapy instrument, may turn out to be less important than the other insights it may develop, and the resolution of conflicts that may be attained by its use.

As the flow chart is built up, often taking a couple of months to put together, the child may come to understand for the first time why she did not remain in the care of someone she remembers with longing. She may, because of the counselling and therapy work developing with the proper use of this instrument, even gain some insight concerning her feelings of fear or anger which have become chronic, and she may develop a wish for a different kind of life experience in the future.

For these aspects of psychosocial development to take place, however, the worker (residential, field social worker, clinician, foster- or adoptive parent) must be sensitive to the child's needs, the signals emanating from the child, and the value of the instrument when certain broad or basic guide questions are put to the child, such as:

Can you remember what (or how) you felt on that day?

Do you ever think about that (or him, or her)?

Would you like to draw a picture of you and your brother at the fair?

What games do you remember playing then?

Naturally, such questions should not come in a bunch in the way I have written them above. They would form part of an ongoing dialogue during which the worker may find him or herself being plied with questions by the child. And the worker must be absolutely honest if for any reason he or she does not know the answer to a question. The offer can of course be made to find out more and let the child know.

I must emphasize that the therapeutic use of the flow chart is something more than merely showing the child a series of moves, changes of address, and so forth. Quite often the children we are working with have no one now in touch with them who is able to share memories with them. Imagine that you are 12 years old. You now have foster-parents whom you have known for 2 years; you have foster-siblings who have known you for the same length of time; but you have no one now in your life who knew you when you were 8 (when that frightening event occurred) and no one who can share with you those games you used to play when you and your friends 'ran wild' in the recreation ground – no one, in fact, who was there when you cried all night or ran away from home.

Apart from giving the child insight concerning the moves in his life, and the people who have come in and out of it, a proper use of the flow chart gives the child a 'little bit' of the feeling of sharing past memories and of having a past – not just a forgotten or half-forgotten other existence, or a jumble of confused memories and fantasies produced by imagination or half-truths that he has been told or just 'picked up'.

As in the case with many third objects designed primarily for awareness experience purposes, the flow chart often has a secondary function for the sensory experiences. This is because some children like to make pictures showing scenes of times or places they remember. They then use paints or felts or crayons and so are involved in a sensory experience. There is no hard and fixed dividing line between the sensory and the insight use of third objects.

In describing the technique of the flow chart we shall first assume that the child and worker have decided to start at the child's birth and then to work forward in time. However, as we shall enlarge on later, you do not always have to commence and carry on that way. With some children we start where the child is now and begin to work backwards, seeing what the child remembers and aligning these memories to facts.

Figure 3.12(a) shows a typical layout for a flow chart and explains the sort of information which would be expected to emerge partly as a result of information supplied by the worker, partly from information provided by the child. It is obviously helpful if the worker has done his or her homework and as well as getting the facts straight, e.g. birth certificate information, has obtained early photographs of child and family members, and place of birth, etc.

Figure 3.12(b) shows how a young child (or an older child who needs to use this approach) might create a flow chart using Jollycraft gummed squares – gummed, of course, to a paper background. We like the idea of using something called Jollycraft, because so often the whole experience of flow charts (and most of the other third objects) is a

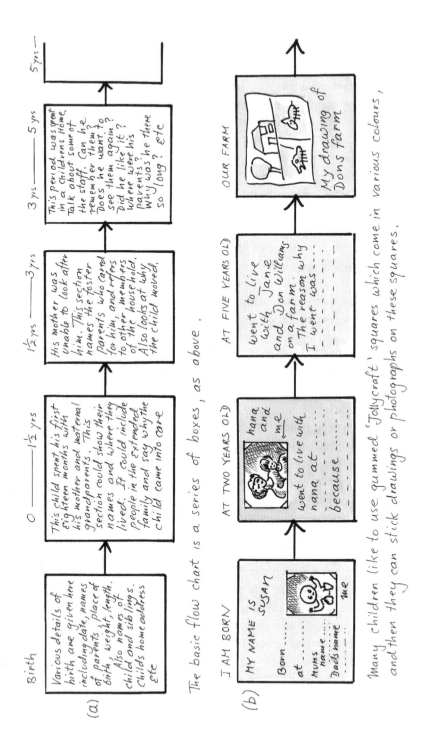

Figure 3.12 (a) and (b) Flow charts

joyful one for the child. But whether there is joy or sadness, or a mixture of both, the experience of direct work should be a rich one. Unfortunately both flow charts and life-story books have been taken out of the context of therapy and often give no more than a shallow experience.

Our illustrations so far look rather too clean and neat. In fact, when a child is using the flow-chart method as a working instrument (not just something to show other people) we will often scribble thoughts and memories outside the boxes, like this:

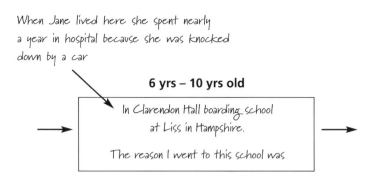

The flow-chart method may be used with children (and adults) of any age from infancy upwards, and like the shield it may be used in different ways and for different purposes. I hope workers will be using flow charts in ways that I have never thought of. Central to the success of direct work is the ability of the care worker to be creative and to help the child or young person to use the third objects in creative outlets.

Figure 3.13 shows an adaptation for a young child. It is still left to the worker to decide whether to start with the whole thing drawn out as a train or, because the child is at a stage when he is being prepared for another move, to start with just the engine and then to look back to help the child to see where he has come from. This is a therapy or counselling matter.

Figure 3.14 shows a very different treatment where the flow chart has mutated (or evolved!) into a bus journey and each of the houses or 'stops' represents a placement along the route of the child's life. The bus, of course, can be an actual little toy bus or one made of cardboard with its features drawn and painted on both sides so that it is still a bus when it turns round the corner. This bus-journey game is painted on a board of about 65×50 cm (26×20 in).

In our modern western society we are producing not only homeless

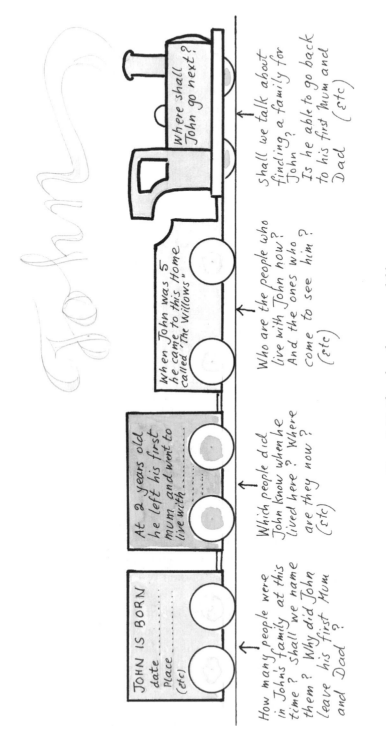

Figure 3.13 Flow chart for a young child

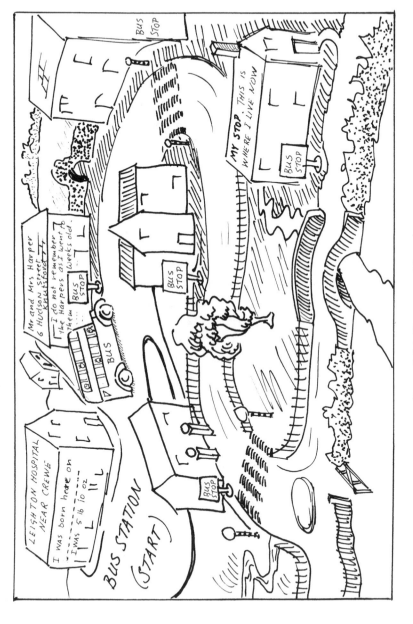

Figure 3.14 'Bus-journey' flow chart

children, the ones that go into night shelters in London or end up as child prostitutes, but family-less children, and children who can't attach to families because help has been denied them and they reach the stage (or the circumstances) when it is difficult to help them.

Selina, an 11-year-old with deep personality problems, had not reached that stage, but she was heading in that direction and had recently been placed in a foster-family intended to be a 'respite' placement which would, it was hoped, be 'short-term'. From there a permanent placement would be found, i.e. the *second* 'permanent' placement in her life! I sometimes cringe when I hear well-intentioned workers telling young children that they are going to their 'forever' family. What do they call the *next* placement or the one after that?

Figure 3.15 shows the working flow chart as it was at the stage when Selina and other people involved had not resolved the difficulties or come to a clear decision concerning her future, so we could describe it as 'open-ended'.

Selina's flow chart is drawn in 'hard' lines up to and including her fourth family, i.e. her third placement after leaving her natural mother's care. When Selina was about 4 she and her two sisters were admitted to a children's home on account of neglect. Because Selina said she was always frightened and everything was scary, she joined the placements up with 'wriggley' roads. In fact they were not roads, they were like waves and you didn't know where the waves were taking you. Selina drew in a 'Magic Carpet' because going from one place to another was like riding on a magic carpet – 'and you might fall off'.

Her next move, at 5½ years old was, with her sisters, to Mavis and Richard. Selina and her sisters were placed with a view to adoption and were later legally adopted by this couple. In passing I will say how perilous it is to place disturbed, neglected children of this age with people who do not understand that they are most likely to be caring for emotionally handicapped children who will need a depth of understanding and tolerance until they are adults, and then to offer no follow-up care for the adopters. So at the age of $10^{1}/_2$ Selina is again 'in care' and is with Don and Sheila.

From this point the flow chart has dotted lines for Selina's future. She is at the 'crossroads' and is talking with the worker about possible directions. It is sad to think that children arrive at a point like this but, having arrived, we must help them to move in the right direction – but what is the 'right' direction? Selina had five possible directions to think about. She could think of returning to Mavis and Richard and her sisters, that is if Mavis and Richard would have her. She could think about a 'small' children's centre (housing about five children) or

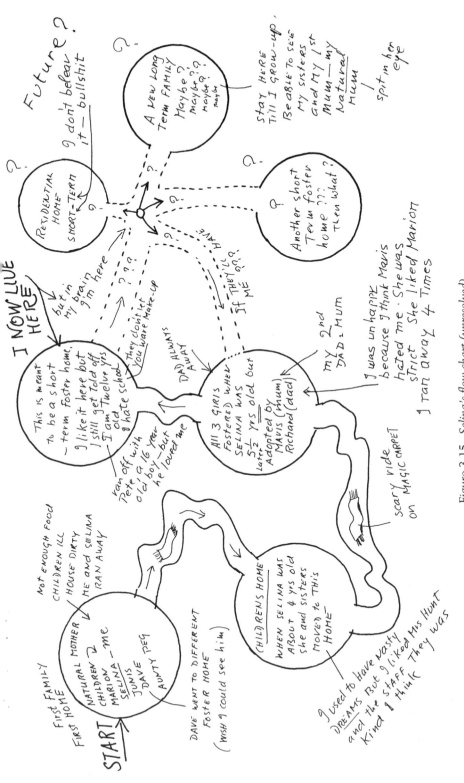

Future?

I don't beleav it — bullshit

RESIDENTIAL HOME SHORT-TERM ?

A NEW LONG TERM FAMILY Maybe? Maybe?? maybe? maybe ?

STAY HERE TILL I GROW-UP, BE ABLE TO SEE MY SISTERS AND MY 1st MUM — MY Natural MUM

I SPIT IN HER EYE

Another short Ter in foster home ??? then what ?

I NOW LIVE HERE

but in my brain I'm here

This is meant to be a short — term foster home, I like it here but I still get told off I am Twelve yrs old I hate school

They don't let you ware make-up

ran off with Pete, a 16 year old boy — but he loved me

DAD ALWAYS AWAY

HAVE

If THEY'LL let ME go?

All 3 GIRLS FOSTERED WHEN SELINA WAS 5½ yrs old but Later Adopted by MAVIS (mum) & Richard (dad)

MY 2nd DAD & MUM

I was unhappy because I think Mavis hated me. She was strict. She liked Marion I ran away 4 Times

Not enough food CHILDREN ILL House dirty ME and SELINA RAN AWAY

FIRST FAMILY FIRST HOME

NATURAL MOTHER 2 CHILDREN MARION — me SELINA JUNIS DAVE PEG AUNTY PEG

DAVE WENT TO DIFFERENT FOSTER HOME (WISH I could see him)

(CHILDREN'S HOME) WHEN SELINA WAS ABOUT 4 yrs old she and sisters MOVED to THIS HOME

scary ride on MAGIC CARPET

I used to Have nasty DREAMS But I liked Mrs Hunt and the staff They was Kind I think

START

Figure 3.15 Selina's flow chart (unresolved)

another 'short-term' foster-home, with a view to finding a long-term family. Bear in mind that 11-year-old girls who smash up their schoolrooms and threaten to run away are not easy to place. She could stay where she is with Don and Sheila. Wherever she went, however, there would be a requirement that she should be able to change her behaviour, and that would require a lot from her, the therapist, and the other care-givers. Using a flow chart in this way helps the child to look back and forward in time. This is not the place to follow individual cases through. Selina did stay with Don and Sheila. Perhaps if more individual therapy (and family therapy) had been available for Mavis and Richard (the adopters) or even at the natural-mother stage, such stressful decision-making would not have been necessary for the child, nor for thousands like her.

Before moving to discuss life-story books I shall enlarge on the 'birth box', the first box in the flow chart in so far as its position in the continuum is concerned, but not necessarily the first one to be worked on. Figure 3.16 gives the reader the kind of information this box or section might hold. However, for some children, especially those discovering this important information, having been in the dark before, a photograph of the place of birth, e.g. a hospital or maternity wing, will help to achieve a feeling about the place. Photographs and drawings can be used anywhere else in the flow chart. The 'being-born' box may also include photographs (sometimes cut-down 'snaps') of the natural parents.

It is very important for children to have information concerning their weight and length (height), etc., especially children who have left their natural families. Apart from the feeling of 'completeness' this information helps to give, you never know how much of an oddity a child may feel without such knowledge. I recall having to trace the details for one child when a teacher at his school had got the whole class, for some lesson, working on those early life details. The 9-year-old in question suddenly felt 'stupid' as he knew nothing, not even where he had been born. But there are other important aspects; for example every child needs to know that there were siblings in the family and that very likely there are brothers or sisters 'out there'. Ideally these days they will be in touch with siblings, or at least know they are there (I'm afraid some cut each other out deliberately!). It is easy to see that the birth box is as important as any other box in the flow chart, and that the flow chart, in so far as it represents a therapeutic instrument, must be used with sensitivity and tact.

There is one important distinction to be made concerning flow charts; it is this: we have discussed, so far, the use of the flow chart as

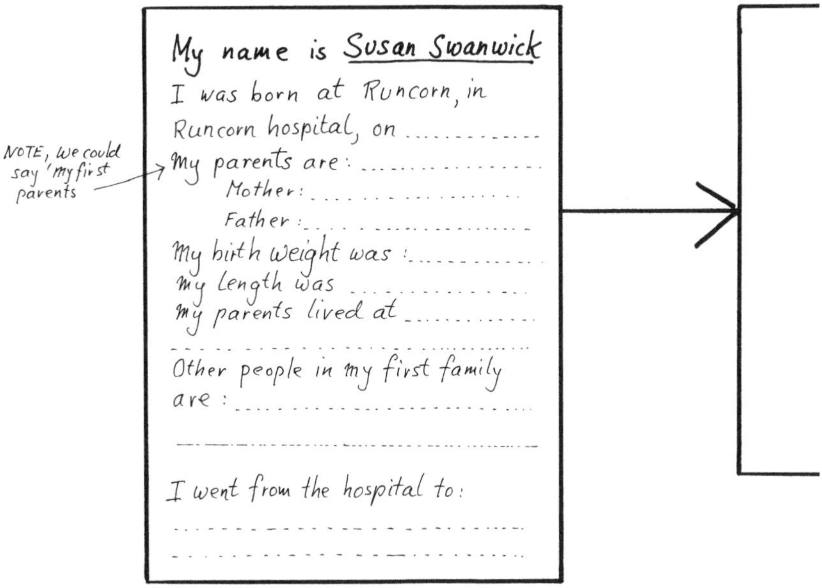

Figure 3.16 'Being-born' box of a flow chart

an instrument or third object when working with a client – child or adult. It is important to distinguish this use from the flow chart which is made by a worker as a guide to his or her own work with the child. When used for that purpose the flow chart is different both in content and structure. Its use is briefly described in Chapter 6.

Life-Story Books

Here is a short extract from a previous book of mine concerning life-story books (and other third objects):

These have been in use for several years now in child care circles, and in fact there is a danger that sometimes they may now be prescribed and used without imagination when some agency decrees that all its children should have their Life-Story Book 'done' in the same way as all children get registered at birth or immunised a bit later on.

I want to talk about them as instruments or third objects which can be of the utmost help when used sensitively, and even selectively. I am not against children making up albums and sticking in photos and other memorabilia just for the fun of it. That's fine, but we must not imagine that this exhausts the use of the Life Story Book in a therapeutic role.

In fact, so adaptable is this method of working with children that it is possible, if you know what you are doing, to cover all the categories I have listed; Starters (i.e. ice-breakers) Focusing On Life Trail (e.g. flow-charts), Discussion Directing, the lot. The way it is used will depend very much on the skill and enthusiasm of the person working with the child. (Redgrave, 1987)

The reader will notice that I was at pains to emphasize the counselling or therapeutic use of the method rather than its use as a photograph album. Before we had gone very far in the development of direct work or care-therapy, people had recognized that many children referred for therapy, especially children who were 'in care', were confused about or ignorant of dozens of life events. Confusion and ignorance often produced conflict. Often the cause of the conflict only emerged in fleeting bits of conversation during counselling or during some relaxed occasion with foster-parents or staff members of a residential establishment.

Because of this we developed the life-story book, which was designed to help the child to ask questions or to be reminded of feelings and events so that in the end the child, and perhaps the worker, would have revelations and the resolution of conflicts. This meant of course that building up a life-story book would be much the same as making a flow chart. There would be ongoing counselling work and the book would become a vehicle for feelings as well as a history of residential and family changes.

As an example of a revelation that came to an 8-year-old boy I was working with, I often refer to Jamie's case. In the course of making his life-story book it transpired that he entertained a fear and an anxiety about going to any new families – it was 'better' (safer?) in a children's home. He emphasized this anxiety when we were working on some photographs and birthday cards concerning a foster-family he was with between the ages of 3 and 5 years. I have recounted this child's story on pp. 12–13 of this book.

It is for the reason of avoiding knowledge blindness that adoption agencies do their best to persuade adopters of very young infants to bring the child up knowing from as early an age as possible that she or he had other (natural) parents. Sometimes, however, children are subjected to untruths about their own environment. We met one adolescent who actually believed she had been responsible for her mother's death. This untruth had been stamped on her mind by her (much older) siblings. The mother had died soon after this child's birth.

Figure 3.17 *Life-story books*

Before dealing further with the theory concerning the use of life-story books, we shall give a few ideas with regard to the practical details.

The adult working with the child will probably have to give the lead in so far as the design of the book is concerned and, depending on the age of the child and his capacity to understand the project, the way the story is to be told. Even the front cover of the book will say something about the individual child. Figure 3.17 shows two covers, one (made from a scrap-book) with some coloured-in lettering by Clare Jones, aged 8, and another of a rather sophisticated type with some nice lettering by artistic Jonathan Williams, aged 15.

There are many ways of telling the story, but whichever way is selected the project must not be rushed. It should be taken at the child's speed, which means that on some occasions a major part of the session is taken up with the book while on other occasions ten minutes is all the time the child has interest or attention span for.

The life-story book may be written in the traditional way, paragraph

Figure 3.18 *Life-story book with matchstick people*

by paragraph, but usually for that to happen we are considering either an older child who likes to write or a very young child with the worker actually doing the writing bits and the child drawing or painting pictures, helping to stick photographs in and generally being involved. Figure 3.18 shows the beginning of a story type of treatment, which actually starts with the well-worn phrase 'Once upon a time . . .' This story book used matchstick people as illustrations. Sometimes even older children, e.g. a child with learning difficulties, will prefer the worker to do most of the writing, but with such children or adolescents some of the more pictorial presentations of life-story books are preferable.

Figure 3.19 shows two pages of a life-story book presented in a pictorial manner by a 10-year-old girl. She is soon to be joining a family either for fostering or adoption so she refers to the adults as 'My new parents (I hope)'. Here, of course, there is room for some discussion among professionals as well as whatever guidance the worker may feel is proper. I am referring to the expression 'My new parents' and I am querying whether the term 'parent' will always be appropriate. However, if in the course of constructing the book that is what the child said or wrote, because that is what she has been led to believe, we must be very careful not to impose the adult (politically correct?)

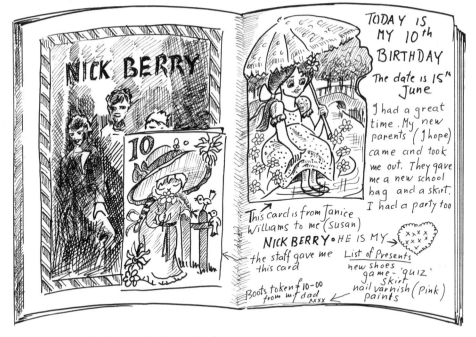

Figure 3.19 *Pictorial Life-story book*

notion on her. In any case the new care-giver will often be acting in a 'parenting' capacity. In this instance the child's comment 'I hope' might lead on to some discussion.

Before launching out on a life-story project with any child, it is important that the adult involved (foster-parent, adopter, social worker, etc.) should have done his or her homework. Besides obtaining facts about the child's history he or she will also have ensured that as many photographs as possible of family (families) and friends, as well as any birthday cards, certificates for swimming or dancing, merit badges, advertisements or other pictures showing pop-stars or football stars the child is interested in, have all been collected and are ready for use on the book. This collecting can be done with the child. Figure 3.20 shows the use of a box file which a child is using for his collection of 'stick-ins'.

As with the flow chart, one of the early pages describes where the child was born and some details about the child as a new-born infant, as well as information about parents and siblings – you can even use rudimentary family trees. Figure 3.21 shows pages used in this way.

If children make drawings or paintings for the life-story book it will not matter if the products resemble not at all the object they are alleged to depict. If the child has made a 'scribble' and says 'this is a picture

Figure 3.20 *A box file used in preparation*

Figure 3.21 *Life-story book: starting page*

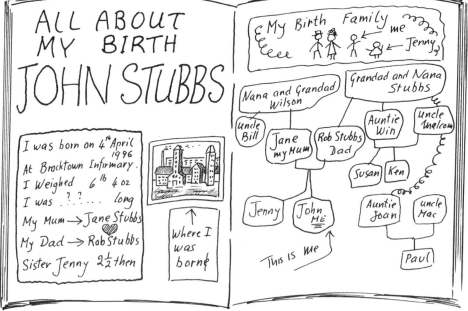

of my dad' then so be it, it is a picture of her dad. Figure 3.22 shows two drawings by Samantha, aged 4 when she drew them. We particularly like the portrait of her 'first mummy'!

We consider that if used as part of a treatment programme, rather than simply as an album or a brief history of movements or placements, the life-story book serves four purposes, namely ontological, clarification, resolving and sharing.

Its ontological purpose fulfils to some extent the child's basic need to 'feel' a past and to know that there were features in that past. Children who have left the care of their natural family at an early age and have been placed in four, six, eight (this happens!) or a dozen placements cannot experience self in the same way as those who have had continuous contact with care-givers from birth or thereabouts. There may be a blank beyond a certain age, or there may be a fuzz. There may be no one around who was 'part of me' even two years ago – and this may refer to a 10-year-old. Ontology is concerned with 'being' (existing). So this aspect and the other three purposes may form part of the answer to 'Who am I?', 'Where do I belong?' and 'What will happen to me?'

The reader will already appreciate the use of the life story in so far as clarification is concerned. For the child who has been 'in the dark' about why certain moves transpired, why she is not in touch with her siblings and a host of other questions, the life-story book is very helpful.

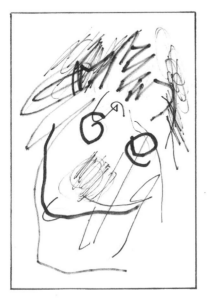

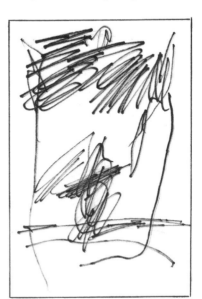

SAMANTHA'S 'FIRST MUMMY'   THE PARK, BY SAMANTHA (AGE 4YRS)

Figure 3.22 *Drawings by Samantha*

Children are made anxious or unhappy on account of factors other than unanswered 'what' and 'why' questions. They suffer as a result of carrying unresolved conflictual feelings or beliefs, just as adults do. In the course of helping a young teenaged girl, and using her life-story book, we became interested in why she was uneasy about moving from a children's home into a family for fostering, as she seemed to enjoy the visits to the family and her prospective care-givers seemed fond of her and were capable parents in their own right.

Gradually she was able to identify and then express the cause of her reluctance to say 'yes' to a move. This teenager's mother had died. They had been very 'close' and very loving. The young girl was troubled by a conflict of loyalty. Deep down she had the feeling that she would be disloyal to her natural mother by joining a family and becoming, as she put it, 'someone else's daughter'. As a result of some wonderful counselling by the care staff of the home, this conflict was resolved. So, even though such conflicts can be dealt with by counselling alone, or by other third objects, it is also true that life-story books may become central to conflict resolving.

This leaves us with the sharing purpose, but we have already described the value of what we might call vicarious sharing when discussing the use of flow charts. It is exactly the same with the life-story book. We are calling it vicarious sharing because we are not referring here to the fact of adult and child working together on the project; we are referring to the child, so to speak, going into the past and sharing that past experience, in fact to some degree re-experiencing the past with someone who was not there on the first occasion. I remember a 10-year-old boy who, while working on a story book with his foster-mother, described an outdoor imagination game he and his mates used to play in a rather rough area of Liverpool. That seemed 'ages ago' to him. It would have been about two years previous to working on his book. He painted a picture of the scene and described how they played the game. He described his feelings when this apparently exciting game was played, involving tree-houses on a piece of waste-land.

He had linked his foster-mother into the past as far as it was possible to do so – and of course it helped to bond the two of them. People have made the mistake of deliberately 'forgetting' (never referring to) the past in the lives of their adoptive or foster-children. Never adopt that policy.

Finally, to conclude our discussion on the life-story book I shall quote from a discussion with Wendy, recorded when she was working on her life story at 7½ years old. The worker refers to himself as 'me':

We need to develop and maintain our skills in discovering what is best for *particular* children and in meeting those needs, Wendy gave me plenty of signals as I worked with her. Here are a few snippets from conversations we had when working on her Life-Story Book:

Me: 'You've got a nice little pile of letters here, do you want to put those in?'

Wendy: 'Let's read them again first . . . I've got three from you . . . and six, no seven from Nana and Grandad.'

She straightens out the letters and then addresses me by using an intonation I've come to associate with her when introducing what to her is an important area for discussion, perhaps something causing anxiety, or some request she wants to make:

Wendy: 'Ke-en?!'

Me: 'Yes.'

Wendy: 'I haven't got any letters from Bob Walters.' (Her stepfather).

Me: 'No.'

Wendy: 'I wish I had.'

Here tears begin to show in the corners of her eyes. A pause follows while I collect the odd birthday card and letter together. Wendy has suddenly 'frozen' and is staring at the floor:

Me: 'Do you want to talk about Bob? . . . Shall we see if you have any photographs of him?'

Wendy: 'It's Sandra Griffith's fault . . . I hate her!'

Sandra Griffiths is the Social Worker who was involved earlier and had to receive Wendy into care when the family broke up.

Me: (After a pause) 'Why do you hate her?'

Wendy: 'She's told Bob not to write to me . . . she . . .'

Here Wendy burst into tears. At this point the temptation was to put the book away for a bit and turn to something else because the session seemed to be too painful, for me as well as Wendy. But it was important, if we could, to follow some of this through because here was a vital mental senario of Wendy's which could be causing problems at the moment and would cause more problems in the future. Wendy was clearly directing her anger at the Social Worker. But how much attachment existed towards Bob, the stepfather?

Me: 'How about drawing a picture of Bob Walters?'

Wendy: (Eyes now dry again) 'I could make him a calendar.'

Me: 'That's a good idea, let's find some pretty calendar things.'

In the middle of the calendar making Wendy seemed settled again. I popped a question which led on to her revealing another anxiety. She seemed to feel Bob Walters had rejected her:

Me 'Did you call Bob Walters "Dad"?'

Wendy 'Yes.'

Me: 'You're making a beautiful calendar . . . is Bob special?'

Wendy: (While cutting out) 'He used to love me.'

Me: 'Doesn't he still love you?'

Wendy shook her head. Whatever she had said and felt concerning the Social Worker she also felt Bob himself had withdrawn his love. (Redgrave, 1987)

And so it went on. We have pointed out before but cannot do so too often, that almost any engaging activity, even going out for a walk, seems to make it easier for some children to converse. To put the reader's mind at rest let us add that Wendy eventually went home to live with her mother and Bob again!

This chapter has considered some of the many ways of helping children to obtain an awareness about themselves, to begin to change ways of 'seeing' (understanding) events and to feel better about themselves: a healing–mending process (or a change process). It has also considered some of the ways in which child and adult may be helped to exchange ideas.

In the following chapter we continue along these lines with further examples of insight work. We shall focus even more on feelings, but we shall also be concerned with the symbolism of 'sand worlds' (or sand-tray work), and we shall provide examples of third objects which helped children in situations involving cross-cultural stress.

CHAPTER 4

More insight work: feelings, sand worlds, 'my world' pictures, cross-cultural stress and more symbolism

'The child who tries to overcome his fear of tigers by becoming a tiger in his play is employing a perfectly healthy approach to the tiger problem.'

Fraiberg, S., 1959

Objects May Mirror the Child's World

It is possible for the child to use objects instead of drawings or paintings in order to get in touch with feelings and beliefs, as well as to obtain a clearer view of how he relates to other people. We do use all sorts of objects, including dolls' houses for younger children and construction sets for older ones. We often make use of whatever is at hand. These objects may stand for something quite material, as when we use a set of boxes to stand for several family dwellings, or they may become symbols denoting feelings. The latter use was described in Chapter 2 for Donna, who was helped by the use of the loving-water method.

'Loving Candles'

Candles can be used effectively in discussing certain very strong feelings, such as grief, loneliness or aloneness, and love. Because we light the candles it will be obvious that some special consideration needs to be given when contemplating their use. If, for example, one is working with a young arsonist it will be necessary to consider their value against the risk. Then again, because matches or lighters may be used, one needs to consider their use with very young children. Having said that, we can also say that we have found this symbolic method very effective and helpful. The case of Patrick is an example.

CASE STUDY – **PATRICK**

Patrick was 7 years old. He had a stepfather but his natural father was also seeing him frequently. His mother loved him but frequently went away for long spells of hospitalization. His natural father loved him and his stepfather was also fond of him and was a good-enough 'father' to him. Patrick also had a half-sister, Jenny, who was only 2 years old.

Patrick was disturbed on account of the separation from his natural father, despite the close contact he still had. He was also very upset when his animal companion, Poppy, a little cat, had to be found a new home because it turned out that he was allergic to cats.

The therapist working with Patrick explained that she was going to let him pretend (imagine) that each of the candles was a person in his life, that is to say 'one for Mummy, one for William' (stepdad) and so on. And also 'we shall light whichever candle loves you and where you love that person. So you tell me if you have a little light (or flame) of love in your heart for William, and we shall light William's candle . . . but because you must never light matches yourself I will strike the match and light the candle . . . now, which candle is You? . . . That one, OK, and which candle is Mummy? . . . OK, is there some love coming from you to Mummy? . . . Yes, right . . .' Here the therapist would like Patrick's candle and the one standing for the mother.

In Patrick's case he joined in enthusiastically and wanted candles lit for both 'fathers'. Then a small candle, a 'night-light', was lit for Poppy, the cat. This piece of work was being done to help Patrick to feel more secure about the content of love within his family experience.

In order to introduce the feeling or to be able to talk more easily, or to share an understanding, the therapist brought up the reality of Patrick's separation from his natural father, and said 'shall we move Dad's candle over there?' (a few feet away). The child was at liberty to say 'No. Keep it where it is', in which case it would not have been moved. However, Patrick agreed to the move.

The therapist then explained that the light from the father candle was still *reaching* the Patrick candle. She explained that love is like that, and that Patrick's dad 'sent his love over to Patrick' even when he was a long way away. Therapist and child had a chat about love and the way it 'doesn't blow out'.

The mummy candle stayed alight when they moved her away 'for a little while to pretend she has gone to hospital . . . but her love-light is reaching out all the way . . . like the light from the candle, and it reaches right over to Patrick all the time'.

Then, and by now Patrick was well into the 'game', they put Poppy's little candle right across the other side of the table, . . . 'but you can still see Poppy's light . . . and you still love Poppy and Poppy still loves you'.

At the next session Patrick bounced in and cried out 'Let's play love candles again, please!' There was a sequel to this candle work. Patrick poured out in detail to his mother and stepfather the whole candle routine, and when next the stepfather saw the therapist he explained how it had made him feel 'good' to learn that Patrick had lit a candle for him too.

With older children and adolescents this symbolic method can be very poignant and healing. Some adolescents seem to make an almost religious use of the candles, but don't think it always turns out that way; some children do not really use the method, and they finish up singing 'happy birthday to you' and blowing the candles out. You cannot be sure what third objects are going to be deeply used by which children.

'My Tree' (Personal Tree)

Here is a feelings exercise which often, like the 'people tree', produces indicators which reflect unconscious as well as conscious material. It uses the tree symbol again, but this time the tree represents the child him/herself. 'My Tree' is another idea which came to me from Violet Oaklander. In her book she refers to some 'wonderful fantasies that can be used in conjunction with drawing'. She goes on to say:

One I have often used is the rosebush fantasy. I will ask the children to close their eyes and go into their space and imagine that they are rosebushes. When I do this kind of fantasy with children I do a lot of prompting . . . I give a lot of suggestions and possibilities. I find that children, especially children who are defensive and often constricted, need these suggestions to open themselves up to creative association. They will pick that suggestion which most fits for them, or will realise that they can think of many other possibilities. So I must say 'What kind of a rosebush are you? Are you very small? Are you large? Are you fat? Are you tall . . . what are your roots like? Or maybe you don't have any? If you do, are they long and straight? Are they twisted? Are they deep? Do you have thorns? . . . etc.' (Oaklander, 1978)

We often ask if the child is a bush or a tree. Most seem to be trees. With older children we do not lead quite as much as Oaklander does in the quote above.

However, the worker should be noting down what the child says about her tree, because once the child has described the tree – described herself – the worker invites her to draw or paint a picture of it. Children should be given a large piece of paper to draw on, not a piece of A4; something about 58×42 cm (23×17 in) is ideal. The worker will sometimes need to remind the child what she described when she was 'being a tree'. Remember, some children may not wish to close their eyes, so make this an 'if you like' thing.

The usual run of trees, if we may put it that way, is not too dramatic, but if you are working with a child who becomes really involved in this exercise, then some really interesting material may emerge. Remember that the exercise itself can 'inform' the child and, even without any observations being made, the exercise may be self-healing.

We do 'observe' things about the finished drawings, such as 'I see you have no roots when you are a tree'. Oaklander, who is a Gestalt psychotherapist, says:

I ask her to describe the rosebush in the present tense, as if she were the rosebush. I sometimes ask questions such as 'Who takes care of you?' After the description I will go back and read each statement, asking the child if what she said as a rosebush fits in any way with her own life. (Oaklander, 1978)

Figures 4.1 and 4.2 show typical trees, one by a young child and one by a teenager, but our third tree illustration is a drawing by Neil, who you will remember came to us burdened down with anxiety, and who completed the bridge (p. 67). Figure 4.3 shows Neil's tree.

Quite often with children the surrounding environment becomes as important as the tree itself and that is why we ask the child where her tree is (in a field? a park? a road? on a beach? etc.). In Neil's case, however, the tree is seen as a small insignificant object. Now let us look more closely at the rest of the scenery and the 'persons' involved.

Figure 4.1 *Tree drawn by a young child (aged 8)*

Figure 4.2 *An unusual 'tree' by a teenage girl*

Notice first, Neil, as a tree, is perched precariously on the edge of a chasm and that, as pointed out by Neil, the tree has 'no roots'. On the other side of the chasm are two 'persons', and one is menacing Neil. He is a hideous character who holds a club in one hand and a whip in the other. Neil had already explained how frightened and anxious he felt about past and future events. The other character appears as a rescuer who is going to attack the menacing character and is wielding a sword.

Figure 4.3 *Neil's tree*

Neil also introduced a church door. He said he was not sure why he had put that in. The picture emerged, rather than being a planned thing. As soon as I asked Neil where his tree was situated, he began to talk about being on the edge of the chasm and feeling that the tree may fall in. Then the other objects emerged as he went on talking.

The frightening monster with the club and the whip has a huge head. Neil coloured this head black and yellow. Now there may be many explanations for these colours being chosen, as well as pure chance, but it is interesting to note that many insects have that colouring, including wasps and bees, and we are told by naturalists that this combination of colours is threatening to predators of these insects.

The following is a guide to the sort of questions we ask the children when they are making their tree. After explaining the exercise to the client, and when he is relaxed, ask:

1 Are you a tree or a bush?
2 Are you a large (tall, small) tree or bush?
3 Is your tree or bush round or tall and thin?
4 Have you any leaves?
5 (If no leaves) Have you any leaf buds?
6 Any flowers?
7 Lots of branches and twigs or just a few?
8 Have you any roots?
9 Small or big (lots of) roots?

10 Where is your tree growing? Garden, park, desert, beach, on a cliff, on a mountain? Where? (With older or more able children you may leave out the prompts.)
11 Are there other trees?
12 Are there any people or creatures about?
13 (If yes) Are they in your tree?
14 What is the weather like? (With young children ask – Is the sun shining or is it raining, or is it hot or cold, etc.)
15 How do you feel?
16 Do you like the people or creatures/animals?
17 Are you afraid of anything?
18 Who looks after you?

Direct Expression of Feelings

Most of the third objects outlined so far will tap into the child's feelings even though many of them will be used for other aspects of awareness or enlightenment, such as the moves the child has made and the reason for these moves. Often, however, certain workers are faced with discussing with children, over a relatively short period of weeks or maybe only three visits, desperately important matters on which decisions must be made, and sometimes reports must be made to courts, concerning parental access or supervision orders. In England, court welfare officers (Probation Service) carry out this duty, but similar roles exist elsewhere.

We have found that some children can be helped by a more direct reference to feelings. Sometimes, quite early on when working with an adolescent, and when the way she feels about events and people needs to be discussed very soon, we have started by suggesting that we should first just think about feelings. We say 'Let's make a list together of all the feelings we can remember'.

We find we usually then begin to contribute alternative words. Obviously, an exercise like this is dependent upon the age and the ability of the child, but with many children of, say 10 or 11, we get feelings such as 'angry, 'happy', 'sad', 'jealous', 'lonely' and other single words. We begin to add some phrases, which stand for what they often actually feel, although they may have difficulty in putting the phrases on paper. So we come up with phrases such as 'left out', 'a long-time-ago feeling' (nostalgic), 'I'm stupid' or 'people make me feel stupid'.

There are many other feelings which it is worthwhile just putting down on the feelings list because children often do not convey how they feel as they do not have a good enough vocabulary. Often, when they have described themselves as feeling 'sad', we go on talking round the subject until we are able to understand that they actually mean they feel 'left out'.

There is no valid reason, if this work is done properly, for people to feel that the child is being directed; on the contrary, a good worker will obtain a much more refined version of what the child wishes to convey. We do not suggest words when children are making or writing out their own statements of events, and of course we are discussing therapy and counselling, not disclosure to the authorities.

Sometimes, when talking with the children later on, we may use the word list they have helped to make so that they can select the words they feel they 'really want to say'. Of course we all need to understand the colloquialisms and slang words such as 'mad' (for 'angry'), and the use of the word 'scary' for frightening. But the children we work with are also very anxious children, so do not overlook the word 'worried' from the list. Then they need to be able to say something about that inside feeling they get when they experience conflict! What shall we say? How about 'piggy-in-the-middle' or 'pulled in two directions'?

Children often have to express feelings in verbs rather than in nouns or adjectives. They often say 'I hate' so and so. Keeping strictly to our starting words like 'angry' and 'happy', we would need to add 'hating', but we may suggest, if it's not already on the list, the 'I hate them' feeling.

Direct Expression of Feelings Game: Beetles

'Let's play beetles!' Beetles is a dice and pencil game which has been around now for many years. We have modified the game to suit our purposes and it seems to have helped many children to talk about feelings, and events attached to feelings. At the same time it remains a game.

Figure 4.4 shows the beetle as it is drawn out 'completed' on a board, for us to use as a guide whenever we play beetles. To play you only need a dice and shaker (we seem to use the plural now instead of die!), some paper and a pen or pencil for each player. In fact we always play with just two people, child and worker, because we turn it into a confidential little discussion. Always explain the rules to the child and ask if they feel they would like to 'play' beetles.

To play, each player in turn shakes the dice and is then allowed to complete that part of his beetle as indicated by the guide. The player must first complete the body parts (head, thorax and abdomen, in any order) shown with the double line round them. No legs or antennae may be added until those three parts are in position (but *do* change

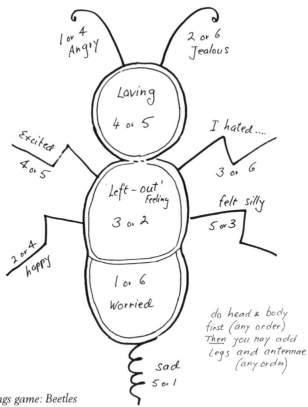

Figure 4.4 *Feelings game: Beetles*

the rules to suit the needs of your work!). So if you shake the dice and obtain 3 or 2 you can draw in the middle part of your beetle, but **wait** – this is where we have changed the game. Before you draw in your middle bit you have to think about any time when you may have felt 'left out'. If you can remember feeling like that you recall the time to your partner. This of course means that the worker has to be open to the child when his or her turn comes round. However, neither 'player' need talk about recent feelings, and if you have never ever felt 'left out' as a child you must have been very fortunate!

Clearly, when using this direct discussion method, a balance has to be struck between making it easy for a child to share his feelings and putting a child in an embarrassing situation of having to disclose feelings that he would rather not disclose. But the therapy or counselling we are describing must always be undertaken by sensitive and emotionally alert people. Note that, having drawn up a feelings list, the worker and child might use the list to select from, when deciding which feelings they may wish to talk about. Note also that the slightest sign of hesitation can be met by a change of rules: 'I tell you what – you choose another feeling from the list and use that one instead'. But, having said that, we must emphasize how helpful some children have found this game. It has allowed them to recall feelings or discuss current situations with ease.

Of course, if you want to speed the game up or make it easier, you can add legs or antennae as soon as you have the appropriate bit of body down, but the main thing is to make it light-hearted and yet capable of expressing depth of feelings. Remember also, that it is important to be aware of those areas which do cause a child to hesitate or to opt out, even if you do not pursue discussion in that direction.

'Bird's-nests'

Here is an exercise which has enabled children to express their feelings, and to inform us so that further discussion followed, concerning their felt relationship within the family or some other group. This has often been extremely confidential material. We have to admit to being surprised at the readiness some children showed in using this exercise, children of 9 or 11 years of age.

Figure 4.5 shows a large, rather hastily done drawing/painting of three nests somewhere up in the trees. This picture is made on our usual size of paper or board (58 × 42 cm), and then we have several card circles (often cut out from postcards). When working with a child or adolescent we usually have the main family members already named, but we have a few 'spare' circles unnamed.

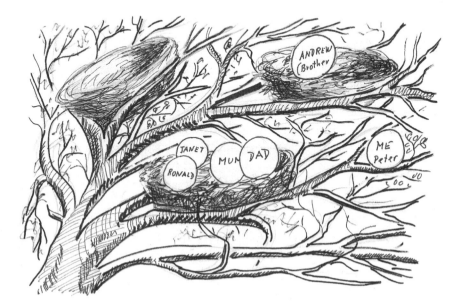

Figure 4.5 *'Bird's-nests'*

We explain to the child, who by the time we are using this exercise we usually know very well, that families or groups can be a bit like nests of birds. Sometimes all the birds, adults and fledglings, are cosily tucked up in the nest, 'maybe that's how you feel in your family most times – perhaps not?'

'Perhaps', we may say, 'you may feel a bit outside the nest . . . or you may feel you are in the nest and someone else is outside – or maybe even in a different nest. Anyway, have a think about it and show me how you feel – or how you feel most times and how you feel only sometimes'.

Even in families which would appear to the outsider to be 'very close', children have demonstrated that they felt 'out on a branch' or sometimes even in a different nest. They take the circles representing the group and they place them strategically according to how they wish to express their feeling about being 'in' or 'out'.

This is not necessarily a terrible thing, this feeling of being 'outside'. Many adolescents will feel this way even in perfectly 'normal' functioning families with good-enough parents. Nevertheless, like most third objects, 'bird's-nests' are helpful for establishing a sharing-of-feelings contact with a youngster, and even in helping him to know that such feelings may be very usual as one is growing up.

The exercise may be used by the child to say something which is indicative of problems in relationships, and bear in mind that many of the children and young persons we are concerned with will be fostered or adopted and may have had many previous placements. They may need to discuss these 'belonging' or attachment feelings as part of the counselling or therapy or, with the care-givers, as part of their growing into the family. Some children may be helped by knowing that these 'separation' feelings are not 'bad' or 'wicked' ('after all we've done for you!'), but are to be expected.

We have certainly found it gratifying when, after a year of contact, a child has been able to say that he now feels all the birds of the family are in the same nest – and the feeling of attachment will go on, if that takes place, even when the young person grows older and moves out to make his own home.

Paints, Pencils and Felts

Paints and felt-pens, and the things which need to accompany them, such as large sheets of paper tacked in some way to the drawing-board, paint-brushes and pots for holding them, are available on most direct-work occasions.

This sort of equipment is on hand for much of the self-choice activity, as is the soft modelling clay. It happens that we are explaining in some detail the use of specially adapted third objects when counselling children and adolescents or treating them in more intensive therapy, but the reader should understand that a lot of time is spent in free-choice activity, and often this choice is for painting.

By 'painting' we do not usually mean anything approaching a work of art, although there are exceptions. The equipment on offer should be varied enough to meet the needs of a variety of children and adolescents according to age, skills and other characteristics. Take, for example, Lucia and James, both aged 8. In defiance of some outdated generalizations concerning the behaviour of the sexes, Lucia's twenty minutes with the paints is a general 'slop-about' which, if done in a living-room or lounge would have required carpet and furniture coverings, and herself to be tented in overalls if not wearing mess-about clothing. The brushes available would need to be strong, rough hog's-hair sort of things – fine points not required.

James, on the other hand, was a born artist who liked to paint delicate detail, using fine-pointed brushes and proceeding slowly. He could not have done his 'work' armed with Lucia's species of paint-brush. On the other hand Lucia would have ruined the fine water-colour brushes used by James. She would 'scrub' the paint on with the brush, abandoning it only to use her fingers!

Both children were benefiting in different ways when they were allowed to choose to operate in the way that they did. Sometimes Lucia would start to squeeze paint onto her hands and squelch it before applying it (partly on the paper, partly on the worker). There are many good reasons, therapeutically speaking, for allowing this free-play. There were other good reasons, incidentally, for guiding both children on other occasions to be different: for James to be able to 'slop' about and either literally or metaphorically to roll in the mud, and for Lucia to begin to learn about motor-control and other forms of self-control, but this is not the place to discuss these aspects.

For most children we use the squeezy-bottle ready-mixed paints. We use Yellow, Red, Blue, Green, White and Black. White is essential for mixing to obtain a whole variety of colours. Some children love to mix the paints to see what colour evolves: some are good at knowing what to expect, some are surprised by what they produce. Sometimes we ask children to choose or 'make' an 'angry' colour or a 'happy' colour, or 'hot' or 'cold' colour, and so forth.

The reader will note that, although in this section we are discussing the use of materials in respect of awareness experience (enlightenment, insight, etc.), the children are also obtaining sensory gratification in the use of paints, clay, etc. Certainly Lucia was! We do have plenty of juicy felt-pens about, and some children reject paint and want to use the felts for their art work. They should always have the choice, but it is important to have paints available because of the much richer sensory experiences obtained by their use.

The ready-mixed powder paints are, of course, a form of gouache and therefore opaque. These are suitable for most children, but if you come across a child who wants to express herself artistically and is able to paint what most people would describe as 'proper' pictures, you will then need water-colours which, if you leave out the white, will be semi-translucent. However, the 'accomplishment' or level of art work is no measure, by itself, of its therapeutic value to the child. Lucia's squelch helped her at least as much as James' 'fine art' helped him, maybe more so!

In this section, however, we are particularly interested in the way in which painting may be used in order to help children 'deal with' their feelings. Children may need to deal with feelings for various reasons. Anxiety feelings which become persistent and chronic, like some obsessional thoughts, may need facing in order to have them diminish in a healthy way. There are often feelings which lie behind anorexic behaviour. The reader will recall Naomi's 'blacked-out' paintings (p. 53) and the symbolism her work carried and which provided a sort of self-healing awareness. We have also described and illustrated Donna's 'feeling paintings' in Chapter 2.

'Feeling Paintings'

Often, when 'feeling paintings' are produced, they can be fairly predictable, but occasionally some very striking features turn up in the paintings. Because a child does not use a third object in the way we have described, do not feel that the exercise has been a waste of time or that you as a therapist or foster-parent have failed. Children, like most counsellees (or patients in some situations) are selective in their use of third objects. Here, however, is a set of feeling paintings we felt readers would value seeing. They were painted by a 15-year-old girl, Christina, who had been committed to care having been sexually abused for some years within her own family. As in many such cases, the abuser remained in the home while she was 'rescued' from that environment but rejected by her own mother. So she received three forms of hurt: sexual, rejection and banishment.

The paintings we are reproducing were made when she was experiencing these feelings or had just talked about them in an emotionally involved way. In Figure 4.6 the two eyes (surrounded by orange and green) represent her feelings of jealousy. The expression 'green with envy' comes to mind.

Figure 4.6 *'Jealousy' by Christina*

Figure 4.7 *'Happiness' by Christina*

Figure 4.8 *'Fear' by Christina*

Figure 4.9 *'Protecting feeling' by Christina*

Figure 4.7 (which is a swirl of colours) represented Christina's feelings of happiness which, she said, she seldom experienced at that time. Occasionally, when one of her aunts took her for a weekend stay, she felt 'a bit happier'. It was pointed out to Christina that she had framed this painting with a black edging. Christina said 'I know, I had to put that in because I never feel *really* happy now. I always feel something is there in the background stopping me from being happy.'

Figure 4.8 shows Christina's effort at expressing fear. It is just a dark swirl, colourless! But there is one spot left white, the worker asked Christina if that was meaningful for her. She said 'Yes, I nearly painted it in but then I didn't because I felt something stopping me . . . I know now that it stands for Hope . . . I still hope that things will be nice one day'.

Figure 4.9 is a strange yet fascinating expression of something more than a feeling: perhaps it represents an attitude of mind. In the course of the therapy with Christina the worker talked with her about feelings of self-blame and also her feelings towards the perpetrator of the offences. At that time she was very confused, partly because of denial – she was almost denying that anyone had committed any offence. She got talking about her tendency (need?) to protect everyone. At that point the worker said 'I wonder if you could express that protecting feeling in your painting . . . I guess that would be difficult'. Christina then painted what you see in Figure 4.9. What can we say about it? It is possible to see something (the central yellow and pink ball) carefully held and protected by – two 'hands'? It is possible to see a womb protecting the developing foetus or embryo. In any case Christina felt good after she had expressed herself in this way. Notice that she still surrounds the protective element with 'darkness'? and a black frame.

Feeling paintings, where the paint is more or less used as the element of expression, are not for every child. In fact children who may be very good 'draftsmen', children who can draw artistically, may find that they have to draw people or objects in order to express their feelings. It is important to remember, however, that they should not be invited to use this feeling-painting way of expression unless they are feeling whatever feelings they need to express, at the time, or they have been discussing events and the feelings in an emotionally involved way just before making the paintings or drawings.

Getting into the Picture (Work with Infants)

Many of the third objects we have discussed can easily be adapted so as to be helpful to young children or to adults. There are some approaches, however, that are uniquely appropriate to infant children – children of 3 or 4, for example. One of these we have called 'getting into the picture'. The reason for this label, as will be evident from what follows, is that we talk to the child in a way which, so to speak, puts both child and worker into the picture.

What helps us to do this is partly the element of magic which young children carry in their minds and partly the lack of clear demarcation in their minds concerning the animate and the inanimate. So, when a child of 4 has drawn a picture with the sun in it, we may ask the child 'What is the sun saying?' or 'What are the trees doing?'

Figure 4.10 shows a painting made by a little boy, Jamie, who at the time was nearly 5 years old. This little boy was in a highly nervous state and was receiving treatment after experiencing terrifying episodes in which he was sometimes locked in a dark cellar and at the same time threatened that various monsters would come to him if he cried out or screamed (a double-bind situation).

In his picture we see 'Big Dad', his mother's third 'partner'. The previous two, including his natural father known as 'Little Dad', had been as cruel as Big Dad, only they had not devised such mental cruelty. We also see Jamie's mother and 'Binji' the dog. Then, underneath Big Dad, we have Jamie himself.

Figure 4.10 *Jamie's picture of 'Big Dad' etc.*

To the question 'What is Big Dad saying?' Jamie replied 'Big Dad says "I'll cut your mouth off"'. When the therapist asked 'What is Jamie saying?' the little boy said 'Hide my mouth, hide my eyes. I'm afraid of Po-Jo'. Po-Jo was apparently one of the monsters who were supposed to live in the cellar. Binji, the dog, was able to talk through Jamie, but Jamie would be silent if asked what his mother was saying. His mother suffered from clinical depression. She was given to overdosing and was often in hospital.

There is no doubt that the painting, and the talk concerning the painting helped to draw Jamie away from his own tendency to withdrawal. Enough has been said here to indicate that the technique of 'getting into the picture' can be fruitful in opening a dialogue with a very young child.

Whether you are working with a 17-year-old, or a 3-year-old, always be prepared to adapt technique, and to use imagination and produce new approaches. Remember, also, that despite the help Jamie received from this approach, the next 5-year-old you ask about the sun talking may say, 'The sun can't talk – silly!'

The reader who is interested in working with very young children will find examples of special application in the text following. It seemed better not to have a section for third objects specifically designed for the under-5s, as so many of these techniques (painting is an example) are usable for all ages. It is the skill of the adult worker which will adapt them to that particular client, 17 years of age, or 4 years of age.

Third Objects in Specific Tasks

We are still concerned here with helping the child in connection with some cognitive aspect, though we recognize that the cognitive will not be separable from the affective. It is important to remember, however, that care-therapy is involved not only with the child who may need two years of sessions to overcome the effects of early rejection or emotional abuse, but also with the child who needs to have his legal status explained to him. Furthermore, care-therapy recognizes, as do most of the modern therapies, that there is a place for helping the child to change, with regard to either attitudes or behaviour, or both. This is an element of what has been called 'brief therapy'. Helping a client to change as a result of insight or awareness does not mean telling a client what he *must* believe. Such a client would not really have changed, except perhaps to have become more antagonized towards the worker. Even so, some workers in a care-therapy team will also have a responsibility to show the child that there are some quite rigid 'do's' and 'don'ts'. Care-therapy is about 'bringing children up', as well as applying psychotherapy or analysis where such help is needed. Here then are some third objects used when the main intention was to help a child who came with a specific problem, or where a change of attitude could help rather speedily.

Options – Peter
Although it should not happen in an ideal world, children, even quite young children, sometimes find themselves in a situation where a decision of some importance has to be made and their wishes are to be taken into consideration. Some of these decisions may affect their lives quite far-reachingly.

Figure 4.11 shows Peter's 'double list'. We have taken this example out of context (as with most of our examples) from the case of Peter, a 12-year-old boy who was faced with a decision either to stay in his foster-family, where he had lived from the age of 2, or to return to the care of his mother and stepfather. He had kept in touch with his natural mother and occasionally stayed at her house. We have previously described several third objects that we used to help Peter (Redgrave, 1987), but here we are seeing just one of them, the double list. I drew up the headings; Peter completed the columns. The illustration is self-explanatory but remember, it was not presented to him in the manner of a school test. We had had a lot of discussion before we got to,

My foster family		My first family	
+ Better	– Worse	+ Better	– Worse
Moore comfort	feel frightened.	I like my step-dad here a lot.	Not so many comforts.
Nice holidays	Not sure what is the right thing to do so I get into trouble.	like going on the ice-cream round with him.	sometimes I'm not sure of the right things to do.
Other children to play with		I laugh much more.	
I like my grandad in this family	Would not be able to see my first mum and stepdad if I stayed here.	I feel nobody is watching me all the time.	
		I like my nana. She has a chat and plays with me.	
		nice holidays.	
		friends to play with	

Figure 4.11 *Peter's 'double list'*

'Suppose I draw up something which will help you to write down the things which you like and the things which are not so good . . .'.

Options – Margo

CASE STUDY – MARGO

Margo was another child with much the same problem. She was about 10 years old when she was referred by the social services. She and her younger sister, Rachel, had been in the one foster-family since infancy and neither had any memory of the parents.

Margo had become 'unsettled' in the foster-family and was also 'giving trouble' at school. She had developed an ambivalent attitude towards her foster-mother and occasionally said she was going to run away, and that she wanted her 'real' mother. She did not get on well with Rachel, whom she teased and bullied. Despite all this she would also attack her absent mother verbally. We were asked to help this child concerning all these feelings about her natural mother, and her foster-family, and to help her to decide if she would like even to meet her natural mother.

We found that Margo had a lot of empathy with the people in her life, and that she put a lot of thinking into the whole dilemma of her situation. She was by no means shallow. We discussed a great deal over a period of three months and in the end she (a), met her natural mother and (b), decided to remain in her foster-family, but here are some third objects we used along the way.

Figure 4.12 shows an options card made for Margo, and the various options we came up with. Of course, Margo – being the child she was – discussed all these options at great length and 'settled' for one or another of them and then came back the week after having thought about all the disadvantages. The point is, of course, that here was something tangible, something she could look at, talk about, think about, something drawn out on a card.

But other things were going on! Margo pressed for information about how she would meet her natural mother ('if I want to'). 'How would it feel?' 'Who would be there?' 'Could she "take" her foster-mother?' So we used the dolls' house people, and used boxes for the different houses and one for 'the office' (the Social Services Department office) and enacted meetings. At one point

I made a 'mistake' (but it was revealing!). I made the natural mother embrace Margo when they first met. Margo snatched up the 'natural mother' doll, flung it across the room and shouted 'Get lost!' and declined to 'play' any longer. The incident was used to warn her natural mother, when they were about to meet, not to be too gushing but to respond as far as possible, at first, by matching Margo's approach.

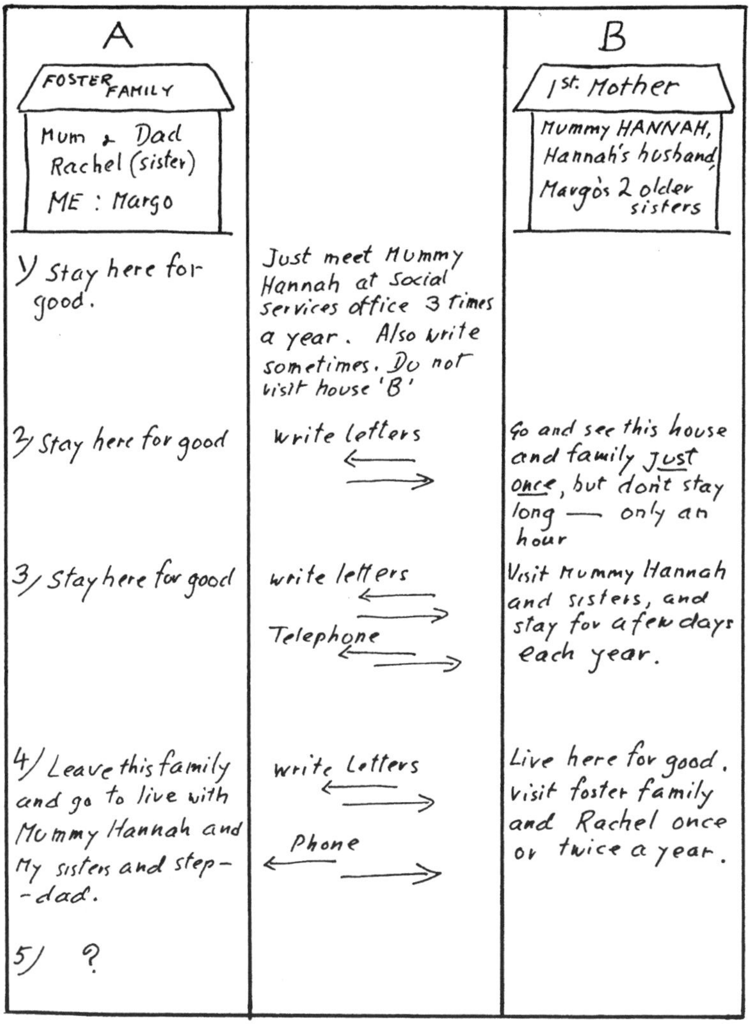

Figure 4.12 *Options for Margo*

Figure 4.13 *Margo's 'I think they think' board*

Margo's mind was very active, and she was clearly troubled and anxious about what everybody involved might feel, and what they might say. I felt she needed to set down in writing even this thinking, so that she could share it and go over and over it. So we made the 'I think they think board' as an anxiety reducer.

Figure 4.13 shows this board and some of the thoughts Margo had concerning how other people might feel and react. The reader will note that she was a 'real little worrier'. Notice that she felt her natural mother (Mummy Hannah) might feel 'worried' and 'shameful' for having left her for so long. She also feels Mummy Hannah might think, 'I hope Margo will like me'. Notice, also, that she sees her sister thinking 'I don't have to meet my real Mum'. Rachel hated the idea and felt that Margo was rocking the boat with all this fuss about seeing her natural mother.

To realize how discerning this child was, note the question she put to me (in the 'Ken' section): 'Ken, can you have two feelings at the same time?'

Cognitive–Behavioural Use of Third Objects (Specific Tasks)

The term care-therapy does not imply a new psychology nor yet another psychotherapy. It may involve a team of workers, even family members, and it may be environmentally holistic – using clinic, foster-family, natural family, school, etc. as places where healing or 'growth' takes place. Under our subheading of 'specific tasks' work (still mainly insightful), we shall briefly describe some third objects and particular approaches used to help a 6-year-old girl, Arabella, whose specific problem was that she became hysterical if the door was shut while she was in a room. This included the classroom doors in school and the bathroom and lavatory doors.

We cannot afford the space to outline the case history, nor the counselling of child and parents involved in this case. However, in Arabella's case the home background and parental interest and attachment gave no cause for concern, but there was a history of trauma or shock which involved a door being jammed. The child had developed panic reactions as a result whenever a door was shut and this problem was leading to agoraphobia.

At first Arabella would enter the treatment room only when accompanied by her mother and her grandmother (maternal). She started happily on the usual free-play things, including painting. The door was open. Inadvertently the door was pushed to. Immediately Arabella began to tremble and whimper.

Doors that Smile or Cry

We opened the door and apologized to Arabella, but then pointed out that this door had a face, and that sometimes it could be happy, sometimes sad . . . we let the door have a smile on it and said 'Look – the door's smiling because you've come'. Figure 4.14 shows the reader why we could say this about the door. We had stuck eyes and mouth (using Blue-Tack) on the door. Of course Arabella, an intelligent little girl, knew this was a sort of game, and she was happy to go along with it. She then went to see faces on several other doors. The reader will note that a quick and dexterous reversal of the mouth made the door laugh or cry. Halfway through Arabella's painting – with the door open – Ken said 'I think the door is not very happy, I think it would like to close a *little* bit' (the mouth was now turned downwards – crying). Arabella got up and 'closed' it 6 inches, and it smiled again!

Gradually, over the next few weeks, Arabella was able to let the doors go nearer and nearer to being closed, and then to be quite calm with the doors really closed – a smiling, laughing door!

REVERSIBLE MOUTH

Figure 4.14 *Happy–unhappy door*

Even more briefly, let me explain other third objects that we used with Arabella:

1 A story about a little girl who had an adventure involving a house with windows and doors that could speak, and how they all became friends.
2 A tape of the story, which Arabella played every evening before falling asleep.
3 A rainbow to be coloured in at home, but she was told only to colour in *half* of each colour arch at a time, and *only* when she had been able to achieve a certain aim (such as having her bedroom door half-shut or the classroom door shut).
4 Telephone calls to Ken each time she achieved any aim – and of course Ken was 'over the moon' every time he got a call; this made her more keen!
5 An exciting 'treasure-hunt', in which she only got the next clue after achieving an aim, and culminating in spending an hour playing in a playmate's house.

6 Imagination games, at home and in the treatment room, in which 'tents' were included – we were in the 'jungle' and the tents were fairly claustrophobic.
7 Pretending, with us, that we were going on a lift and Arabella could open the doors by pushing a button. We used a small boxroom for the 'lift'.

We used other approaches, including imagery, when Arabella would sit and *think* about closing a door or walking to next door's house. When she did this she was asked to make herself relaxed ('make your arms and shoulders all floppy') and she held a little flag. She was to raise the flag if ever she felt afraid and we would immediately think of door opening, or imagine her going back to her own house.

Within three months Arabella was over the problem and became proud of all the things she could do, even to the extent of going on real lifts without a murmur. Of course the counselling or therapy dealt with the actual frightening event, and her parents were asked to do things differently. We don't pretend that all such cases will respond as well as Arabella did, nor would we say that the behavioural–cognitive approach would be what we would choose for many children, but the case illustrates the value of third objects which can be used for children with minimum emotional damage as well as for our deeply disturbed and maltreated children. It also shows what we mean by the worker coming up with new ideas to fit particular situations.

Faces for Little Ones
As we have been discussing work with quite young children such as Jamie and Arabella, this may be an appropriate place to mention another third object that we often use with little children.

Figure 4.15 shows six face-cards. Writing elsewhere about these cards I said:

> With young children who find it had to say what they feel about certain things, I have used one of the methods devised by Dr Vera Fahlberg, the method of using face-cards. This is a set of cards which has the same face but showing different moods. One face is crying, the next card has it smiling, another has it looking very cross, and so on. I may say to the young child something like this: 'When I show you this photograph (perhaps we are doing her life-story book) how do you feel? Does it make you sad, like that face, or does it make you cross, like that one, or do you feel happy like that one? You point to the one that feels like you do'. (Redgrave, 1987)

HAPPY, PLEASED   SAD, UNHAPPY   I FEEL ALRIGHT, O.K.

I'M NOT SURE   CROSS! ANGRY! MAD!   A BIT ASHAMED, SORRY

Figure 4.15 *Face-cards*

There are many other ways of using these face-cards. For instance they can be used quite by themselves, simply to stimulate a discussion. The worker may ask the child 'What is that one saying?' 'Tell me something about that one', or 'Would you like to draw some faces yourself?'

Never make the mistake of believing that these objects are restricted, however, to young children or to older children or adults, or that they serve only this or that purpose. I was very interested but not surprised when a client of mine, a young woman, saw the faces and then proceeded to work out several of her own relationship problems by drawing her own set of faces. Admittedly this client had a special gift for drawing – quite a genius in fact – but it was this set of faces that sparked off her exercise, and she was 24 years old!

We've Had 'My Tree', Now 'My World'

In discussing this next approach let me say, as we have said concerning life stories, that it is possible for the 'My World' third object to deteriorate into 'just drawing'. As a matter of fact this can be quite a difficult object to use, but if used properly and with the right children or teenagers, a lot of insight can be gained by the client and worker.

A lot of the third objects discussed in this book were devised by the author, but others have been 'lifted' from the works of other writers or have come to us via our colleagues. 'My World', which we have used with adults as well as children, was pilfered from Violet Oaklander. This is the way she introduced the subject in her book:

A very effective exercise is to have children draw their families as symbols or animals. Now think of each member of your family. If you were to draw them on a piece of paper as something they remind you of, rather than real people, what would that be? If someone in your family reminded you of a butterfly because they flit around a lot, is that what you would draw them as? Or maybe someone reminds you of a circle because they're always around you. Start with the one you think of first. If you get stuck, close your eyes and go back into your space. You can use blobs of colour, shapes, objects and things, animals and whatever else you can come up with. (Oaklander, 1978)

We explain it somewhat like that, but also show them an enlarged drawing of a 'My World' which we have actually taken from Violet Oaklander's book. Some children, we find, need more help than might be thought just from the extract above; otherwise they can't readily conceptualize. However, this becomes an opportunity to simply discuss people in their lives. 'Tell me about your brother.' 'What does he like doing?' 'Does he play sports?' 'How do you and he get on with each other?' Then we might ask, 'So what does he remind you of?' 'What can we draw to remind us of him?' The ideas still come from the child, although the therapist has helped the thinking process. We are aware

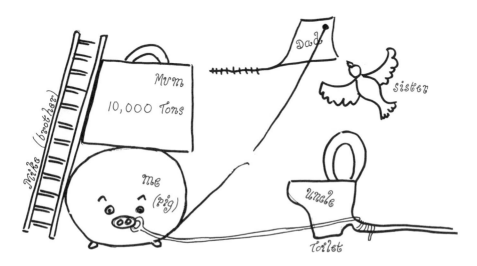

Figure 4.16 *'My world' drawing by a 13-year-old girl*

that some therapists will want to avoid any leading whatsoever; we prefer to use both methods on different occasions. So in the sand-tray work (which is much easier for a child to use), it is left completely to the child.

We don't, as a rule, ask children to shut their eyes, as Oaklander does. They seem to manage quite well without doing so, and some abused children could worry about what is going on while their eyes are shut.

We have also introduced other variations into our 'My World' object. This has come about as we have found ourselves responding to the needs of different children. With some children who enjoyed saying what the various people were like, but who were then reluctant to draw (and sometimes directly asked us to draw), we would draw the object they asked us to draw. We would then cut them out and the child would place them on the large sheet of white paper provided. This often gave them the will to add other 'people' or to draw in roads or join-ups.

Figure 4.16 shows a 'My World' made by a 13-year-old girl who was anorexic. She has drawn herself as a very fat pig. This concept of the body-self is typical of the anorexic. In fact at the time of the drawing she was emaciated to the extent that her legs and arms looked like sticks and her face was sunken and hollow-looking. This girl had been severely sexually abused by an uncle, and she could not get out of her mind the belief that she herself was the 'dirty' one and the 'guilty' one, despite the fact that she was between 9 and 12 years old during the period of abuse and therefore was the injured party. Nor could she get the uncle out of her mind. If she saw someone resembling him she would get panic attacks. So, in her 'My World' picture she is tied (through the nose) to him – he is depicted as a lavatory bowl.

She could not get on with her mother, whom she blamed for not protecting her. This is another common but often irrational belief, the belief that the parent *could* have done something. The mother is depicted as a heavy weight upon her back.

The father was happy-go-lucky, seldom at home, all over the world, so he's a kite. But notice that the cord which should have connected the girl to her father is broken! Then there is her 'beautiful and successful' sister, whom she drew as a bird (father's favourite!), who is able to fly up to dad and needs no cord. Her brother tries hard to 'climb' up to mum and dad but seems only able to get close to mum, so he's a ladder which has to do with climbing, and is leaning against mum.

In passing, although we are not dealing with case outcomes here, it is worth reflecting on the systemic view which the 'My World' can often reflect – and can let the client understand more deeply as a result. We see in this 'My World' the family system. Beyond that of course are the sub-cultural and cultural systems.

Focused Therapy

We have had many discussions concerning 'directing' and so-called 'non-directive' forms of therapy. Readers will appreciate the need that some children (and adults) have for a 'focusing' process. Such a process can help the child to utilize the therapeutic situation. We accept that with certain children a purely 'stand-off, say almost nothing, allow the child to emerge in the situation and focus on the transference' practice is ideal. It so happens that in many instances, especially where the child has to make decisions on practical matters, that kind of approach alone is often not helpful enough. Therefore, as we illustrate in this volume, a wider choice of approach is favourable, and here we emphasize the word choice. To some extent this is analogous to what happens in many professions, including medicine, where one aim (to heal) will be met by a diversity of techniques and medicines.

Discussion Rosette

It is important that when offering to help the child or young person to express her/himself no pressure should be used. As a result of this notion we developed a third object which we call the 'discussion rosette'. Figure 4.17 is a picture of a discussion rosette.

When the rosette is used, the child and the therapist agree to write out possible discussion subjects on small cards and place each one in one of the sections or cells in the rosette, taking turns to come up with

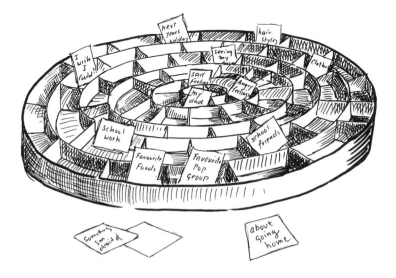

Figure 4.17 *Discussion rosette*

a subject. It is agreed that the child in fact *places* the cards. It is also agreed that the more difficult the subject to talk about, i.e. from the child's point of view, the nearer the centre of the rosette it is placed. Therapist and child may then take it in turns to ask permission to discuss any of the subjects. It is understood that each may decline to discuss a subject. While it is unlikely that the therapist (who may in fact be a carer or social worker) would decline to discuss a subject, the 'rule' that either may decline puts the child in a safe position. She can say 'No' without embarrassment. On the other hand she may say 'Not yet'.

The outer ring of cells is, of course, likely to contain subjects which are innocuous, such as 'pop-groups', 'last year's holiday' or 'hair-styles'. When using a rosette with a young child it may be made 'playful' by using some little toy figure – such as a replica of Pooh Bear – to represent the worker. The worker then makes the toy figure do the asking and at the same time jump into the cell holding the subject she wishes to discuss. The child can say 'No' and throw the little figure out!

Sand-tray Therapy

Although this form of therapy is easy to describe, some writers argue that its use is best left to therapists who have been trained in the therapy, because it may reach deep into the psyche. The child is invited to select from a wide variety of small objects, set out on shelves, and to make any scene or 'picture' she wishes to within the bounds of the sand tray. Figure 4.18 shows a typical sand-tray picture.

The results from this simple procedure, especially if the sand-tray work is extensive and a whole series of trays is made by the child, may be both enlightening and profound. It happens that Jungian analysts have made more use of this third object than have others, and perhaps the reason for this becomes clearer when we note that the small objects used, and the way they are used as part of the picture, together with the way the sand is used, all add up to a deeply symbolic function which, in Jungian terms, taps into the archetypal strata of the personal and the **collective unconscious**.

Dr Margaret Lowenfeld, who devised this form of therapy, writes:

My own endeavour in my work with children is to devise an instrument with which a child can demonstrate his own emotional and mental state without the necessary intervention of an adult either by transference or interpretation, and which will allow of a record being made of such a demonstration. (Lowenfeld, 1979).

Figure 4.18 *An 'orderly' tray picture by an 11-year-old girl*

We usually introduce the child to sand-tray work by showing her a few photographic examples and explaining that she may like to make a sand picture herself. With older children, teenagers for example, we usually tell them that although we are using sand and lots of objects, some of them being 'toys', this is really something which grown-ups do (which is true) and that most of our 16- and 17-year-olds have done this 'work' and have enjoyed it.

We show them the objects and point out 'Over here you'll find lots of different people, notice that some are "small" and others "large" (different scales), and here we have things you would find inside houses, while over there you'll see trees. Then of course there are all these houses, as well as a bridge . . . Down on this shelf there are fighting men (soldiers) and here are some wild animals . . . Oh, and these things are a mixture of objects. Look, there's a strange little African mask. There's an ornamental vase; an old Chinese man in prayer (the old man, the wise man?) . . .', and so on.

Then we tell the child she can make any pictures she wishes to make: 'It could be some place you can remember, or a dream you had, or you may simply like to collect the things you are attracted to – maybe you like the feel of them – and just put them in and see what picture turns up'.

We explain that while the child is making the sand picture the worker will make a drawing or sketch of it, if the child agrees. The worker tells the child that she will only begin the sketch when the child says it is OK to start. It is as well to do this because children often start a tray and then decide to shift things round before really settling for the true picture.

The therapist does not have to be an artist. He or she can make a ground-plan drawing simply putting in ovals and oblongs and naming them. However, we always try to obtain a photographic record of the tray. A series of such drawings and photographs becomes a useful source of analytical information as well as a record of change. It is really interesting to trace the change in the pictures and compare it to the change in the child.

This can be demonstrated in a series of sketches I made during many months of sand-tray work with a boy of 10, an intelligent child but one who had been 'unhappy and troubled since birth', according to the parents. This child seems to have experienced a birth trauma. The actual birth was very difficult and the child was reported as being 'in distress' during the birth. The amniotic fluid had been lost some days before the actual birth, but there had also been a condition known as oligohydramnios in which the fluid is always short of what is comfortably required. Marvin, the child concerned, had become a semi-recluse by the time I met him: partly being forced into a hostile world, but retreating to his own bedroom and his fantasy life as soon as he could.

Figure 4.19 shows my speedily made sketch of Marvin's first tray picture. There are several features here which are important when reviewing his series of trays. I shall discuss four of his trays covering a period of three months, during which time changes began to take place in Marvin's behaviour and outlook. I shall discuss the first tray, and then three others. Readers are asked to remember that other trays (with the same theme and the same design) intervened between those I am discussing. So I am discussing four out of a series of twelve trays.

Notice, first, that the tray in Figure 4.19 is divided into left- and right-hand sections. We shall notice that this division is carried through into the following trays and only slowly disappears – or resolves. But there is another interesting continuing feature. It is that the left-hand section contains a picture which carries a theme of violence, while the right-hand picture does not have any violence. This idea was carried forward, only really fading around tray number eight. By the time he reached tray twelve (our Figure 4.22), both the left–right division and the violence had almost disappeared.

Now take a closer look at Marvin's first tray. Look especially at the right-hand section. Notice that the child has mounded up the sand to form a 'defended' and 'safe' area, a sort of bulwark, with a large piece of rock or stone planted in the middle of it. Within the bulwark are non-fighting people as well as animals. There is a gate (closed) between the left- and right-hand sections. In the left-hand section we see soldiers fighting. The left-hand section is the dangerous section. The right-hand section is safe and contains an enclosure – the bulwark.

What is going on in the mind of the child as he makes the sand-tray picture? It is hypothesized that the picture constructed, and the objects selected, reflect at least two levels (probably more) of psychological function. On one level the child is conscious of the picture and what is happening in the picture; on a deeper level the child is attempting to resolve what we might call 'inner problems'. Estelle Weinrib, a specialist in this form of therapy, writes:

> I believe that the making of a sand picture is in itself a symbolic and creative art. Provided it is happening within the free and protective space [which she describes], symbolic active fantasizing by the patient stimulates the imagination, freeing neurotically fixated energy and moving it into creative channels, which in itself can be healing. (Weinrib, 1983)

Before leaving Marvin's first tray, readers are asked to look again at the sand bulwark. What does its shape and outlet remind you of? Whether or not we are reading too much into this, there is a distinct impression of a womb. The womb is normally understood to be a safe and protective place for the young life of the foetus. However, there is yet another remarkable 'coincidence' associated with this tray. The stone (in the middle of the 'womb' in the tray) is usually a very dry object. The children are usually given a small amount of water – a cupful – and a baby-feed scoop in case they wish to dampen some spot in the sand. Marvin told me that in order to keep the space really safe he must scoop small amounts of water over the stone to dampen it – it must not get totally dry! Could this have any connection with the oligohydramnios condition of his mother's womb, and the early loss of amniotic fluid?

This is not the place to expand on the symbolism of the objects used in Marvin's sand pictures, but do note the absence of certain features. There are no trees. Trees may have a positive significance psychologically. They hold the idea of 'renewal', of 'growth' and of 'strength'. Notice also the one soldier on the right-hand side, the 'man with the gun'. This is a defensive gun.

A few weeks later Marvin produced the tray picture shown in Figure 4.20. Here we still see the division of the tray into distinct left- and right-hand sections and once again there is violence and fighting going on in the left-hand side while the right-hand side has the 'very safe

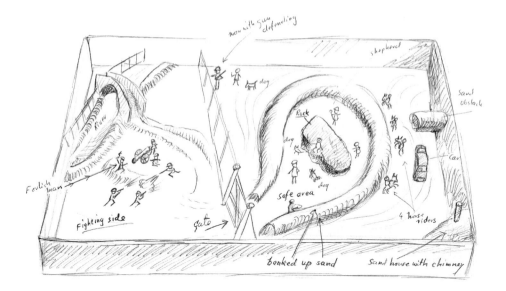

Figure 4.19 *Marvin's first sand world*

Figure 4.20 *Marvin's sand world a few weeks later*

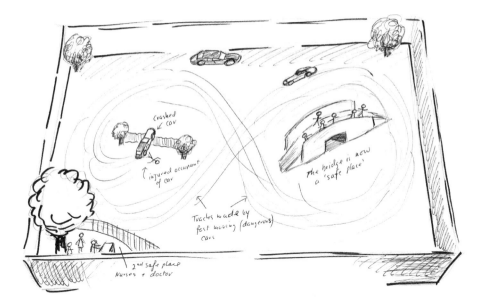

Figure 4.21 *Marvin's sand world after 2 months*

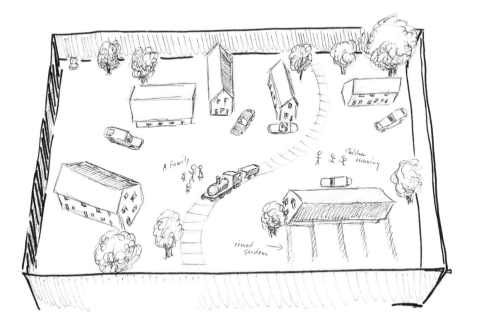

Figure 4.22 *Marvin's sand world after 3 months*

area', which is now made by using walls. Within this very safe area there is a family with children at play with a ball. Again there are animals.

Now look at the left-hand side, the violence side of this tray. Note two meaningful changes – additions. We now have trees. We also have nurses and an ambulance. Something is occurring to overcome the worst effects of the violence. The idea of 'care' and even 'tenderness' is being allowed to emerge.

Figure 4.21 shows a tray made by Marvin about two months after his first tray. The distinct separation of left and right is beginning to break down, but it still remains. However, the fence no longer divides the tray. Fences of course may be used in various symbolic ways. They may enclose or entrap, or they may protect or demarcate. Yet, even without the wall the safe and unsafe sides are still preserved. Now, however, the cars are racing round on a figure eight circuit and one of them has had an accident. Note that the hurt has come about by accident this time, not by shooting. Now, also, there is a second 'safe place' in the bottom left-hand corner, and a doctor is provided as well as nurses.

The right-hand half of this tray uses the bridge (note how certain objects are used frequently by some children) but the bridge now becomes a 'safe place'. Despite the apparent speed of the cars leading to hurt, there is a concept of movement. The idea of movement may indicate change, and certainly Marvin was responding in a way which indicated a desire to change to a more positive way of thinking.

The last of Marvin's trays that I shall describe is seen in Figure 4.22. This was in fact his twelfth tray, though by no means his final one: it was made about three months after his first tray. This tray illustrates the psychological change taking place in the child, although we were still only at the beginning of his being in therapy, which in his case covered at least two years.

In this tray there is a totally different 'feel' from that of the first tray. We are looking down on a village. There is no fighting; there is no violence, not even in accident form. There are houses, plenty of them. There is a family which now is able to be out in the open and not hemmed in as we saw earlier. There is a lot of movement. Some of the cars are meant to be seen as moving; there are two running children; and there is the little engine. This last is interesting because its railway lines stand for a vestige, the only remaining sign, of the dividing wall between left and right, but cars and people can cross the line in comparative safety. Marvin was eventually able to take his place fairly comfortably in school, college and society.

Figure 4.23 *Robert's sand world*

Figure 4.24 *Sand world (by a 7-year-old girl)*

On the preceding page are two more sand-tray pictures taken from our own practice and also taken 'out of context', in that we are showing these to our readers without them having the advantage of a complete case history or full discussion on the treatment provided. Our purpose here, however, is to introduce this important form of treatment, and to encourage readers to make further studies of sand-tray therapy and to undertake training in the subject.

Figure 4.23 shows a typical tray (the theme was recurrent) made by a 6-year-old boy whose neurotic behaviour and school refusal sprang mainly from 'separation anxiety'. This child's natural mother had deserted him about eighteen months' prior to our working with him. The child, Robert, would 'bury' his mother in the sand at the spot marked (Y). Robert is represented by the teddy-bear (X). In Robert's fantasy game, the mother has to break out of the sand and head for the ship (Z). To do this, however, she has to run the gauntlet of the armed men and the two lions, not to mention the cannon. On reaching the ship she must sail across the river and land safely on the lower bank thus uniting with her son.

The symbolism is richer than it may seem at first. The armed men and the threat from the lions look very much like the anger generated in the child towards his mother. A teddy bear is a cuddly object and the mother should want to cuddle him. The child at this stage lived in fear that his foster-mother would leave him, as his natural mother had done.

Figure 4.24 may seem quite unsubtle in that this child, a girl of 7, has openly presented a tray picture of couples, as she put it, 'snogging'. She made this picture, with variations, on a number of occasions. The couples were always lying down. Notice that she has one doll who she said is just 'watching'. Only by observing a series of trays by the same child would it be safe to conclude that this doll represented either herself or someone or some*thing*, for example some Power, watching her, unless of course she said to the therapist, 'That's me', which in fact she did. Notice how she also uses articles which imply a higher moral or ethical tone: the cross and the 'dove of peace' stone. This sexual theme completely died away as the therapy continued and as she became 'safe' in her adopted family. Notice the bridge ('safe place') planted firmly in the centre of this tray.

This is not the place to dwell on this child's background or to discuss further the revelations and our own conclusions. Readers will be aware that a series of such trays carried some significance. What it does help to show, however, is the value of sand-world (sand-picture) work for non-verbal expression of feeling and other factors within the self-healing scope of this particular approach.

There is a lot to learn concerning the use and effects of sand-tray work. For those who wish to study the subject under an experienced tutor, details of a number of books are given in Further Reading.

Third Objects and Cross-cultural Stress

Most of the third object examples we have presented so far have been discussed with relevance to person-centred and often unique events in the lives of individual children and adolescents. This is as it should be, but there is always a danger, in such descriptive accounts, of overlooking important broader factors such as sociological aspects and the dynamics of group and social psychology.

It is, for example, imperative that adults working with children who have lived through the sort of life experiences we are describing should have some training in the psychology of racism, and should be fully alert to the dynamics of cross-cultural stress. In our work we have found that the greater the 'cultural empathy' of the adults involved, the more positive has been the response from the children. For this reason we are including two examples of third objects which were used in cases involving racial and cross-cultural problems.

Loretta

The first example concerns a teenage girl who was anorexic (anorexia nervosa). Like most anorexics, Loretta experienced deep feelings of conflict and anger. She also experienced what has been called 'double consciousness' (Roy, 1997). Loretta was a second-generation Indian immigrant on her mother's side. She experienced 'multi-cultural parenting' as, although her mother was a high-caste Indian by birth, her father was a self-styled 'working-class Marxist from Liverpool's dockside'. He was white and Anglo-Irish. The 'double consciousness' was experienced, not only on account of the cultural clash between the parents, with each encouraging Loretta to disown aspects of the other's culture, but also because Loretta saw herself as being English, and yet felt 'part of herself', as she put it, was unacceptable to the main-line (majority or macro-) culture.

Loretta's loyalties, ideas, beliefs, attitudes and feelings were embedded in conflict and contradiction. She was helped partly by a simple way of 'sorting out' this mixture of cultural and sub-cultural conflicts by being able to 'stand back' and review what was going on, and by being able to share with a care worker all this 'muddle' in her life and the feelings it generated. In her case the care worker was well-practised in similar cross-cultural cases, and was from a minority ethnic group herself.

Three 'Clash' boxes were used to help Loretta. They were labelled in this way:

1 Mum – v – Dad.
2 Parents – v – other people.
3 Me – v – other people.

During each counselling session, material would emerge concerning Loretta's three conflict areas, which were:

1 (Corresponding to box 1) The cultural differences, prejudice, bias and misunderstanding between her parents. These included differences between ideas and attitudes about the meaning of life and about aspects of family and social life.
2 (Corresponding to box 2) The cultural differences between her parents and the macro-culture of the district (white English, urban society, occupational groups IV and V, i.e. partly skilled and unskilled).
3 (Corresponding to box 3) The cultural clash between the macro-culture and the ideas, beliefs and practices Loretta had accepted from each of her parents.

During counselling, and at other times, Loretta would write her thoughts down and put them in the 'appropriate' box. The insights she gained, and the continuing conflicts she endured concerning the relationship between her parents were put into box 1.

Box 2 was reserved for insights concerning the difficulties existing between her parents and the society in which they and she moved.

Box 3 was used for what was perhaps her most difficult experiences as they involved prejudice and antagonism directed towards her (as she saw it) by 'friends', teachers and other people she met up with.

This third object proved extremely helpful. It was so much better than simply 'writing down' in a sort of essay form, or even a diary form, the thoughts and conclusions emerging from counselling. It clarified the social interaction for Loretta and enabled her to ponder each category as she resolved her difficulties.

Robert

Our second example concerns a little black (African) boy of about 6 years old on referral. This little boy had 'lost' his natural mother when she 'left home' eighteen months prior to our meeting him. We will call him Robert. We have referred to him earlier. Robert was being looked after by very loving white foster-parents at the time of our work with him. He had not got over the traumatic loss of his mother and was exhibiting 'separation trauma' where the foster-mother was concerned. This showed up in his school phobia or school refusal. He was afraid when separated from his foster-parents (even for an hour or so), and afraid that they would not show up at the end of the school-day to collect him.

However, Robert was also angry that his natural mother had 'left' him. He was now at his second school, but he had been affected by racial prejudice and ignorance existing at his first school. He had been the only black child in the class, in fact the only ethnic-minority child, and had been upset by some children calling him 'Golly' and 'Niggy', and by a class-assistant who spoke crossly to him and reprimanded him (or so he felt) for colouring angels' wings black instead of white!

It may be helpful, here, to mention certain psychological features which were revealed during this child's treatment. 'Treatment' here is not a term restricted to clinical practice, but includes the work of the foster-parents and the teachers in Robert's (second) school who also worked in liaison with the therapist. In Kleinian terms (Melanie Klein) for instance, it was found that Robert was projecting 'badness' away from himself. But 'badness' included his black mother (who in his terms had abandoned him), and his own blackness. His own unresolved feelings of inner conflict were becoming more confusing as a result of the sort of behaviour we have described concerning the children in his first school, who intimated that he was different, 'funny', 'niggy'. This difference was all to do with skin colour – called 'black'.

Then again, angels are 'good' and 'good' creatures do not have 'nasty' (implied) black wings. How dare he make them black. Black like himself; black like his ('bad') mother – confusion and conflict! But he was also in conflict because he was attempting to form a true attachment to his white foster-parents, especially the foster-mother, yet he felt part of himself did not belong to the white family.

Making 'pictures' in various media, and talking about them, seemed the most helpful approach for Robert. He used sand and clay but he most readily expressed his feelings and conflicts through the medium of drawing and painting, although he was not fully aware of just how he was using the media.

Robert would often draw a picture, or as he said, 'a photo', of himself. Sometimes these self-portraits would be of himself alone; at other times 'at school' with other children. While all the other children remained 'white', which is to say their outline in felt-pen was not coloured-in, the 'photos' of himself had parts of his body filled with black or with any dark colour if no black was available. He usually left his face 'white' and made his legs and hands black. His hair was also black.

Obviously, this use of art medium helped the worker to talk with the child about his feelings. It also helped Robert to 'externalize' his problem while grappling inwardly with it. Robert once drew a picture of his mother (all in black felt-pen, all filled in with black) lying on the ground with a 'big heavy stone' on top of her, and on top of the stone was a rough drawing of a cross.

Readers will be interested to refer to Figure 4.23, which shows one of Robert's sand-tray pictures in which he had buried his mother in the sand. This child had to deal with one major problem, the loss of his natural mother, while experiencing another gross problem of cross-cultural prejudice. Direct work and care-therapy helped him, but it was some time before the wounds became only scars.

We have now presented and discussed a selection of third objects which, although many of them involve the client in sensory experiences, were illustrated as examples of third objects used together with counselling or therapy to help children to understand, relate to, reappraise and gain insight concerning themselves and others. We shall now consider third objects used mainly as sensory experiences, bearing in mind that the senses connect with memory and with emotions.

CHAPTER 5

Sensory experience: direct work using third objects particularly for sensory stimulation, also poetry, play-acting and bridging

' . . . sight, sound, touch, taste and smell. It is through these modalities that we experience ourselves and make contact with the world.'
Oaklander, V., 1978

There are two ways of viewing the involvement of sensory experience when considering the subject matter of this book, and we trust that both ways are being adequately represented. One way of viewing the importance of sensory experience is to consider its value as an aspect of healing, as an element in therapeutic work with child or adult.

The other way of viewing the function of sensory experience is to take into account its importance in terms of the child's physical and mental development. There is evidence, perhaps sparse at present, but mounting, to indicate that the actual physical development of the brain may be affected positively or negatively depending upon the amount and quality of physical stimulation an animal receives in infancy. The number of connections made between brain cells, for example, may differ as a result of different early sensory experience. Susan Greenfield (1997), the pharmacologist and university professor, states:

> For example, adult rats were exposed to an 'enriched environment' where they had an abundance of toys, wheels, ladders, and so forth with which to play. In contrast, other, similar rats were kept in an ordinary cage, where they received as much food and water as they wanted, but no toys.

> When the brains of these two groups of rats were examined, it was found that the number of connections in the brain had

increased only in the animals in the enriched environment, not in those from the ordinary cages. (p. 117)

We must remember, however, that sensory stimulation energizes activity, so that the opportunity to 'experiment' with objects is part of sensory stimulation. Greenfield goes on to say:

In the study with rats, it was found that it was the activities that involved learning and memory, not mere physical activity, that resulted in the greatest changes in the brain . . . Thus, as we live out our lives, we fashion the connections between neurons that endow us with an individual, unique brain. (p. 117)

Of course, apart from evidence of physical development changes, there is a mass of evidence to indicate that physical stimulation affects behavioural development in mammals and some other species, and we have given some examples, in Chapter 1, of the effect on human infants of the lack of physical stimulation. It seems that even passive stimulation is necessary for the proper development of some species. Ashley Montagu, who has written extensively on the importance of touch and skin stimulation states:

As soon as I commenced my inquiries among persons with long experience of animals I found a remarkable unanimity in the observation they reported. The substance of these observations was that the newborn animal must be licked if it is to survive, that if for some reason it remains unlicked particularly in the perineal area (the region between the external genitalia and the anus), it is likely to die of a functional failure of the genito-urinary system and/or the gastrointestinal system. (Montagu, 1978)

There may be another important mental development function associated with early sensory experience. Papousek (1969) (quoted by Margaret Donaldson) argues that young infants and babies have a built-in tendency, not only to gain control over environment (objects) but, as Donaldson puts it, '. . . are already engaged in building some kind of "model" of bits of the world – some mental representation of what it is like' (Donaldson, 1978, p. 111).

It is important to remember that many of the children we see, i.e. children who have been nurturally deprived in infancy, have not had the opportunity to experience sensory (and sometimes motor) experiences in the rich way that we are stipulating as important. Then there are those children who, because either the adults have provided only sparse sensory involvement or they have been over-protective, are not encouraged or permitted to enjoy sensory experiences. Again, quoting Donaldson, 'It is arguable that in some ways we do not encourage competence – that we keep our children too dependent for too long, denying them the opportunity to exercise their very considerable capacity for initiative and responsible action'.

Let me emphasize again that when I am using words such as 'exploration' and 'control' I have in mind, as well as later cognitively connected experiences, the most basic sensory and motor experiences, such as the baby's senses of touch, taste, smell and warmth, which go along with breast feeding and even bottle feeding. We are thinking of the effect of movement in the life of the new-born and the toddler, and of the effect of light, colour and sound. And let us not forget that more and more evidence becomes available to convince us that all the senses are probably active (or activatable) from eight weeks of pregnancy. We know now that babies start to hear after about 20 weeks in the womb.

This chapter, however, will be concerned chiefly with the use of third objects where the main (but not the only) objective is to provide the child with sensory experiences which will become part of the total therapeutic experience. It is interesting to note that therapeutic work involving materials such as clay, paint, wood and sand is helping adults as well as children. Andy Sluckin refers to therapeutic work undertaken with two mothers who had experienced 'bonding failure' with their infants following severe post-natal depression. The outcome in both cases was good, and Sluckin reports:

> One of the most striking aspects of the therapeutic process in these two cases was the power of the visual image to create a context for growth. Both these women worked with art materials and placed great emphasis on the art therapy process. As artists they allowed novel connections and new meanings to emerge; (Sarah) 'I could express my emotions in a safe place . . . It showed me how to relate to my family . . . It allowed me to decide what others could see (of me) . . . (Catherine) 'I got strength through painting . . . It helped me sort out my feelings . . . I could make a tender fleeting moment last longer . . . The pictures acted as landmarks along the way; that's why I hung them up . . . But they didn't always turn out as I want (or expect).' (Sluckin, 1998)

Remember, however, that along with sensory impressions go memories, and along with memories go feelings. The reader will observe the way these elements are bound together in experience as we discuss the various sensory third objects. As we have already explained, this is not a textbook on any particular school of psychology and therefore the extent to which the material is used and the interpretative outcome resulting from the client's use of the material, or his resulting behaviour, will reflect the worker's understanding of psychology, and of his or her particular therapeutic approach.

For example, Jung saw the neuroses resulting not so much from the repression of ideas (although that was accepted) but as the 'splitting off' of parts of the psyche. Whole complexes, in this view, may be split off. Also, elements of the **personality typology** may become 'lost' or split of so that, whereas 'naturally' a child may develop a 'sensation (sensory)–extrovert' psyche, the 'sensation' element may, for example, be split off. Many of these split-off elements, according to this view, become or remain unconscious and yet act as separate psyches within the individual, causing further conflict.

We have touched on this 'deeper' aspect of sensory work because we want to emphasize that whatever hypotheses we may hold on these matters, one thing grows more certain daily: it is that the quality of early motor and sensory experience has a profound effect upon development and behaviour. In providing experiences later than babyhood or infancy, where there has been a lack of good-quality experience or even an experience of painful (emotional and/or physical) sensory life, we have been able to see children make amends for the deficiencies of their earlier experiences.

Take a Broad View

Care-therapy involves more than the work in clinical settings that is mainly described in these chapters. It is important for the reader to keep in mind that the sensory experiences that we are describing in this chapter should echo what is being provided in the 'real world'. Apart from the special treatments such as the Infant Nurture Programme described in Chapter 2, and provided within Donna's daily milieu, we should provide a richness in everyday experience. Even with the children we treat clinically we like if possible to take advantage of a walk or a run outside.

Fortunately these days most children do get plenty of body movement enjoyment in running, swimming, roller-blade skating or whatever. But some children who come for treatment may need help in actually relating to their physical environment, so it can be wonderful, for example, to run through the woods and rustle through the dry leaves, or to pause after a run and listen, to hear what sounds you can pick up – 'I can hear the sound of my heart beating!'

The Gestalt psychologists are particularly interested in the individual's relationship to his physical environment, as we have indicated in Chapter 1. So we find Violet Oaklander (1978) describing part of her treatment with a child:

> We have taken off shoes and tried feeling a variety of textures with our feet. We have taken a walk barefoot indoors and out and *talked about* how our feet can feel. We've compared the feeling of our feet on cardboard, newspaper, fur, rugs, pillows, sand, grass, leaves, metal, cement, brick, dirt, felt, rice, water. (p. 110, my emphasis)

Earlier, in the same book, she had written:

> Throughout this book I write about giving the child experiences that will bring back to herself, experiences that will renew and strengthen her awareness of those basic senses that an infant discovers and flourishes in: sight, sound, touch, taste and smell. It is through these modalities that we experience ourselves and make contact with the world. (p. 109)

The Five Senses

Once we have assessed that it will help the child to have a focused experience of the senses we may suggest that she draws a person – a man, woman or child – on a large piece of paper so that we can then talk about what the eyes, ears and other sensory areas 'do'. An alternative is to draw round the child while she lies on a very large piece of paper. Figure 5.1 shows such a preparatory drawing. This one is an example of the first method, i.e. the child drew a picture of a 'girl', and then the worker began asking questions or making comments. She asked, 'What can her mouth do?' Naturally, the child came out with what came into her mind. She said, 'It can talk', and then, 'It can eat food'. Interestingly, not many children immediately say 'It can taste'. The reader will see from the illustration that we did eventually get round to touch (feel), taste, sight (see) and sound (hear).

We then (perhaps in the next session) do some sensory 'work' (or play?), concentrating on one of the senses, but of course all the other senses will be involved although not highlighted. Because in babyhood taste (and of course the mouth – oral phase!) is a highly focused experience, we usually start with that sense.

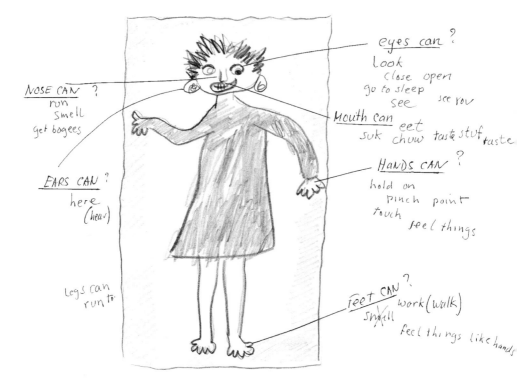

Figure 5.1 *A preparatory drawing executed at the start of a sensory-work programme*

The 'Taste Tray'

Most children love this experience even though some of the tastes are 'horrible'. The 'taste tray' consists of small quantities of different edibles, just 'tastes', some unusual, some sharp, others bitter, salty, sweet, and so on. We usually manage to include one or two substances which give other than taste experience, such as sherbert or some other 'fizzy' mixture: sorbet powder is an example. This adds a bit of fun. I would not be surprised if readers are at this very moment recalling childhood memories of 'fizzy' things!

We should also mention 'hot' tastes, although with a caution not to overdo it, and of course to adjust the tray to the age and other attributes of the child. Some things, like chilli sauce or fresh chillies, except in the minutest speck, would be too hot. In any case, when we use the taste tray we always have a 'spitting bowl' for the child so she may spit out any 'horrible' substance immediately. Another rescue substance is water; have a mug of water always at hand just in case the hot was a bit too hot.

We usually arrange the 'tastes' in a set order (see below), and behind a screen on the table so that the child concentrates, and we do, on one taste at a time. Mind you they usually take a peep just to see what is behind the screen.

Usually we start with mundane foods, but in an unusual state. Small pieces of diced raw potato are offered, 'Guess what this is . . . we'll both taste and then talk about this taste'. Raw potato is unusual, and it has an earthy taste. We tell each other what the taste reminds us of.

Another 'ordinary' vegetable is green peas. Most children in the western world have cooked (previously frozen) peas, or tinned 'mushy' peas. Seldom do they have freshly picked green peas, and even more seldom do they open the pods and eat the peas raw. If they are in season we obtain peas in pods and taste them raw; if not we share the taste of defrosted green peas – raw.

Again we share the taste experience. Some children say they taste like grass. I wonder how much grass they've eaten! We always ask if the taste reminds them of anything. This is important because as well as concentrating on the sensory experience we want to link that experience with any memories. Very often children are reminded of a place, a person, a particular time in their lives. I remember a child tasting some Marmite on a very small square of buttered bread – only use a *trace* of Marmite, it is strong. Immediately he recalled times he used to have with his grandmother. He recalled the little back room they sat in, and the buttered 'Marmited' toast. We decided to have a special talk about grandmother, and that time in his life, at our next session.

We gradually move over to sweet things, but only after trying out other kinds of vegetables or edible herbs – fresh herbs of course. We chew a small piece of, say, rosemary, and then put the chewed or tastes piece into the spitting bowl. Another surprise in the summer-time is nasturtium leaves straight from the garden with their minty–peppery taste.

Here are some tasty ideas for you, probably in this order of introduction after the vegetables:

Sharp tastes. Thin slices of lemon to suck
Vinegar to dip a finger in and put on the tip of the tongue
Worcester Sauce, ditto
Pomegranate cells
(Can we think of any 'sharp' people, or 'sharp' moments or 'sharp' feelings?)

Salty tastes. Salty water, an eggcupful. Again, dip finger and taste. What does it bring to mind? (The sea? The baths? Anything else . . . ?
Seaweed if available
Marmite
Crisps, just one or two tastes

'Hot' tastes. Root ginger, cut to minute pieces – ready to spit out and take a swig of water! (I mean the raw root stuff not the stuff in syrup)
OK – stem ginger in syrup – very nice, hot and sweet!

Bitter tastes. Lemon peel
Orange peel

Sweet tastes. Sweet fruit
Brown sugar (makes a change from white)
Honey
Chocolate spread

And I am sure the reader can think of many others. Sometimes, in order to have fun and concentrate at the same time, we get the child to 'close eyes' and tell us which yoghurt is the strawberry, which the peach, and which the banana. We spoon-feed the child from each pot – the worker will often be obliged to have his or her three spoonfuls in return.

There are many other taste games you can play. Once again, we appeal to the reader's imagination and ingenuity but, and this is important, valuable as are the actual sensual experiences in sensory work, do give the child an opportunity to express herself concerning whatever feelings and memories may be conjured up in connection with the sensory experience.

From Lavender to Old Socks: Smells

'What can the nose do?' we might ask. 'Yer nose can run', might be the reply. The sense of smell is closely associated with memory, and of course taste and smell are connected. If you have a bad cold, or if you pinch your nose while eating, you lose much of the taste.

We may have a 'smell tray' and use it in much the same way as the taste tray. Think of the many scents or odours it is possible to collect for this exercise. First, we can simply use a variety of edibles which might grace the taste tray; our friend 'Marmite' may return. But with the sense of smell we often play the game with a guessing element involved. So the child might first have a sniff with eyes closed. We might offer the pot of honey and say 'Tell me what this is'. Another way to guess is to look at about three or four articles, and then close eyes for a moment and try to sniff which one is which.

Nice and Nasty Smells

We usually have a few 'nice' smelling essential oils, as used in aromatherapy. These oils, in small bottles, may be purchased from drugstores, pharmacists and other shops. Of course, as for taste, 'nice' and 'nasty' are very subjective matters so far as smells are concerned. Don't forget the herbs as well as the oils. Actually one of the nastiest smells in our box of smells is some herbal cough medicine, 'nasty' that is to most children, but I remember one boy who 'loved' that smell because it reminded him of some strange brew his grandfather used to concoct.

Another smell game is to go round the house, or the permitted areas of the clinic or school in which the therapy sessions are held, and discover various smells as you go – include the garden if there is one. Have a sniff in the cleaning-materials cupboard where the polishes and sundry smelly articles are kept.

Play 'I remember' with smells (you can play it with taste, sound, or colour as well). 'Can you remember a special smell from the seaside?' or 'Can you remember some smells you used to like when you were little?' 'What did your grandmother use which used to smell nice?' (With grandfather it often turned out to be tobacco!)

The Eyes Have It

There are many obvious activities concerned with the sense of sight, and yet unless you, so to speak, capture a particular sight phenomenon, sight is the more easily overlooked even though most children are using their eyesight all the time they are awake.

We made great use of colour. We allow the child to mix paint colours and to see how many hues and shades or tones s/he can produce. With many children the mixing goes on and on until a darkish grey is produced. It is helpful to have at least two plastic palettes, the sort which each have about nine 'cups' or mixing saucers in them. Have plenty of white paint available.

There are games to be played with colours. Try playing 'memory matching'. The therapist or other worker will need to have prepared strips of various *shades* of green, red, blue, etc. An exactly similar set (colourwise) is produced at the same time, using the *same* colours. The child chooses which red he will remember, and which blue, for example, then five minutes later looks at the matching set of colours and chooses the one he has 'remembered'. He takes this and compares it with the one he previously selected.

There is also fun to be had with 'seeing'. We collect various optical illusions, or even create some just to show that we can't always 'believe' our eyes. 'Touching the pencil' is another sight-involved exercise. The child holds her hand over one eye and keeps that eye closed. She is invited to touch the pencil the worker is holding up, but she must bring her touching finger (index finger) sideways on to the pencil. If this 'trick' is performed properly, the viewer will usually miss the pencil by a few centimetres. The point of the finger must come in sideways, aiming for the pencil.

If you can get hold of a few gadgets it will also help with the sense of sight. We use a modern 3-D viewer to give the child the sense of 'being there'.

No, we have not overlooked the computer and 'painting' using the mouse. That can be fun as well, but it has become ordinary for many children, so try putting the colour arrow on an object and colouring it in either with eyes shut or (the child's choice) by looking away or having a piece of card blocking out his view.

We play 'memory seeing' as well. The child is invited to remember anywhere he has been to in his life and to try to name as many objects as possible which he can 'see' in his mind's eye. This of course may spark off all sorts of feelings going along with memories.

What about a 'seeing stroll'? Walk a short distance either along a street or round a garden and agree that at the end of the stroll you will compare notes on what you 'saw'; see how different your lists may be.

Very quickly let me suggest some other sight objects: try making a peep-show in a shoe box; see what patterns emerge with a kaleido-scope; see how big you can make things with a magnifying lens and how small you can make them with a reducing lens; see things through binoculars, then look through the wrong end.

Touching Moments

In recent years, whenever I have been talking on our subject to groups of carers or social workers, this aspect, touch, has always produced the most questions as well as highlighting the feelings of concern and even confusion existing in the group. Most readers will know why this is. Schools (European, UK, USA?) now work to strict codes concerning the way staff touch children, or strictly speaking, the way they avoid touching children.

These schools codes seem to have come about as a result both of the revelations concerning child sexual abuse and the tendency on the part of some children, or the adults responsible for them, to make accusations against staff, sometimes bringing lawsuits. This is not the place to debate this matter in great detail, and we hope that in the text which follows there will be given a number of examples concerning touch which everyone will feel are 'safe'. However, even without much debate, it will be agreed that there is both reason for feeling thankful and reason for regret that our society is now so confused over touch, or even over some forms of care. We know many very caring people who now avoid approaching a child at a busy road crossing in order to see the child safely across. Yes, they *could* be 'kidnappers', and yes, some child might be killed in crossing. It is difficult.

In various ways it has already been noted, in this book, that actual touching, individual to individual, is an important aspect in child (and therefore ultimately adult) development. We have at least implied that in the early months of infancy it is important as part of the nurturing process – untouched babies appear to suffer psychologically and physically. Then again, many adult clients of psychiatrists and psycho-therapists break down and weep over the realization that they were never hugged as children.

Before moving on to examples of 'touch' third objects, however, I want to emphasize that many children (and adults) *cannot bear* being touched, and touching the wrong client, even offering to hold hands to cross the road, could send more than shivers down the spine of the touched child. Some psychological and/or brain-abnormal conditions cause the person (child or adult) to suffer torment if touched by another person, particularly if affection is implied. Donna Williams, an autistic, but highly intelligent autistic, tells on her audiotape how she felt when she and a young man who had 'befriended' her touched hands by mistake:

> There was no desperation to reach out and touch each other in the real world. The only thing that mattered was that someone had touched me emotionally. One day as we sat (having a picnic) and without any deliberateness, our hands touched. I was terrified . . . The pain of this emotionally touching touch was almost more than I could bear . . . I felt as though I was going to die. (Williams, 1994)

Third Objects Focusing on Touch
The reader will note that we have already described some of these third objects, as several of them were mentioned in Chapter 2, in the case of Donna. For example, we described in some detail how Donna used foot-painting, and how the worker washed her feet. We also

described the Infant Nurture Programme which was designed for Donna.

Also in Chapter 2 we described Donna's enjoyment in using the clean potter's clay. We shall take a further look at such materials and the use made of them. Certainly the clay has an important place in our therapy room, and also in the foster-homes and schools where care-therapy is to the fore. We do use other touchy/squeezy materials, especially for younger children, including Plasticine and Play-doh. However, even with clay, which is a clean material, some children abhor the dry feeling they get on their hands, so we need to be careful. Always have a bowl of water available for dipping fingers in, in order to stroke the clay into something smooth and touchy, if not slimy! We encourage foster-parents and other close carers, where a young damaged child needs to experience touch, to actually help the child to wash her hands after clay – provided this is clearly acceptable to the child. Sometimes this is seen simply as a 'hurrying up' procedure, but it can be a good caring experience. Clay, unlike some of the other materials, does not stick in clothing, and when dry can easily be brushed out.

While we are thinking about clay and touch we shall mention two examples in which the sensory and the insight aspects came very clearly together. The first concerns a 16-year-old who was heading in the direction of becoming anorexic. In our counselling discussions we were talking about the different aspects of his behaviour, and he had been able to visualize these different aspects as if they were different people sometimes pulling in different directions (see Rowan, 1990).

He had also been working on a 'My World' (see p. 120) but had not been able to decide how to symbolize himself. Then, when using the clay he discovered that without planning to do so he had shaped it into a polygonal figure which presented many 'sides'. He used the clay figure to symbolize himself once it had set hard. He cut pieces of paper and glued them onto the surfaces and then added the names we have used in therapy. He was then able to complete his 'My world' drawing by adding this symbol. So, although the clay was used in the first place as a soothing form of touch therapy, it also became an insight third object.

Our second example is drawn from the work we did with Neil. This is the young boy we described earlier and whose bridge we have already discussed (p. 66), as well as his 'my tree' picture (p. 100), but as well as being burdened with anxiety Neil had a need to express a destructive, aggressive aspect of his personality. He used to like films or videos which showed violence, and one of the films he liked was *Jaws*, which has to do with a killer shark. When using the clay he fashioned a scene in which Jaws was swimming, open-mouthed, towards a struggling swimmer who was about to be crushed between the upper and lower rows of dagger-like teeth. Neil made the wavelets of water in the sea, and he painted the whole scene once the clay had set. As we do not kiln-dry these models we usually glue them onto a very thick cardboard to lessen the likelihood of breakage.

Another touchy, clay pastime is what we call the clay 'pizza'. For this pastime, which often seems to help some children relax and talk, you take balls of clay, about the size of a large orange, and roll or flatten them out into 'pizza' bases. Next the child selects from boxes containing an assortment of coloured bits and pieces: beads, buttons, coloured stones, shells . . . and sets them into the clay making whatever patterns she wishes. Although on the face of it this seems like simply making a 'pretty' object, the mind of the child will often be using the clay pizza to relate unconsciously to deeper, possibly archetypal, material which Jungian therapists would be interested in.

Other Touchy Materials and Games

The 'feely-bag' is, I think, quite well known among workers. There are many ways of using the feely-bag and similar feel–touch articles. A common way is to place articles of different textures into the bag (which should have a pull-to opening like a sponge-bag so that you can ensure the things remain hidden from view), and then during the session the child is invited to 'feel and describe' them. Another way is to ask the child to pick out objects; this method is sometimes better with very young children.

We also have a variation for school-aged children, when we use thick plastic letters or numbers. We show the child these letters and numbers before putting them in the bag, and then say something like 'See if you can find a "T"', or we may just invite the child to dive in with one hand, feel a letter (or a number) and say what it is before bringing it out of the bag.

Water-play is fun, and of course there is a special feel to water. We use a large tub or basin (we have used a baby-bath) and we provide various 'toys' or water equipment related to the child's age or interests. These include boats, and 'people' who can swim, but water-wheels and gadgets may be available. Some children discovered a way of 'munching up' newspaper with their hands and turning the pulp into articles which they called 'mats' – there's no end to the watery touch. Then, of course, there is the bubble-bath liquid which can heighten the sensory experience with picking out all the rainbow colours seen in the bubbles.

Water touch should be a part of actual living in foster-homes, children's homes and families in general. So if a child is being treated by us and he needs an enriched touch experience, then swimming is part of the expected 'at home' treatment. Remember to call the child's attention to other sensory experiences when water is used: the splash, the squelch, the bubbly noise made when you blow down a tube into the water.

Touch–Taste–Smell Regression
We know of some very loving and competent parents who adopted a family of three children with disturbed psychological backgrounds. At one stage, to meet with the children after two years with these parents would have meant meeting three lively children of normal intelligence who were engaged in many activities such as swimming, music, gymnastics, dancing, football, etc., children who were sometimes 'up' and sometimes 'down', in moods and behaviour. However, had you been privy to the more domestic and private life of the family you would have discovered that, at that time, when the children were aged about 7, 9, and 10, all three owned and used their own baby-feeding bottles. If they felt like it, perhaps when in a 'down' mood, they would have a private suck at the baby bottle, which might contain orange-juice.

This was part of an Infant Nurture Programme. Readers will recall that Donna (Chapter 2) had one designed for her, although in her case it did not feature a feeding bottle. If it is felt that a child in therapy will benefit from this form of touch–taste, we may leave a bottle in a prominent place. If the child, of any age, asks to 'try it', which often happens, we let him use the bottle – usually with a fruit drink.

Clearly, this third object may be used to capture a regressive experience. However, with most children, it will be used (experimented with) over a short period of time (two weeks to two months) and then discarded. The child's 'worker' (residential worker, foster-parent or clinician) will be involved in work which will be designed to ensure that the child moves forward (see Chapter 6) and does not get emotionally stuck with the object. The lay carer (if not professionally qualified as a therapist or counsellor) will seek professional advice on this matter.

Finally, there seems to be a case here for allowing some especially needy children to be treated by a professional aromatherapist.

Sound Advice

We have considered touch, taste, sight and smell as aspects of sensory-experience treatment, and have stressed the importance of attaching the sensory experiences to events in the child's life. Reflect for a moment on sound and your own private memories. Consider what an important part a piece of music may play in evoking the past. A tune, a song, a symphony, may have you recalling times, incidents, people and, above all, feelings.

For some it may be the tune of what was (or may still be) a popular number; a dance-band song, a film theme music. For others it may be a hymn. In fact all these musical genres may awaken something in each of us.

But do something else. Close your eyes and recall a time and place in your life: Christmas Day when you were a child; a seashore; a private memory of place and time. Recall sounds associated with those memories. Quite likely you will also experience an affective change: you will begin to experience feelings related to the sounds, especially if you recall the sounds of voices – voices of people special to you. You could become quite 'emotional'!

Let us not overlook sound then, even when we are working on life-story books or flow charts: 'What are the sounds you can remember, the sounds you heard in Nana's (Grandma's) house?' 'I've just remembered, she used to rattle the fire about with a poker and make the cinders fall underneath the fire' or 'There was a big clock in the hall that went ding-dong all night.'

Sound Games

Just as we used touch games so we often use sound games when working with children. Remember, it will not be all children who need intensive sensory-work therapy, only those whose early nurturing experience was poor. But sensory work may help children and adults who are experiencing psychosocial problems. In some cases music-therapy is indicated (referred to below).

In our 'ordinary' clinical and at home (or school) work, however, we may use the hearing–guessing game. In this game the worker has a collection of everyday articles and makes ordinary sounds with them. The child has to be somewhere quite near but not where she can see the objects. The worker then makes the sounds and the child has to guess what the sound is coming from. Here are some examples: putting the lid on the teapot; stirring some beverage or liquid in a cup or pot, with a teaspoon; shutting a cupboard door; running a tap; opening a brief-case, and closing a heavy book. Usually the child then wants to have a go, so you have to make sure there are plenty of possibilities.

There is also a sound-memory game. In this game we ask the child to see how many sounds she can recall from some recent event (visit to the zoo, holiday by the sea, etc.).

We can do a bit of science and sound with children. If you have a substantial wooden post at hand get the child to put her ear to one end while you tap the other – see how vibration travels! OK, so you haven't got a spare post in your house or clinic! Better still then, when out for a country or in-the-park walk (or run) if you do come across a big log, a fallen tree, try it out then.

Perhaps more practical are musical instruments, especially percussion instruments. Anyone working with or bringing up children (of any sort) should make musical instruments available. We are in the same league now as when we were talking about art and painting. We are not teaching children music any more than we were teaching them painting. There are some children who are brilliant artists and they should be helped to develop their art. The same goes for music. Some children will turn out to be very clever, if not geniuses. But music or musical instruments used in our therapy setting are there to alert the senses (and maybe memories) of any child. Usually, in fact, we are not making 'music', we are making sounds. We may take three drums and give the child three drums and we will try drum talking: 'try making your drums be angry with mine . . . OK now my drums will shout back at yours . . .' 'Now let's pretend they are friends and are both laughing together . . .' 'Now my drums are going to be sad' (make 'sad' single drum beats) 'and your drums are now cheering me up . . .' and so on.

Then of course we put an audiotape on and leave it to the child to beat time (or just beat!). There are so many things you can do with just a few instruments.

Outside sounds are important because most of these alert the child to her immediate surroundings. Usually, we are unaware of most sounds. This seems absurd if we are talking about people who have good-enough hearing but in fact it is true because our focus (of interest) is elsewhere. When I had a ticking clock I used to try out a little experiment with people (adults and children). I would stand near the clock and say, ' . . . listen . . . isn't it quiet, see if you can hear anything'. Often they said 'No – nothing'. Then I stopped the clock and only then did they become 'aware' that it had been ticking.

So when our children are out with parents or foster-parents we encourage the parents (or others) to play hearing games with them. It is amazing how many, these days, don't hear the birds; or they don't hear the river rippling (even splashing) along, or the raindrops reaching the puddles or the window-pane. If all this seems quiet and gentle, then how about *screaming*! Yes, screaming where it is OK to scream.

There are some very exciting 'modern' things to do outside when we can combine the extremes of sensory experience and make a big noise by screaming. I am thinking of the modern funpark, with the 'rides' that fling you in the air and whirl you round, the roller-coasters that give you the impression you are diving vertically to the ground, and the virtual reality (strapped-in, mobile) film experiences.

It goes without saying that not every child or teenager wants this but for those who do, let them have it. But we like to provide the opposite extremes of experience. That is why we often have a background of classical music, or 'mood' music, when a child is painting or using clay, etc. I remember one 9-year-old boy who came from what people describe as a 'rough' background. Session after session Schubert's *'Trout' Quintet* was softly playing. He never mentioned the music. On one occasion, however, I left out the music. That child suddenly stopped his clay-work and said, 'Where's that nice music we always have?'

Music and Art Therapy

These are specialized therapies. It is important to mention this because some children will benefit by referral to specialist therapists. No one is prohibited from using paint, or drums, or clay, and people should not try to set up 'new' therapies every time some third object proves helpful, otherwise we shall soon have diplomas in Yo-Yo therapy, or roller-blade therapy. However, music therapy (like art therapy) training involves knowledge and skills in the arts, integrated with counselling and therapy skills.

There are children, some of them autistic, who have been able to relate to the world outside them, and begin to use language as a result, clearly because of their music therapy experience. In the case of extremely withdrawn and/or traumatized children, consideration should be given to such specialist treatment.

Creative 'Hands-on'

I have so far been emphasizing what we might call sensuous objects such as clay and the taste-tray. Some children love to make things. In making things the media used may not be so sensuous. They may use balsa-wood, cardboard or paper (as when making papier-mâché). We often combine a making-things operation with a game-playing activity. Dolls' houses are constructed from cardboard boxes and the furniture from thin card or matchboxes, the carpets being paper either painted over or coloured with felt-pens. Then of course we use them with the doll people to enact events.

We have made theatres, cardboard ships, cardboard villages and so forth. One little boy (and therapist) spent many hours making a farm. Large flat boards (throw-outs from shops) became covered in green paint to represent green meadows. That little boy had a special thing about farms. These were rather idealized versions of the old-fashioned 'mixed' farms with cattle, horses, hens in the farmyard, a farmhouse, ponds, cottages – you name it.

Depending upon the age, abilities, and keenness of the child, these models tend to be either unrecognizable sloshes of colour; or scale-model cottages and churches carefully planned in one-piece bend-and-stick models. Sometimes gardens are made in boxes using either artificial flowers or dried flowers, but sometimes actually planting seeds. Do not forget that creativity itself is healing (in emotional terms) and generative (in intellectual terms).

Before leaving the hands-on creative third objects, let me once again place in juxtaposition a game which some will see as the very opposite of creative. I shall call this game 'bombardment'. We each, i.e. child and adult, have half the wooden building blocks (intended for very young children) and each build a 'castle' or 'barricade' on the floor, hiding our 'men' (toy soldiers) in different parts of the structures.

We then take it in turns to bombard the opposition's castle using a solid, but not too hard object for the purpose, e.g. a potato of about 4 cm in diameter wrapped in several layers of tinfoil. The last one to have a man standing is the winner! I'm sorry if this sounds bellicose. I can only say that many children who have played it, and used all the other creative experiences, have gradually moved from a destructive mode of general behaviour to a more creative and calm mode. Clearly, such constructive/destructive activity used clinically will be related to the therapist's understanding of the child's needs.

Imagination, Imagery, Drama and Dance

In this book I have given these activities a separate section because, although we use them therapeutically, they are characteristically different from the activities so far discussed. Some of them involve the thought processes in ways very different from the cognitive skills already outlined. Yet many of these activities appeal to very young children. As with all the activities and third objects, children will be selective about their use of them.

Poetry and Stories

Some children who have had disturbing life experiences, or have experienced sudden loss and trauma, are able to help themselves by expressing feelings or recording events through the creative activities of story or poetry. Such 'work' may be crude and not necessarily pleasing to those schools or teachers who are only after grades. Occasionally one meets a child who has a writer's gift.

What is important here is the use and development of imagery and 'pretence' behaviour, which either reflects society or allows for the child to retain some 'magic' and to step outside the real world and control a pretend world (or other worlds, e.g. playing at spaceships!).

We have taught some children to play imagination games. We did not teach formally, we merely introduced them to that kind of play. Many of the children we meet have three types of 'play'. One is sports play (usually football), another is crashing things into each other or making them, e.g. toy cars, zoom about, and the third is computer games, using the mouse. This sort of play has its place, and of course sports play is very valuable.

However, some children have discovered a 'new world' when we have introduced acting-out story-adventure. When, for example, I have said 'Let's pretend we are going to another land to find a treasure – we'll hide these jewels (a box of artificial jewels) in the other room first, then we'll make these chairs into an aeroplane (or a ship) and you can be the dad of this child (a doll) . . .', and so on.

This sounds like 'directing' (anathema to some therapists), but we see it as encouraging the development of a lost part of the child. It is the same with the dolls' houses: some children just move the furniture round but soon get bored and want to go outside and kick or do somersaults (excellent activities in their own right); but many of these children have discovered, as a result of watching the therapist or foster-parent for half an hour, that the doll people can 'talk' to each other, fall out with each other, obey or disobey, and so forth.

Clinically, of course, such play can be healing. It can also provide insight, not only for the child but also for any adult watching or participating. I remember a 9-year-old girl who was playing a dolls' house game with me. I made the doll mummy see her little girl into bed, tuck her in after a short stay and kiss her goodnight. Helen, the child playing with me suddenly paused and said, 'I wish I had a mum like that'.

Another girl, a girl of 12 whom these days we normally wouldn't see as playing with a dolls' house, took this kind of play back to her foster-home. Everyone involved knew that this child had been abused, but she had never talked about it. One day, when she knew her foster-mother was watching, she enacted a scene in great detail. She had been able to 'tell' someone by using a 'game' when in fact no one was asking for information.

Such talking or acting games are really alternative ways of story-telling, but some children and adolescents are good at actually writing stories. Some find that poetry is a way in which they can express feelings and ideas. Here is a poem written by a 9-year-old boy to his natural mother (Mum 1) and to his foster-mother, whom he calls Mum 2. The first verse is to Mum 1:

Red, like the berries, like fire

Reminds me of you, now higher

In Heaven, my mother.

Red was your favourite colour.

and the second is to Mum 2:

Blue, like the sky, like your eyes,

Makes me feel safe, and ties

Me close to my other

But very sweet mother.

Some children love play-acting and will enact certain scenes time and again. We have sometimes combined play-acting with music and suggested that we try to do three very short acts, i.e. one story, set to three pieces of music. These pieces of music have often been pre-recorded on a tape, in which case the 'happy' bit (Act 1) comes first, then the 'sad' bit (Act 2) in the middle, with a rousing bit or a dance for Act 3.

Sometimes a child makes up the whole three acts and tells us what to do and who we are in the play. I have been both handsome prince and evil designer; I have been imprisoned beneath the table and married on many occasions!

We often invite the younger children to act one of the fairy-stories, sometimes after reading one of them. So we enact *Goldilocks and the Three Bears* or the story of the *Three Little Pigs*. However, when children become used to acting we can then, if the child seems to need it, invite him or her to enact whatever they wish. If we know that there are some matters between the child and parent, for example, that are unresolved (what the Gestalt psychologists might term 'unfinished business') we can give the child a chance to 'tell' the parent, in a little vignette, how he feels or what he thinks.

Of course it helps a lot if you have a 'dressing-up-box, and some small 'props', such as the jewellery I mentioned above in the treasure. So collect a suitable assortment of hats, shoes, and coats as well as jumpers and dresses. Collect pieces of cloth or curtain material (including old net curtains) – dressing up makes it much more real. Also have make-up, old spectacle frames, a moustache or two, and even a few wigs if you can run to it. You can also use dolls, teddy bears, and those enormous stuffed creatures, as big as real children, creatures such as Bugs Bunny, to 'act' as extras.

It is important that, wherever possible, these forms of 'play' should take place at the child's home, i.e. natural family, foster-home, children's home, etc., and with his parents or other carers. However, where the play is being used in a way closely associated with counselling or therapy, the guidance of a professional therapist is necessary.

Feeling–Caring

There are some third objects which can best be associated with the home or school setting. Some children are referred for treatment and it is evident not only that their ability to empathize is under-developed, but that they have never been helped to care for another living thing. We have said a lot concerning the child's need for care, affection and friendship, but in fact that is only half of what is necessary. Nobody is really complete if they are only the receivers of care or affection. People need to satisfy another human potential, that of caring, or giving or contributing. Many professionals will go for that word, 'contributing'.

To want to contribute to society (to the family, to the group), however, the care-giving, nurturing self needs to develop. How do we start? In the good-enough family with good-enough parenting this care-giving potential is able to develop without any special arrangements being made, but with the nurturally deprived, self-centred or egoistic child it may be necessary to 'arrange' things as well as setting examples.

For this reason we have often advised the residential staff to encourage a child to take an interest in a 'young thing' and look after it. We do not always mean an animal – that may be going too quickly. No, we often start with two or three potted plants. Or we may obtain some bulbs or young seedlings and provide the child with the necessary materials to grow the plant, to feed and water it (not killing it with water), to begin to develop 'tender care'.

Of course, the adults at this stage must maintain an interest. They must express pleasure at seeing the progress made by the plant. One of the finest things we saw done at a boys' remand home was the encouragement given to some 'rough lads' to grow food on a small plot of land. These youths not only discovered a connection with mother earth, a sort of meaning attached to work and care-giving, but they felt good about being able to contribute to the remand home 'nosh'. That lettuce had been grown by them; those tomatoes had been grown by them. This is all part of a living therapy . . . care-therapy.

Animals represent another step up in the care-giving world. So often do we find, when a child does an exercise such as the 'My World' painting, that a cat or a dog (perhaps owned by the child) is the creature which is nearest to him both in the painting and in real life. In this work we are going to be disappointed time and time again. Hours, months, may be spent helping a child to 'settle' with a family – a loving, caring family – and the child appears to repay the family by stealing from 'home' or running away. Yet the affection toward, and the attachment to the cat, dog or horse remain. Even if the family placement breaks down ('disrupts') do not feel that the experience was all a loss in terms of development. If the child has even felt affection ('love') towards an animal, it means that the spark is there; the embers are there. Affection, the entity itself, can develop and eventually transfer to people. So do not forget this caring–feeling work.

Bridging

'Bridging' in this section, refers to the process, sometimes lengthy, of establishing a child in a family. At any rate it is usually into a family, although on occasion it may be into a residential establishment or, with an older working adolescent for example, it may refer to setting her up in a job and a bed-sitter.

We have in fact described Donna's preparation for moving into her foster-family, and the reader will find several third objects for that purpose described in Chapter 2. Bridging is an essential element of fostering or adopting an 'older child', by which we mean any child who is not a very young baby! It is a very serious operation and is still taken far too lightly. In fact, in recent years there has been a deterioration in the preparation work with children due to be 'placed'. This may be partly due to the disappearance of 'reception centres', residential establishments which spent months studying and preparing children. Bridging is given as focus number 7 on our list in Chapter 2.

Recently in the UK there has been a trend, overlooked by authorities who 'looked the other way', to move children from foster-home to foster-home regardless of the enormous psychological damage done to children who, by the age of about 10, may 'boast' of as many as 10, 15, 20 or even 30 placements. Fortunately, in 1998 the British Government (Health Committee) awoke to these facts and published a Report, 'Children Looked After by Local Authorities'. Paragraph 86 of this Report states:

> One problem which appears to be very widespread is that of *instability* in children's lives caused by the sheer number of separate placements an individual may experience.

And when the Committee members asked Sir William Utting, former Chief Inspector of Social Services, to comment on the cause, he replied (Paragraph 89):

> It will be a combination of lack of thought, lack of process, *inadequate assessment*, resources not being available so that the next best thing, or perhaps the only thing, has to be done within the particular circumstances of the day . . . I think that it is absolutely devastating . . . Although children are pretty resilient by and large, they do need continuity and security if they are actually to thrive. (HMSO, 1998, my emphasis)

There is no doubt that the preparation of children for fostering and/or adoption, and the support offered to the care-givers once the child has been placed have both decreased in recent years. Skills and resources have both been lost. We now need to treat this part of the work as of the utmost importance and not as something tacked on to the 'care system', but by and large overlooked or ignored. Readers who are involved with children who need to move to a 'new family', or to be rehabilitated (after extremely careful thought) to the natural family after years of absence, are advised to read again that part of Chapter 2 which deals with Donna's preparation and to note afresh our Appendix 2. (See also Further Reading.)

As will by now be appreciated, we are not able in this volume to discuss the detailed work and problems arising case by case, whether to do with placements or receiving children into care in the first place. We are working on a broad canvas and indicating the value of certain techniques to those who are trained to work with children or who are members of the public supported or advised by professional workers.

Clearly, however, as well as the basic psychosocial needs, and the harm which can come from clumsy childcare work where preparation, placement, and support are concerned (a running theme of this book), there are many fairly obvious factors to bear in mind. There may be a great deal of anxiety experienced by any child in this position: the position of knowing you are going to be found 'a family'; you are going to leave people you might (once again) have begun to attach to; you may or you may not like it when you get there.

There may be other indescribable fears and feelings associated with previous placements. Perhaps the child has a fear of getting emotionally or physically 'too close'. There may be basic 'shameful' reasons for anxiety. 'Suppose I start to wet the bed again!' or 'Will they be told about those things I did?' Because of these states of mind, and many more besides, the bridging process is very important.

The bridging process should start well before the actual placement occurs and should continue for at least a year after the child has moved into the family. Preparation is only a part of bridging; continued support (of child and care-givers) after the child has moved in is also a part of bridging.

The process may be even more complex than I have so far intimated. We tend, for example, to think of a child, i.e. a single child, or a group of siblings having to adjust to a new set of carers, and a set of carers having to adjust to a child or to a sibling group. What we have learnt, however, is that the groups themselves may need to undergo an internal dynamic change. Here we are dealing with a systems aspect.

If, for example, a group of three siblings is placed with a family, internal stresses may be set up within that sibling group. Previously, for example, the oldest sibling may have acted in the role of 'parent' or 'boss'. That child may discover that she now has to make a role-change. It is now the foster- or adoptive parents who will 'parent' all the children. The 'boss' child may be required to alter her role, especially as the other siblings discover the role is no longer valid.

Then again, the adult carers may find that the roles previously held by them and the ways they related to each other need to change. If there are already children, even young-adult offspring of the carers, in the home, then there could be additional complex relationship and role-changes required.

As these required changes take time and may be fraught with danger, it is extremely important that all involved should, first of all, be aware of the possible (likely) need for change, and that advice and support are readily available to children and carers; and of course the study of such changes in family dynamics should have been part of the training of social workers and of preparation for foster-parents and adopters.

We referred in Chapter 2 to 'wall building', an exercise used to help

Donna (see Figure 2.7). When introducing that third object we stated that 'even before a firm idea of fostering had generated itself within the team the therapist began to use wall building'. This is important. We are talking here about preparing children for all those possible role-changes just spoken of *and* being faced with new ways of doing everyday things, making new friends, going to new schools and so forth. It is useless to start to deal with these aspects of life two weeks before you intend to 'transplant' a child. I use the word 'transplant' advisedly. We are used to the idea of organ transplants, and the complex physical process involved. We do not yet treat the transplanting of the whole child with equal care and respect.

Figure 5.2 shows a variation in this method of working through the many issues associated with relating to other people in diverse situations, and when involved with diverse feelings. Instead of a wall we have a foundation. Most normal children above a certain age will be able to appreciate that, if the house in the picture is built upon a wobbly foundation, it will collapse. Such children will be able to extrapolate from a collapsing house to a collapsing family. This sort of third object must not be used as a threat but as a way of learning about

Figure 5.2 *House with foundation*

the value of loving and caring for each other. The bricks or stones in the foundation are painted-in over a period of months (not days), a small portion of the brick at a time, until the subject has been well thought about.

Another very valuable aid is the 'loving steps'. This third object was also used in helping Donna and so is discussed in Chapter 2 (and shown in Figure 2.8). When using the loving steps it is important to let the child know that from time to time she may feel that she has gone either up the steps or down a step or two, but that going down does not mean that things are getting steadily worse – very often something has happened to make her feel in a different mood. However, it is also important to accept that the child is on whatever step she says she is on, even if you as the adult feel that that is not the true position.

Quite often, a week or so after the date of the actual placement start (as against the many occasions when the child has arrived for a contact period), a child will tell you that she is on the top step. Discuss round this. Say what is really meant by the top-step feeling, and, if the child persists, leave her there. It is more than likely that when you are talking with the child, and maybe with her carers, two weeks later you and the child will be able to obtain a more accurate step! The child may then be assured that this only fits in with your much earlier discussions and that she can again feel (this time with more understanding) that she is further up, even if not yet on the top step. Eventually, however, many children make it to the top step and just feel they 'belong' in this family. To be really useful, however, the steps must be started well before placement (but later than wall building) and continue to be looked at and discussed well into the placement.

We now have an alternative to the steps. We have used the idea of the elevator (or 'lift'), with the ground floor representing the moving-in time and the other floors being equal to the steps previously described. We can then make the elevator move up and down as required to reflect feelings. We find this is often more easily understood by children who know about elevators. When presented with steps, the idea of progress (always upwards) seems to stick in the mind, whereas the elevator is expected to change floors, and this symbolism is much nearer to what really happens.

Bridging with a Bridge

As we are discussing the process of transfer to long-term placements under the heading of 'Bridging', it will be appropriate to mention a third object which (once more) uses the bridge idea, and combines it with the wall- or foundation-building idea. Figure 5.3 demonstrates this technique. The child starts out with a few bricks (or stones) in place on each side of the bridge. On one side of the bridge we put a representation of the child, and on the other side, representations of future carers. Apart from the few bricks actually drawn in, however, the rest of the bridge is done in dots or dotted lines.

The idea given, and discussed, is that the child will be going to live with the carers (provided he wants to, but see below) and that there are things to talk about before this happens. Sometimes there may have to be a waiting period on account of practical reasons. However, by using the bricks to discuss all the things that need to be discussed, it will be helping child and carers to build the bridge and eventually come together (as a foster- or adoptive family, etc.). Future carers can be involved in this work. It may be helpful for children who can understand these things to know that the carers will also have to adjust and maybe change some habits. To give a rather trivial example, they may have to give up spending all Sunday morning resting in bed! Carers can actually 'do' bricks on their side of the bridge, and talk with the children about their own adjustments. The bridge can be used not only to reach to the day the child arrives 'for good' (is placed) but, like the stairs or the elevator, may continue to be built after the placement date. Older children and teenagers may use it in this way because they can often understand the adjustments both they, the carers, and in some cases their siblings are having to make.

I said above that the child would be going to live with the carers 'provided he wants to'. Sadly, it is not always such a simple choice. Practitioners in childcare and 'court welfare' will be aware, in cases involving divorce, separation and other complications, that sometimes the child wants to live in two places at once or does not wish to move from the family he already shares a home with, but for some reason that family, or perhaps an individual carer, can no longer perform the parental role. Nevertheless, we must still help the child literally to 'make the best' of what is possible, and careful preparation is needed for this.

One last comment concerning this bridge third object: the representations of child (and maybe siblings) and future carers and other family members may be drawn in by the child, or we can use cut-up photographs, or they may be drawn or painted on separate paper so that they can be cut out and then moved across the bridge as it grows. The adult will negotiate this with the child.

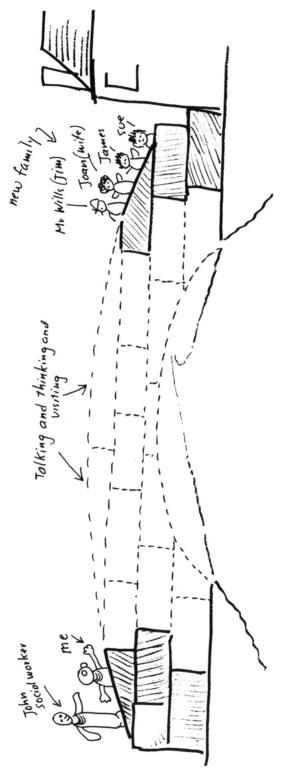

Figure 5.3 *Bridge to a new family*

The Umbilical Cord Idea, Contacts

Anyone may feel anxious about going to a new job or a new school. Imagine how a child may feel about moving into a new family? It is not only that she will be meeting new people, apart from the foster-parents or adopters (or the staff and other children if they are moving to a residential placement), but also that she will be leaving the people she is already living with! The child may have been with them for six months, two years or all of her life. There are very natural reasons for children to feel worried, because they may still want to be 'in touch' with children, foster-parents, social workers and others whom they have come to trust. They may actually have formed an attachment bond.

Despite the fact that the child has 'accepted' the move in hand, she may feel she needs some sort of insurance, at least for the time being. The insurance referred to here is the knowledge that the previous care-givers are still in touch and that there will be ways of keeping in touch. We may know, as adults, that these umbilical-cord connections will, in many cases, be ultimately broken off: indeed as the child becomes attached to a family and becomes part of that family, the child may very well allow the connections to wither. In the meantime, what third objects can we use to help children feel less anxious and more secure about the future?

The reader will recall that in the case of Donna, a device referred to as a contact indicator was used. By using this third object and putting in the names of anyone the child is anxious to keep in touch with, various possibilities may be illustrated and discussed. This may need to happen many times in order to reduce the feelings of anxiety.

Picture-Contacts

With children who may not be able to conceptualize using such ideas as contact bars (as in the contact indicator), pictorial third objects are probably going to be more helpful. One such object is shown in Figure 5.4. In this case the worker has talked with the child concerning the various ways he will be able to maintain contact with people he feels he needs to be in touch with after he has moved into the new placement. Obviously this object may be used (or the game may be played) in many ways. For instance, the child may be asked to think about how he will be able to talk to Auntie Hannah (real aunt? member of staff? previous foster-mother?) in the future. Eventually the idea of the telephone will emerge – perhaps with hints from the worker – so now the child may draw a telephone, or cut one out of a catalogue and stick it in the appropriate section, and

Figure 5.4 *Ways of keeping in touch*

sometimes of course the worker may be asked to draw a telephone.

There are so many ways of playing this helpful third object, and of course some workers will enact these contact moments by using a toy telephone set, or pretending they are visiting the child in his new family.

Sibling-group Dynamics – Change Indicators

Earlier in this section on bridging I referred to the fact that dynamic changes take place within sibling groups once such a group is placed in a new setting. Figures 5.5 (*a*), (*b*) and (*c*) show an instrument used during discussion with a sibling group some months into a placement.

In the case of these four children the natural mother had deserted some two years prior to the work we are describing. The fathers were not involved in the lives of the children. The siblings were: a girl of 15, and her sister aged 12, and brothers aged 9 and 6.

The three younger siblings had been placed, as a sibling group, with a married couple with adoption in view. The bridging work was going on prior to any court hearing for adoption, but after the children had joined the family. The elder girl had been placed separately, also with a view to adoption.

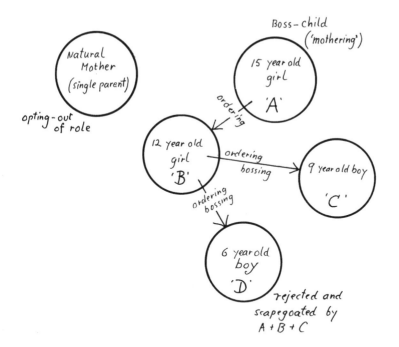

Figure 5.5a *Dynamics of natural family*

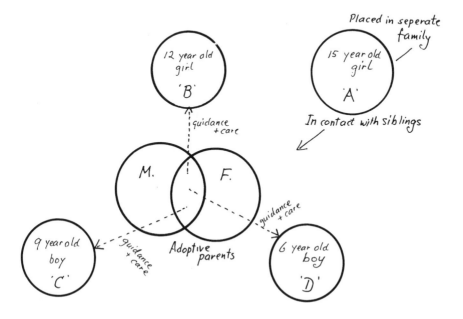

Figure 5.5b *Concept and experience of guidance and care*

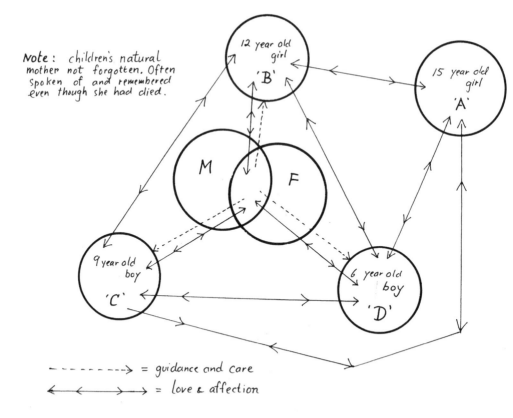

Note : children's natural mother not forgotten. Often spoken of and remembered even though she had died.

- - - - - - -> = guidance and care

<- <- -> -> = love & affection

Figure 5.5c *Dynamics of care and affection*

The interactive dynamic of the whole sibling group while they were in the natural mother's care is shown in Figure 5.5 (*a*). This was worked out with the children: it was how they described the relationships. The reader will see that there was a 'boss' hierarchy. The oldest child actually bossed all the children, but delegated to the 12-year-old girl. The mother was a drug addict and most times was non-operational. However, the youngest child was also scapegoated by the rest – he had a different father and a very different personality.

When we were working with the group it became clear that the existing dynamic was clashing with the concept of a family group with the parents at the head of the family. The 12-year-old girl felt that her role was being challenged by the adoptive parents. She continued to 'parent', or rather to boss the younger children. Also, although the 9-year-old lad was beginning to realize that the parents should be 'in charge', he was also in conflict because of the previous set of family dynamics. The 15-year-old had lost her role within the sibling group.

Together, the adoptive parents and the worker (during the counselling/therapy sessions) helped the children to see what was happening (enlightenment). Figure 5.5 (*b*) emerged as a result of discussions with the children, using cardboard pointers to show that guidance (not bossing) and care were now coming from the parents through to each child.

As we went on talking and counselling it became 'agreed' that there was something else about this family experience. It was, of course, love. So we made a new set of pointers, and this time it emerged (as a result of more thinking and talking) that the 'love' pointers would be going in *both* directions in every case! [See Figure 5.5 (*c*).]

Now this looks rather idealistic, and indeed the illustration is idealistic. Of course there were plenty of fights and sulks and protests, but gradually a new family dynamic emerged which was such as to produce a stable, good-enough family life.

This third object emerged! It came about because of what was happening. At the time, I suppose, it was unique, but this is the way care-therapy should work. The worker, whoever he or she is, should be continually searching for new interactive paths, in order to both convey information to and receive information from the child. Child and worker gain insight.

Life Can be a Jigsaw Puzzle

Sean was 14 years old and was about to move into the family of Fred and Sue Devises for the third time. The social services had placed him with the Devises twice previously and twice it had broken down. We were very doubtful as to whether this placement would succeed but Sean pleaded that he wanted to return and that things would be different. In fact the situation demanded a change (of attitude and behaviour) on the part of both child and prospective foster-parents. This need for change became, as I think it should have, an open discussion. With a 14-year-old like Sean, who was discerning, it was better to be open concerning the change which the adults needed to make, because he was pointing out some of their weaknesses. The incorrect alternative so far as true insight was concerned, would have been to help him to see his need for change and then to discuss (in a private session with the adults) their need to change. This is often what is done and may lead to the child feeling that all the problems are his alone.

In order to illustrate more clearly the importance of the need for this dual change (adjustment), we made the 'wrongly cut pieces of a jigsaw puzzle'. Figure 5.6 shows that in order to get a 'fit' both pieces had to change shape.

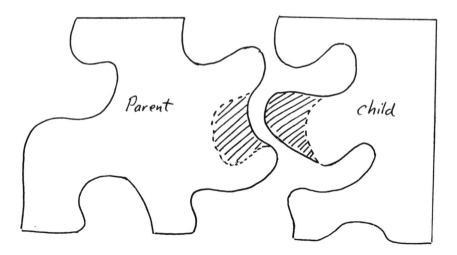

Parent child

Figure 5.6 *Wrongly cut jigsaw pieces: both need to lose the shaded parts*

Conclusion

In this chapter we have looked at the third objects concerned with what we have called sensory work. We have considered the importance of sensory experiences in infancy and the value of using sensory experience within the therapeutic setting. We have also touched on the importance of creative 'hands-on' experiences, and of imagery and acting, and poetry, as well as the physically exciting, even 'scary' experiences, all of which may have a part to play in care-therapy. These valuable experiences should never be confined only to a clinical setting. They should belong to home and school and holiday settings, but may need to differ according to the setting, and will also be used differently in different settings.

We have also discussed bridging and have stressed the importance of this aspect of care-therapy starting before a child is placed and continuing for about a year into a placement.

However, not every child who needs counselling or psychotherapy needs a clinical sensory-work programme; and of course in many situations there will be no call for bridging. In Chapter 6 we shall look closely at the appropriate use of these various classes of third objects and we shall consider the psychosocial factors which may emerge during counselling or psychotherapy as the third objects are used. We shall also be noting the way the objects may be selected (or invented) as new feelings, memories, hopes, and perhaps anger experiences emerge.

We shall also look at 'corporate parenting', 'parenting', that is, by state or charitable organizations, by proxy. Even now, and even in our western society, it is difficult to get this right – 'right' for vulnerable and exposed children.

CHAPTER 6

The assessment process: the selection of appropriate care-therapy approaches (a spectrum of objectives and methods) and corporate parenting

'One of the early tasks in work with children is to obtain enough information to assist us in arriving at an assessment of their needs.'
Triseliotis, J., et al., 1995

The idea of using various media to help child and worker to communicate and to express feelings and thoughts during counselling sessions is not new. We have referred elsewhere to the work of Margaret Lowenfeld, who as early as the 1920s was using the sand-tray technique which we have described in Chapter 4. Lowenfeld's treatment approach was psychodynamic.

We have referred, also, to the work of Violet Oaklander, who used a wide variety of media. Oaklander is a Gestalt therapist. More recent writers have stressed the value of using the various media, and being selective in their use. We can name Kathryn and David Geldard (1997), Sharp and Cowie (1998) and Triseliotis, Sellick, and Short (1995). This form of help for children is clearly becoming an expectation within the caring professions. Moreover, some of the recent writers have found that children may be helped by what is called 'brief therapy', using the media selectively over a shorter time span.

Clearly, when we find therapists of different schools of psychology, and of high standing professionally, able to use the media, we must no longer write off the use of these materials as merely a 'directive' approach. Of course, anyone can be too directive with or without the use of the media, but used in conjunction with appropriate knowledge, skills, and positive attitudes to the basic rights and needs of the child they may become wonderful focusing and communicating channels.

Having, in the previous chapters, introduced the reader to a 'spectrum' of alternative media of both types, insight and sensory, we shall shortly discuss some of the main counselling and therapy objectives, and will relate these to various third objects discussed in this book. This list of therapy objectives we have called 'The spectrum of experiential and therapy objectives'.

Before we describe the spectrum and the order in which the various third objects might be used in helping a child, however, we need to say something about the process of assessment. We are referring here to something more than a mere case history. Assessment as we see it is an ongoing process which gives us information about a child's psychosocial needs, which are going to change even as care and treatment proceed. This process, therefore, will be concerned with obtaining information about a child's history (developmental, social, medical, educational, behavioural, spiritual and psychological) up to the point at which she is referred for treatment, and will continue for as long as we are concerned with the care of the child.

Assessment

At the time of writing it is estimated that out of the twelve million children in England, some four million may be said to be 'vulnerable', and approximately 600,000 may fall into the category of 'children in need'. These terms, 'vulnerable', and 'in need', apply in various proportions to psychological, physical, medical, economic, family dynamic, moral, educational and social factors. The picture is similar in many other 'developed world' countries. In New South Wales alone, in Australia, where 5,500 children enter the 'care system' each year, 'Many children today experience the disastrous combination of family breakdown, domestic violence, poverty, social isolation and frequent moves' (*Sydney Morning Herald*, 25 September 1999).

In order to know how vulnerable a child is, to know what her needs are, and how far these are from being met, information on all the aspects of life mentioned above must be reviewed. But this is a process we are referring to, not a one-off check-up. It may well be that in the course of making an assessment of needs it is discovered that some aspect can be met without further delay. It may be that the child's vulnerability is so acute that urgent action must be taken at once – but that is not the end of the assessment process.

In our own work with children certain principles have been upheld when the needs of children and families were being assessed. These echo closely a similar set given in the document 'Working Together to Safeguard Children' (see Further Reading) and include:

- assessment is grounded in child development
- assessment is concerned with human ecology
- assessment is concerned with the child's history
- assessment is concerned with the child's present psychosocial condition
- assessment involves a multidisciplinary approach
- assessment involves (where realistic) communication with, and observation of the child
- assessment is family inclusive but child orientated

Certain sequels spring from these principles. Some of these are as much to do with the training of child therapists and social workers as they are to do with counselling and treatment.

Child development (physical and psychological), for example, should be to the fore in training, but this should include a basic knowledge of what to look for in terms of physical malnourishment and/or ill health.

Family therapy should be an approach well understood, if not practised. In so far as 'history' is concerned, professional people working with children who are being cared for by state or charitable organizations should have been intensively trained to recognize both the psychopathological and **ecological** factors relating to placement breakdowns and the danger of drift, i.e. the child who is frequently moved from placement to placement and can never attach. And finally, it is clear from some of the principles set out above that the professional childcare worker should be well trained in direct work with children.

Concerning the child's history, it is often possible to learn more about her by using the flow charts, as described in Chapter 3. But now the flow chart will be used only by the adults concerned, who will chart the child's moves from place to place, i.e. changes of address, including hospitalization or periods when she was in care. School changes will also be charted. Along with all these changes will go 'events', i.e. anything occurring which may have any connection with the child. So any illnesses (either the child's or parents' or siblings') are recorded; the reasons for any address or school change; and family or friends' deaths, and so on.

By setting out the child's history in flow-chart form and questioning (adults as well as the child) we often 'see' more than when we read through a thick file. It is rather like seeing a landscape from the air; sometimes features are highlighted which are missed at ground level.

We have emphasized the importance of a full assessment concerning environmental and historical aspects of the child, and including an interdisciplinary element. Such an assessment might be described as a 'wide-lens' assessment. However, once enough information is available and it has been decided as a result of the wide-lens assessment that the child is to be offered counselling or therapy, it is then necessary to make a 'narrow-lens' assessment, i.e. to decide what kind of counselling approach is going to be helpful, and what third objects are going to be helpful. We now come back, therefore, to the whole spectrum of third objects which have been fully discussed in this book.

The Spectrum of Experiential and Therapy Objectives

This spectrum is in fact a list of therapy, counselling and psychotherapy practice functions. They are drawn from a broad field of practice and theory background. Although, when put in the form of a list, there will be a set of figures alongside, from 1 to 10, we want to emphasize strongly that these figures in no way refer to the order in which work with a child should necessarily be undertaken, nor are they intended to convey the idea of 'least' important and 'most' important. As will be explained, the workers helping the children may start with subject 9 with one child and subject 1 with another. They may also find themselves using approaches associated with 1, 5 and 2 all at the same time, or at least in the same session. Here is the list – the spectrum:

1 Sensory experiences (as described in this book).
2 Outward expression of the unconscious and the preconscious (seen, for example, in the sand-tray work, Chapter 4).
3 Understanding events. Helping the child to attain awareness of events, and as far as is possible and helpful, the significance of events.
4 Differentiation of feelings (emotions, affect). Listening to the child's awareness of feelings, moods and reactions.
5 Expressing feelings (affect), needs and wishes. Feeling free to share feelings, memories, beliefs, fears, etc.
6 Getting in touch with the self. Introspective and reflective processes dealing with feelings and meaning concerning events.
7 Reflecting upon interactive behaviour. For example, why are people responding in this way to me?

8 Change focus. The child is helped to think about changes taking place, or the value of change which may take place in ideas, beliefs, behaviour or environment.

9 Bridging (as described in Chapter 5).

10 Specific attachment/bonding work.

Spectrum (1): Sensory Experiences

For the purpose of explaining the spectrum we shall start at number 1 and work our way through to 10, but when presented with an actual case this is unlikely to be the only order for working with a child and using the various third objects. Furthermore, as already stated elsewhere, there are many children and adolescents who do not need the clinical use of sensory third objects where the focus is specifically on giving the child that kind of experience. She may very well, of course, experience sensory pleasure from items used to help her focus on insight issues.

When, therefore, shall we consider sensory-experience work to be an essential part of the treatment programme, and when might such work be peripheral? Three case types should be borne in mind:

1 Cases in which it appears that the child has missed out on a good-enough early nurturing experience, i.e. as a baby, toddler or pre-school child.

2 Cases in which it is felt that some sort of Infant Nurture Programme is required. These programmes were described in the case of Donna (Chapter 2) and referred to in Chapter 5. These cases will include some children from 1 above.

3 Peripherally, in order to help certain children to relax and to focus away from the eyeball-to-eyeball contact, we may make available separate items of the sensory third objects, such as clay and other manipulatable products, or of course background music.

The selection of sensory third objects will depend, also, on the age of the child and on her interests. At this end of the spectrum it is good practice to provide several sensory third objects so that the child may choose to enjoy whichever media she wants to spend the time with. It is not necessary to have everything lying around at the same time so that the child flips rapidly from one thing to another. We may have two different media out (at one time) and invite the child to choose from, say, painting and clay work, or clay work and water-play. On the previous session we may also have had the drum kit out. If the child says 'Oh, I want to play the drums again', then we will either promise them for the next session or, if it's not too difficult to arrange (or the set is not in use elsewhere), promise them for before the end of the current session.

We like to start off a sensory treatment programme with the less formalized objects such as I have described above, and then if judged an appropriate part of treatment, to bring in the more organized and focused sensory third objects, such as the taste tray (see Chapter 5) and the specially designed touch, sound, and sight 'games'.

The reader will notice, as we go through the spectrum, that we shall refer back to this first phase of the treatment programme, and that although we shall be discussing third objects as being used mainly for, let us say, sector 2 (outward expression of the unconscious and preconscious), we shall also be suggesting that there are many cases where such work will start on the very first session with the child. For example, sand-tray expression may be used.

Spectrum (2): Outward Expression of the Unconscious and the Preconscious

It might be argued that this represents a function which therapists would be hoping to be implicit in any and all the work they do, so far as aims are concerned. However, there will be a differentiation, whether this comes about as a result of the particular 'school' to which the counsellor or therapist belongs, or because of the particular problems brought to the situation by the child; and of course, depending on the nature of the case, there is likely to be a greater or lesser need for such outward expression.

There are, as we have demonstrated in these pages, case referrals which will demand much more in the way of counselling concerning decision-making, and much less, and sometimes very little time directed at work concerned directly with unconscious elements. However, with most emotionally disturbed children, there are unconscious elements which need to be taken into account, and therefore this aspect of treatment has been placed towards the elemental wing of the spectrum.

The experienced worker, drawing upon the extensive assessment work and case history (flow charts, etc.) that we have recommended, will be the judge as to whether or not to introduce early on the sort of 'depth' work which may be the outcome of sand-tray work, but there are many other 'tools' which, while they help child and worker to communicate and 'get to know each other', will also function as a means to express unconscious and preconscious factors.

Take for example the paintings of Naomi (Figure 3.2), which were then blacked out! What unconscious (as well as conscious) factors were involved? Or take the 'people tree' (Figures 3.4 and 3.5). Here the child is often revealing aspects of the unconscious through the positioning of people on the tree.

Nevertheless, some third objects are likely to be used by more children (and adults) than other third objects as a means of expressing unconscious 'wishes', 'projections' and 'fears'. Where appropriate, i.e. considering the age and personality of the child, etc., the 'my tree' drawings or paintings and the 'My World' drawings (Chapter 4) seem to fall into this category. Having pointed that out, however, it is equally important to emphasize the fact that the children may use any of our third objects to express the unconscious and the **preconscious** even though they may be using them, consciously, for quite another purpose.

The way in which third objects are used will depend very much on the child's own private motives and drives. It is, however, important in most cases to build in the opportunity to use materials which facilitate the child's expression of the unconscious and preconscious. Remember, however, that expressing oneself in this way is not the same as interpreting the symbolism of the various paintings and other media outcomes. Do not interpret. By all means ask the child if he'd like to say something about his work, and it is certainly all right to ask what *this* person in the picture (or sand tray) is doing, or what *that* one is saying, etc. It is useful if you are experienced, or you are working under the supervision of an experienced therapist, to 'discern' unconscious motives and wishes, etc., but do not directly interpret. When you are using materials for ordinary insight work on a conscious level, then the child can be asked questions sensitively. Such questions as 'How do you feel about meeting your mum?' or even observations such as 'I noticed that the last time you were here you said some angry things about your dad' are in place, but such questions and observations are not attempts at interpreting to the child what is going on in his unconscious.

Before discussing Sector 3 of the spectrum, we need to say that when work is being undertaken with a child, even when the aims in mind may be very practical and have to do with such matters as whether or not a child wishes to be fostered, there will in most cases be both indirect reactions in the child and needs which the child will require to be met, and of course if he is experiencing, however vaguely, anger, guilt or other feelings as a result of impulses from the unconscious, these indirect reactions ('indirect' because they emerge from the unconscious) may well be stronger.

At the same time there are certain needs which have to be met. He needs to be helped, for example, to 'make sense of' (understand) past and present events in his life, and to understand the 'signals' being directed towards him or to other family members. Sometimes children are confused by 'signals' because the signals are often diffuse and even inappropriate. Is it a signal, for example, if a parent repeatedly promises to visit a child in residential care, and repeatedly (for no apparent reason) leaves a distraught child to wait, and wait, and finally burst into tears or to lash out at someone? Or is it not a signal at all? The child is clearly interpreting it in *some* way.

So, it is important to remember that various effects will be triggered as a result of the work being undertaken. It is often necessary for these effects to be triggered if far worse reactions are to be avoided 'further down the line', as the child becomes adult, but obviously we want to help the child to avoid bad hurts (emotionally) and that is why sensitive 'empathetic' people are needed to undertake the daily care and guidance of these children; and the same requirement stands for those offering counselling or therapy.

Spectrum (3): Understanding Events

A very straightforward example of a child being helped in this regard was given earlier (Chapter 3), concerning the 8-year-old boy, Jamie, who had experienced many fostering and residential care moves and who had lived for several years believing that he was removed from the family of his happiest memories because he wet the bed. The significance for him had to do with rejection on account of his 'nastiness'! While it did not reverse the course of history, the information he gained, revealing that his removal was unrelated to bed-wetting, and that both foster-parents would have liked to keep him, certainly helped him to improve his self-image and self-confidence. The significance of the event changed.

In counselling terminology we are talking here about change of frame or change of reference. Sometimes we may be dealing with what Gestalt therapists refer to as 'unfinished business'. There was the case of the teenage girl involved with two 'events', the first being her natural mother's death and the second being a plan to place her in a foster-family. She at first refused to consider fostering despite her glowing reports of her 'holiday' experiences with the proposed foster-family.

As a result of the work undertaken with this young woman she was able to express her feelings of guilt and anxiety, which had to do with her feelings of 'disloyalty' to her deceased mother, 'If I go to *another* mother'. In her case the significance of both events needed to be looked at again, and she needed to 'understand' (not just acknowledge, but feel different about and really accept) a great deal more about fostering, natural parenting, and her natural mother's desire for her child to be happy.

So what sort of third objects might be especially helpful for understanding events? The reader may recall examples already cited. We can point to two examples immediately, and there is a nice distinction in that one example focuses on past events (while still coming up to date) and the other focuses on the developing situation.

The first was used to help Donna (Chapter 2) and is referred to as the loving-water technique. Readers will recall that Donna and the worker rehearsed certain events in her life, some of them concerned with sexual abuse, and that she was also helped to understand how those events had affected her behaviour.

The second example (also described in Chapter 2) is the use of the loving steps. I have purposely selected this example because it is likely to be used towards the end of a programme of therapy and I wish to remind readers that the various aims and objectives listed from 1 to 10 in the spectrum are not necessarily approached in that order. Understanding events is a function which may need to run right through a therapy or preparation programme.

However, whereas the loving-water third object focused clearly on Donna's history, the loving steps are more focused on 'current' events concerned with moving into a new family and relating to people. Of course, as the child looks back he will recognize that he has either moved slowly up the steps or that he has gone up and down, and up again. He will be helped to understand that feeling low, or feeling that people's moods and interactions change from time to time, does not mean that they are unable to grow fond of one another.

Spectrum (4): Differentiation of Feelings (Emotions, Affect)

Although we are concerned here with focusing on feelings, by which we mean emotions and moods, the discerning reader will be aware that this element of the person, this psychological factor, has been involved in some way or other in the parts of the spectrum that we have already described, and moreover will be involved in the following sections of the spectrum.

Nevertheless, we may sometimes find that a child is confused about feelings, or that she may be required to let certain people know how she feels (or felt) and would find the task confusing and difficult without help. We may have to help children who are going to be cross-examined in court (or perhaps videoed in order to avoid actual court appearance). Then again, some children are not sure about matching words to feelings; they may use the word 'sad' when they want to convey to the listener that they are unhappy (but not actually sad).

Furthermore, some 'feelings' describe complex emotions relating to the actions of others and perhaps to how a person experiences a social situation, and some children don't find it easy to recognize these feelings or to express them in words. These are feelings which usually have to be expressed by a sentence or a phrase rather than a word like 'angry' or 'happy'. The real meaning of how the child feels may only be expressed by a group of words such as 'I feel left out' – we might call that the 'left-out feeling'. Because of this complexity it is sometimes useful to help the child to differentiate feelings.

However, when it comes to differentiating feelings some third objects are more suitable for younger children (or children with a younger mental age) while others are more readily used by older children and adolescents.

Readers will recall the use of 'faces' or face-cards in Chapter 4 (Figure 4.15). These faces have different expressions and the young child can use them to indicate how she felt, or feels.

In Chapter 4 we also introduced the idea of discussing feelings and making lists, quite unattached to a discussion about any incident or event. This was done jointly by child and worker, each contributing words which indicate feelings. This sort of exercise is useful when working with older children – it 'loosens up' ideas about feelings in general, and it helps the child to say more accurately how she feels. It is very important, of course, that when a child does say what her feelings are, or were, we accept what she says and do not impose our ideas (or our feelings) upon her.

'Feelings-cards' are also helpful for some children. Each small card has the name of a feeling (or an emotion) on it. This may have resulted from thinking about different words and feelings, so that the set of cards has been made by the child or jointly with the worker. Later on, perhaps a week or so later, some event or situation or memory is being shared between child and worker ('worker' will include foster- or adoptive parents) and the cards will be available for the child to see if any of those feelings 'belong' to that event. Remember, these third objects are there to help in communication. Any discussion may 'take off' and leave the third object behind. Third objects should never restrict; they should, so to speak, only oil the wheels.

It is important that people bringing up vulnerable children should themselves be very aware of the complexity of feelings. Apart from anything else, the feelings and the moods of the child so often affect behaviour and the way other children react to the child in question. For example, there are 'associated' feelings (a child may say she feels 'two things at once'), so often we get anxiety and panic, or anger and guilt. Then again we may often come across 'consecutively attached feelings', where one feeling (or state) develops from a previous one, so we find anxiety . . . fear . . . panic.

Basic teaching in psychopathology, and supervision or guidance from those advising the lay carers, will also make people aware of the development in the child of what seem to be inappropriate feelings. A common example is that of the abused child who develops feelings of guilt. Similarly, the child who has lost an attachment 'other', e.g. mother or father, may develop such guilt feelings. This is not the place to expand on the deeper psychological reasons for the development of these feelings. However, readers will appreciate that the differentiation of feelings is often helpful so far as one can take it with a child or young person.

Spectrum (5): Expressing Feelings (Affect), Needs and Wishes

Providing various means for children to express feelings is, it seems, easier than differentiating feelings. Once again we are moved to point out that although we are here focusing on materials, games and media aimed at a particular aspect of counselling and indeed an aspect of children's normal behaviour, i.e. expressing themselves, this particular function (the expression of feelings, wishes, etc.) will not be confined to these specially selected third objects nor to any particular spot in the treatment or upbringing continuum. One hopes the child will express his feelings by various means in early counselling sessions and in the bridging process to a new family – at any time in fact.

We can therefore say that this entire book, and especially Chapters 3, 4 and 5, is concerned with helping children to communicate with adult carers (foster-parents, natural parents, therapists or social workers) and also helping the adults to 'get in touch' with the children. Violet Oaklander's book has the very perceptive title of *Windows to Our Children*. I think it is as important to remember that we are using all these instruments to discover, 'get to know', the children, as it is to think of children getting in touch with us.

We could go all the way through Chapters 2 to 5, pointing out ways in which we have described different children using the media to express aspects concerned with their emotions, wishes, memories, moods and, putting it generally, feelings. We could take Donna's 'feeling-paintings' (Chapter 2); or the 'My World' drawings from Chapter 4 (Figure 4.16) by the 13-year-old girl, who reveals her feelings about her whole family; or that 'my tree' painting by Neil (Figure 4.3), in which he expresses his fears and hopes by almost forgetting the tree itself but filling in the tree's environs. All the way through these chapters the reader will find examples of the expression of feelings.

There are, of course, some more focused third objects, such as the beetle game described in Chapter 4. In that game the child is invited to share experiences when they had experienced certain feelings or were involved in particular behaviour, and the adult is expected to share similar memories with the child.

Even when the third objects were focused on sensory experiences, feelings (often associated with memories) emerged. The taste tray in Chapter 5, for example, produced feelings associated with memories. There was the child who, when he tasted the Marmite, was immediately 'in touch' with his grandmother and the feelings he had for her. Smells and sounds evoke memory-associated feelings.

Perhaps some of the most poignant moments concerning feelings have emerged when we have been involved with children in play-acting (psychodrama), either with their real selves involved or using toy people and letting the child play-act the toy people, making them 'talk' to each other.

Interestingly, practically all these illustrations would involve our next category in the spectrum, 'Getting in touch with the self!'

Spectrum (6): Getting in Touch with the Self
This, no doubt, would be the place for a long review on what is meant by the 'self', and indeed it would be a long review. I'm afraid I am going to cunningly resist that temptation and ask the reader to allow the following examples of work with children to 'explain' what we mean by this heading. Then again the phrase 'getting in touch with' must carry a heavy burden when it comes to getting in touch with the self!

However, before going further I shall take one very short quotation from a dictionary of psychology in which 'self' extends to many pages, and for the time being ask readers to be satisfied with that. Here it is: 'Self as inner witness to events. Here self is viewed as a component of the psyche which serves an introspective function' (Reber, 1985).

In Chapter 1 we listed three attributes of what we have called care-therapy, the subject of this book. In our first attribute we used this word with a capital 'S', stating that care-therapy would help in the development of the Self. Although it may be difficult to conceive of the self developing, readers may accept that the 'introspective function' can 'develop', i.e. improve functionally. So, before the philosophers clamp down on us, let us retreat to some examples of third objects used in order to help the child 'get in touch . . .', etc. We are concerned with a special aspect of insight here.

Readers will again find that we shall deliberately make use of third objects which we have already used to illustrate another sector of the spectrum. By doing so we are emphasizing the point that the child and the worker will often be scanning a number of psychosocial dimensions during one encounter. This of course is where the value of training and experience comes to the fore, enabling the worker to discern and to help the child to obtain insights.

Two examples spring to mind: the first is the sand-tray work, which we spoke of in connection with sector 2 of the spectrum, and the second is Naomi's method of blacking out her paintings, which we also used in connection with sector 2, the 'Outward expression of the unconscious and the preconscious'. Both these examples may also relate to introspective and reflective processes and therefore to the sector we are now considering.

Depending upon the use made by the child, and on the counselling and guidance the child receives, shields also become media for more self-awareness. In Chapter 3 (Figure 3.9) we looked at Judy's shield. Clearly, she was, at the time of working on the shield, reflective concerning her relationships as well as her more overt self-image. Judy actually kept some of her feelings in an envelope (attached to her shield) marked 'Private'.

Provided it is used in the way we have described in this book, and not merely as a photograph album, the life-story book may be used in conjunction with therapy to help the child to meet this need to reflect and introspect. We said in Chapter 3 when discussing this third object, that one purpose served by the life-story book can be described as 'ontological', that is to say, concerned with 'being', and concerned with obtaining answers to the question 'Who am I?'

It would be possible to discuss a number of other third objects with this particular aim in mind, i.e. becoming more aware of self. I hope enough has been said to indicate that although objects (games, instruments) may lend themselves to specific objectives, and some objects may lend themselves more readily to meeting specific objectives, there is no third object which fits rigidly to only one aim or objective. Much depends upon how the child wishes to use an object and upon what particular objects (and activities such as psychodrama) may conjure up in the child's mind.

Before looking at the next sector of the spectrum it may be helpful to remind readers that during counselling or other therapeutic work with children, various changes will be taking place which will affect the child in a number of ways. This, of course, is to be expected in any treatment or care programme which has the potential to heal, to rectify, or to change. In this book we have provided some very powerful media, and it is important that anyone using them should do so within a training scheme (where not already a trained professional) or under the supervision of a trained counsellor or therapist who has used these or similar third objects.

Spectrum (7): Reflecting upon Interactive Behaviour

There are many facets to the work related to children who are not only vulnerable in general psychological terms but have also in many cases experienced loss of family, rejection, constant upheavals and change of school and address, let alone change of family by fostering or adoption.

Such children often exhibit an ambivalence towards the adults who look after them and 'bring them up'. This is something much stronger and altogether more devastating than the normal, 'love–hate' relationship said to exist between most children and parents.

Sometimes this pathological ambivalence commences with the generation of a protective rebuffing process. Children have been so hurt by (sometimes only apparent) rejection or abuse that they protect themselves from any close loving. After all, it may again turn into 'rejection' and pain. This later becomes the general mode of behaviour.

Sometimes, quite often in fact, the children we work with are having to change their social role or they are anxious concerning the expected need to change roles in the very near future.

Apart from ambivalence and role-change, however, there are children whose socializing skills are undeveloped. There are some children who are dyssemic. A dyssemic child has a disability in the realm of non-verbal 'messages'. In the words of Daniel Goleman:

> The problem can be in a poor sense of personal space so that [such] a child stands too close while talking or spreads their [sic] belongings into other people's territory; in interpreting or using body language poorly; in misinterpreting or misusing facial

expressions by, say, failing to make eye contact or in a poor sense of prosody, the emotional quality of speech, so that they talk too shrilly or flatly. (Goleman, 1996, p. 121)

In Chapter 7 of this book the reader is given other examples of dysfunction and the possible causes of dysfunction related to attachment problems. It is easy to see that these various interactive difficulties will be exhibited in the home (natural, foster- or adoptive), in the school, in the residential establishment and anywhere else. Care-therapy must therefore extend to all these situations.

In so far as our third objects go, our first example is the so-called Loving Water and the way that this was used to help Donna (Chapter 2) to reflect on the way that she was rebuffing any affection. The reader will recall that the therapist went through 'Donna's story' with her, and showed her how the water (love) could not enter the vessel (Donna) because she had put on the 'suffering skin' (the 'cling film'). When a child has become aware of such a rejecting state, we may talk about her having put on the 'suffering skin', a skin which can be taken off again. Three illustrations which show the reader third objects concerned to a greater or lesser degree with role-change are given at Figure 2.7 (wall building), Figure 5.5 (*a*), (*b*) and (*c*) (changing dynamics and roles within a foster-family) and Figure 5.6 (the wrongly made jigsaw part).

There are of course many other examples within this book of third objects used either deliberately to help the child focus on interactive behaviour or where the child uses the object or activity in this way herself. An example of a child so using a third object was demonstrated when a sexually abused teenage girl suddenly made the dolls' house people become herself and others, and used them to demonstrate what had happened to her and how she felt.

Spectrum (8): Change Focus
The emphasis here is on the word 'focus'. The reason for this is that 'change' is something which care-therapy aims to bring about, and, once again, any of the third objects may be utilized by the child to bring about change. Indeed the whole care and upbringing of the child may do this. Often, however, concerning the children we are working with, the awareness of change or the desirability of change is to the fore.

There are two dimensions of change we need to consider, and readers will note that some of the third objects lend themselves to one dimension rather than to the other. These dimensions are: (*a*), change in external circumstances, or in the environment; and (*b*), change within the person or concerning the way the person interacts with others. Of course, in human affairs matters are not so neat or so simple, so that often change is likely (or necessary) in both dimensions at once. If a child is fostered or adopted, there are enormous external or environmental changes which impinge upon the child (and adults) so that interactive changes, or even habit changes, may be implied. This is often where the stress comes from in adopting or fostering older children (by which we mean any age, right down to eighteen months (i.e. not a very young baby).

Several of the third objects already discussed were focused, or helped the child to focus, on external, environmental changes. Figure 2.6 shows a board with movable 'characteristics', which was used to help Donna understand more about the changes which would be involved in being legally adopted. It also helped her to see that some aspects would not change.

But as well as changes in her legal status and in the responsibility for her care and upbringing, there were other changes (friends, school, neighbourhood) which would involve her feelings. For this the worker used the third object shown in Figure 2.9, the contact indicator. Clearly, if the work is being done thoroughly, there will be emotive aspects involved in the use of both these objects.

Other third objects, however, may effect a greater change so far as person to person interaction is concerned, or at least they may lend themselves more clearly to that aim. This goes for some of the third objects already discussed, such as the jigsaw pieces (Figure 5.6) and the third object we discussed when considering role-change (Figure 5.5 (*a*), (*b*) and (*c*).

Another example in which change was very much to the fore on referral is that of Arabella, the little girl who could not cope with doors being closed. We discussed her problems in Chapter 4 and we illustrated the work which was undertaken, including the 'doors that could smile' (Figure 4.14) and several other third objects. Her behaviour did change remarkably. It must not be thought, however, that a purely behavioural approach was used. Arabella was given the opportunity to reflect on and discuss her feelings, memories and fears. Nevertheless, in her case, a cognitive–behavioural approach aimed towards change of behaviour was helpful, but her behaviour would not have changed so long as the fears remained, and some of those arose from a 'forgotten' episode.

The Spectrum (9) and (10): Bridging, and Attachment/Bonding Work

There is no need for detailed accounts concerning these sectors of the spectrum, for we have dealt in detail in Chapter 5 with the process of bridging and have examined typical examples of third objects that we may use during that process. As for attachment and bonding, the whole of this work is concerned with these aspects to a greater or lesser degree, and attachment is a process (and a condition) which takes place between individuals and depends, not on counselling or direct work, but on what happens between individuals when they actually share a part of life together, either living together or frequently coming together and sharing life's experience (as with child and grandparents). The same applies to bonding, by which in this work we mean a parent's feelings towards a child, the words 'parent' and 'child' being inclusive and extensive, and going beyond 'natural' parenting. In Chapter 7 we deal more extensively with the phenomenon and process of attachment. Usually, these aspects of the spectrum will be important towards the end of a period of preparation, counselling or therapy aimed at helping a child to become established in a long-term placement, no matter what the placement outcome finally is, including rehabilitation into the fold of the natural family.

It should also be clear that as preparation and counselling proceed, and as the child moves into a situation in which strong friendships develop between child and carers, and more so where attachment is developing, the important changes will be taking place within the care and upbringing milieu, not in the clinic or counselling office. More often than not, however, a professional – social worker, psychotherapist or residential worker – will be in the essential role of co-ordinating, as far as he or she is able, all the life-experience elements which impinge upon the child. Care-givers need support and sometimes encouragement; schoolteachers have a vital role; the child's natural parents are meaningful persons; there may well be social work and adoption agencies involved; the courts may be involved, and all of them may be entitled to information concerning the child.

Before we conclude our discussion concerning third objects, and the appropriate times for using these, we shall remind the reader of the ways in which children (and adults) may be affected along the way, and we shall see that, even in the most careful practice, children may appear to regress or to become a little more 'disturbed' while they are coming to understand events or are 'coming to terms' with difficult memories or feelings.

Emergent Effects During Counselling and Psychotherapy

It is a widely held view that some children present new or escalated behavioural problems shortly after going into treatment. This may be so, although many accounts are anecdotal. Nevertheless a behavioural change is what one would expect to follow from an affective (emotional) experience if that experience is in any way connected with meaning or with self-respect or, to use a psychological term, a narcissistic aspect of the self. Such behavioural changes, often seen as temporary phases of regression, will usually be 'worked through' as treatment continues and as the child loses the tensions and stresses underlying her original referral condition.

Of course, as we have said above, deeper and permanent changes will take place as the child becomes positively attached to others. When counselling a child, however, it is important to be alert to the emergent effects of psychotherapeutic treatment. Alongside the work involving the various sectors of our treatment spectrum therefore, the following effects must be considered:

1 Memories will be triggered. These may be positive as well as negative, but the negative ones are hurtful and workers must therefore be careful to note changes. Memories of violence and of previous guilt feelings could be involved.
2 A sense of loss or grief may be aroused or re-aroused.
3 Anger feelings may emerge or re-emerge. They may be generated by insight; or repressed anger may be expressed in behavioural idiosyncrasies.
4 Surprise may be experienced.
5 Negative feelings may be temporarily generated. These may include feelings of having been cheated, e.g. not told what really happened, or guilt feelings may temporarily take hold. Then we could meet with suspicion, mistrust, feeling 'not wanted' or 'of no account'.

If such feelings are generated even in the most careful and child-centred work, it follows that behavioural changes of a temporary nature will be the outcome. Children may become quieter (even withdrawn) or excitable, aggressive, moody or secretive. It is vital that carers, social workers and therapists remain alert to any behavioural and mood changes during treatment. We see this as an essential part of treatment.

As we are nearing the end of this review of counselling approaches, it will not be out of place to say again what we have already said several times: allow things to develop according to the child's natural pace:

do not pursue a line of counselling which is destructive of the child–counsellor (or carer) relationship. Never 'dig' for information and do allow, even if you are keenly aware of 'the unconscious element', for 'therapeutic forgetting'; allow some things to 'sleep', unless important for the child's well-being and happiness.

Of course, the general movement or change during careful professional counselling and selective foster-care will be positive. Also, the therapy itself will encourage positive emergent effects so that children will gradually, sometimes quite soon in the process, experience feelings of:

1 Relief
2 Liberation
3 Support and assurance
4 Exuberance
5 Understanding (insight)

As the treatment proceeds, and as the child begins to feel self-assured within a supporting environment, other negative feelings and 'negative' behaviour (which once was 'functional' to the child) are dissipated, so we see the following behaviour lessening and being replaced by socially acceptable and personally satisfying behaviour:

1 Testing out, but remember, this may last on and off for a long time
2 Self-hate
3 Secretive, aloof behaviour
4 Denial
5 Affection and friendship rebuffing (rejecting)

We also note that children lose troublesome feelings such as:

1 Conflict feelings
2 Rootless, non-attached feelings

However, it cannot be stated too often that the changes we have outlined here, the positive growth changes, *may* take several years in the case of some severely maltreated children and young persons. For many children it will call for enormous patience, wisdom and, yes, suffering on the part of care-givers (parents and professional workers) across many years.

When we use the term 'maltreated', we are using it in is widest application. Maltreatment applies not only to what physical abusers may have done, but also to what social-care agencies and governments have done or have stood back and not done, and so our final section of this chapter will be concerned with a brief study of the corporate parent.

Corporate Parenting

From all that has been written in this book so far we can say with emphasis that children need the experience of a consistent family experience which will provide for an attachment and bonding process between child and at least one adult. The literature appears to support the proposition that the adult does not need to be the natural parent of the child. It also supports the proposition that the attachment experience is enriched if there is more than one parent figure able to give good-enough nurturing, and that sibling attachment is a very important experiential factor which should be considered seriously and not put lightly on one side in considering any child's welfare.

Many of the children discussed in this book will have been the subject of corporate parenting. By this we mean they will have been cared for ('looked after') in legal terms, by a social-care agency, either a state or local-authority agency or a voluntary (charitable) society, although for day-to-day purposes, and ideally for child-rearing purposes, some will have been fostered or placed for adoption, while others will have been cared for in residential establishments – the older term was 'children's homes', but with a capital 'H'.

Sadly, much of the corporate parenting today, even in Britain, Australia and the USA, is so bad that the basic welfare and developmental needs of the children are not being met. Even the foremost need mentioned above, of a consistent family experience, is in many cases denied to the child in corporate parenting, so that the care system itself often helps to produce the vulnerable unattached child.

There is evidence that, at the time of writing, children cared for by corporate agencies are experiencing a childhood of short-term family life, and what we might call a serial family experience, in which they move from family to family, placement to placement. With this experience continuing over the childhood years, the attachment and bonding process is disrupted. Sometimes a child remains with a declared 'short-term' fostering placement just long enough to begin to form an attachment, only to be uprooted and shifted yet again to a new family. In our own practice we have evidence of children of 10 years of age who have experienced up to twenty moves between the ages of 3 and 10. The reader will not need much imagination to realize how emotionally and developmentally devastating such a progress must be to any child, let alone those whose early infancy was fraught by the trauma of deprivation.

So why, with so much research over recent years, is such bad corporate parenting being offered to the most needy children within the twenty-first century? Despite the fact that, as we said in our first chapter, some excellent childcare is being practised by individual adopters and foster-parents, and despite the fact that there are many devoted and nurturing professionals, social workers and residential-care staff, the corporate parenting experience for many children is proving crippling in terms of mental health. Why?

In many respects childcare as practised towards children in care has deteriorated over the last 30 years. This can be said in spite of the damaging and insidious sexual abuse to which some children were submitted up until the present time. Corporate parenting is not left to a group of high-minded, child-caring and scrupulously moral persons; nor is it left to the professionally trained workers or the enthusiastic amateurs. Corporate parenting involves the politicians, the governments, and, for the last 50 years, the academics.

Loss of Children's Homes

Let us take one factor which seems to be responsible for some of the frequent moves made by children in care – the closure of most of the residential care establishments. We have already accepted that family life (of good-enough quality) is the preferred care style, so there's no argument here. We must also accept, however, that *some* children will need (for shorter or longer periods) care in a residential setting with well trained, reliable staff looking after them and providing counselling and training. Rather than divert here in order to provide all the reasons for saying this, we ask the reader to bear with us on this point.

The closure of hundreds of residential establishments, some specializing in assessment, forced state and voluntary care agencies to place children in foster-homes – foster-homes which 'weren't there' and foster-homes which could not cope with the behaviour of the children. Throughout the last ten years it has, in certain circles, been quite *de trop* to argue for a balance or a mixture of care facilities. Residential care (children's homes) was 'out'; no child should reside in 'a Home', even for a short time. The idea of residential care was 'Victorian'!

In Britain there have been recent official and other reports indicating that an awareness is creeping in, to the effect that we may have gone 'too far' in closing down these establishments. For those interested in studying the actual documents the information on 'Reports' in our Further Reading section should prove helpful. Here we shall mention and give brief quotations from the House of Commons Health Committee Report 'Children Looked After by Local Authorities' (HMSO, 1998), which in Paragraph 170 states:

> Secondly, the reduction in residential home capacity has gone too far. There is a clear need for an increase in the number of children's homes countrywide, to enable local authorities to make appropriate placements . . .

Elsewhere, the same Report in one of its recommendations now accepts that a mixture of care facilities is required and that:

> We counsel against any automatic assumption that foster care is preferable to residential care, although in many cases this may be so. A variety of options should be available to SSD's (Social Services Departments) so that placements can be suited to the needs of the individual child. (para. 85)

But it is not necessary even to think in terms of either A or B, foster-care or residential. Some children need to make use of both facilities at different times. A 'very disturbed and disruptive' child will, if we are going to provide the best care for that particular child, need to be carefully and skilfully assessed. This means making a study of the child: his personality, social, educational, and psychological needs; readiness to either return to parents (if they are not unsuitable) or to consider a foster-family; and many other factors. At the time a child is either received into care or placed in care by a court, we may not know very much about him – and we shall not have a flow-chart history.

Using a foster-home for such a child very often has a number of drawbacks. First and foremost of course, what has happened in practice is that there has been a quick perusal of 'short-term' foster-homes available. The discovery is made that only two beds are vacant, and the child is placed in one of the two homes. In fact neither is suitable but nothing else is available. The child may have been 13 years old and wanting to stay with her 11-year-old brother also coming into care, but he had to go to the other available 'bed' so the children are split and upset. This sort of childcare service often results in stress being placed on both child and care-givers, because nobody could possibly have *matched* the children with the placement facilities.

Despite the usually fine and altruistic motives of most short-term foster-carers and despite the fact that there are, here and there, some outstanding people who have a gift for childcare, there are many children who need at first, when they are removed into public or voluntary-society care, a larger group of people around them so that they have psychological and social space as well as the feelings of safety and reassurance.

Furthermore, some children also need to be assessed concerning long-term outcomes, or plans. This calls for a co-ordinated study by a number of specialist professionals. We do not want to see children 'drifting'. We do not want to continue the record of the last ten years or so during which time there have been terrible records of placement movements that have damaged children, some of them now adults, who can speak of ten, fifteen, twenty and (at least one child) as many as forty placements during a childhood of being 'in *care*'!

We are still urging, and this book as a whole does so, that children and their natural families should first receive all the help needed to maintain them as a unit, but that if children *have* to leave the natural family, then we should do everything possible to find *suitable* (a very far-reaching term) alternative families and that in order to secure the best match of child and family, we may also need specialist units (residential) for proper assessment and therapy. Remember, some children need treatment before being placed in a long-term foster-home or adoptive family.

Sadly, in many 'developed-world' countries there is a serious deterioration in the quality of corporate parenting at the same time as society is generating social problems affecting children and young adults. In Central Europe there has been an increase by 75 per cent over the last ten years of children requiring corporate parenting. In New South Wales, Australia, in 1999, social-work staff of the Department of Community Services 'cited the critical shortage of foster carers and residential places as their most pressing need' (*Sydney Morning Herald*, 25 September, 1999), while in the states governed by Russia the suicide rate of teenaged lads is now twice the rate of ten years' ago. The corporate parenting of the nation's children must not remain a hidden backwater in the nation's life: it is far, far too important.

Corporate Parenting and Multicultural Issues
Elsewhere in this work we have raised questions concerning cultural and ethnic minority problems, and in Chapter 4 we briefly outlined two third objects used in counselling certain children. We have also referred to the importance of the careworker's (or therapist's) attitudes to cultural differences in so far as outcome success is concerned.

The value of any counselling or caring service provided appears to be related to the ability or otherwise of therapists and care-givers to relate sensitively to cultural and ethnic factors. This involves not only being aware of cultural differences in society but also being aware of ('in touch with') one's own feelings, possible prejudices and shortcomings concerning these sensitive matters.

Since we are here concerned with 'corporate' parenting, it is important that we should include consideration of the function of management. It is as important for higher echelons of management to be concerned with multicultural issues, as it is for the face worker. In fact the importance of this issue reaches beyond units of local government and chief executives of welfare societies, right up to government ministers. We must therefore be concerned with all these aspects both at the level of individual care-givers and at service-delivery level. This observation also has a message for training organizations.

Rawson *et al.* (1999) say that service managers should build trans-cultural considerations into the basic economic equation of demand and supply and that in particular they should ask the following questions:

- Is there a clearly defined ethnic/cultural catchment client group for the service provision?
- Has this catchment group been surveyed?
- What distinctive cultural demands are there in this catchment?
- How can the service respond effectively to such groups?
- Does practitioner provision reflect the cultural diversity of the catchment group?
- Does the service monitor effectiveness of service provision with respect to cross-cultural sensitivity?

In so far as individual workers and care-givers are concerned, here are some of the 'tentative' guidelines provided by Lago and Thompson (1997).

- Attempt to gain an awareness and knowledge of your own culture and cultural style, race and origins.
- Attempt to gain knowledge of the client's culture, cultural style, race and racial origins (avoid simplistic beliefs and views based on inadequate, biased, or limited accounts).
- Hold in mind that any breakdown in communications may be attributable to the dynamic process between you (and the client).
- Remember that many concepts like truth, honesty, intent, politeness, self-disclosure and so on are culturally bound.
- Be alert to your usage of language.

- Monitor your own attitudes during the interview, especially in relation to feelings of superiority or power over the client (associated with areas of racism and oppression).

There are of course certain problems which are germane to corporate parenting in multicultural states such as the USA, Australia, or the UK and elsewhere in western society. These problems may be ethnically bound but that will not necessarily be so. In Northern Ireland, for example, they may be bound into the so-called Protestant–Catholic divide.

The sort of thing we are thinking of has been highlighted in Britain recently, with certain agencies developing the policy of placing black or Asian children for adoption or fostering *only* with 'appropriate' black or Asian families. Until then many children had been placed in ethnically and culturally dissimilar families. The controversy resulting from placements which became headline news caused some navel contemplation, which was not a bad thing.

Government policy in Britain now shows an attempt to balance the ethnic and cultural background factors (important in any placement) with the attachment and bonding needs emphasized in this book. This adjustment came about because large numbers of children were being denied a family upbringing because of difficulties associated with cultural/ethnic matching when looking for adoptive parents.

The Department of Health circular issued to local authorities in Britain, LAC (98) 20, attempts to define the balance by a series of statements, which in effect say (when matching a child for an adoption placement):

- It is important to take into account the child's ethnic origin, culture, religion, language and her wishes. (Sec. 12)
- Other factors, however, should be taken into account. These will include concern about 'drift' (i.e. child waiting for appropriate placement as the months and years drift by). No child should be denied the chance of placement for adoption solely on the grounds that the child and the (otherwise only suitable) family do not share the same racial and cultural background. (Sec. 1 and 14)
- Great importance is placed on the wishes of the child's natural parents. Their wishes concerning age range of adopters, religious upbringing and cultural factors should be taken seriously. However, the wishes of the parents cannot always be met. They may be too restrictive. The needs of the child must be the *first consideration*. (Secs. 19 and 20)

- The child's wishes may also be too restrictive. (Sec. 13)
- Children should be prepared to meet forms of racism and cultural prejudice. Families caring for children placed for adoption should receive guidance on this matter.

The same message is spelt out concerning fostering (The Children Act 1989, Guidance and Regulations, Vol. 3: Family Placements).

Most of the voluntary (or charitable) societies concerned with fostering and adoption appear to be working along the policy lines outlined above. Most, if not all, rightly emphasize the importance of ethnic and cultural matching, but also warn against drift and children being deprived of family care.

In our final chapter we shall consider more deeply the phenomenon and process of attachment. It is important that people caring for children, those who offer counselling to vulnerable children, and those in management positions in childcare agencies should understand the importance of this process. We also have a brief look at the 'survivors', i.e. people who, as children, suffered many set-backs but who nevertheless grew up to take their places in society as stable adults, and we ask 'What factors were involved here?'

CHAPTER 7

The attachment process: child development as affected by attachment experience and poor nurture: types and sub-types in 'Reactive Attachment Disorder' and survivors.

'Sensitivity, consistency, stimulation and responsiveness are some of the qualities important to the early relationships in a young child's life.'
Sylva, K., and Lunt, I., 1982

Attachment, Nurture and Good-enough Parenting

This chapter deals almost exclusively with the attachment process mentioned in Chapter 1. It is important to our study because so many of the children requiring care-therapy treatment have experienced attachment problems in their infancy. Furthermore, the theory of attachment in human infants is central to understanding the full treatment approach described in this book.

First, a word about terminology. The terms 'attachment' and 'bonding' are often used as synonymous and are interchanged. In the present work I shall restrict the term 'attachment' to the child's orientation toward another (e.g. parent, sibling or foster-parent) and shall use the term 'bonding' when referring to the parent's (or sibling's, etc.) orientation toward the child.

Semantics are important in this discussion as it is easy to overlook the powerful developmental influence of the attachment phenomenon on account of the common usage of this word. People talk about being 'attached' to some particular article which they favour. They might say 'I'm attached to my little automobile', or to 'my little cottage', and this means they are very fond of and keen about these things. But that is not the same as a child's attachment to a good-enough parent. Even when we say we are 'attached' to a good friend, a 'bosom pal', it does not have the same power nor anything like the same meaning as when we talk, in technical psychological language, about attachment in child development. It may help if we give a quotation from John Bowlby who states:

> What for convenience I am terming Attachment Theory is a way of conceptualising the propensity of human beings to make strong affectional bonds to particular others and of explaining the many forms of emotional distress and personality disturbance including anxiety, anger, depression and emotional detachment, to which unwilling separation and loss give rise . . .
>
> Advocates of attachment theory argue that many forms of psychiatric disturbance can be attributed either to deviations in the development of attachment behaviour or, more rarely to failure of its development; and also that the theory casts light on both the origin and treatment of these conditions. (Bowlby, 1979, p. 127)

We shall be advancing the view that the attachment experience, together with the whole nurturing experience, even when no physical separation takes place between child and parents, is a vital aetiological factor which has a connection with the subsequent development both physiological and psychological (cognitive and affective) of the child and later adult.

As the human being grows and develops and experiences the various social pressures, the effect of a poor attachment experience may become more generalized, or it may adversely affect certain important psychosocial developmental variants. The paediatric psychotherapist, Dr Vera Fahlberg, argues that a satisfactory attachment experience enables the child to

1. attain his full intellectual potential
2. sort out what he perceives
3. think logically
4. develop social emotions
5. develop a conscience
6. trust others
7. become self-reliant
8. cope better with stress and frustration
9. reduce feelings of jealousy
10. overcome common fears and worries
11. increase feelings of self-worth

(Fahlberg, 1991, p. 14).

It is easy to skim through this list and to miss the tremendous message it gives. If we take the first and the fifth items on the list and consider what is being said here, the importance of a good-enough attachment experience will be emphasized. The first item states that a poor experience may adversely affect the intellectual development. Barrett and Trevitt, who have made an extensive study of attachment behaviour as it affects the child's school performance, have stated:

> Our third category of children who are resistent to learning is the most puzzling group of the three that we have identified. They have no learning disability as such; nor have they lost their capacity for learning. They appear to resist learning: they can learn but they won't ... they appear to be angry, sad or depressed and we place them, emotionally speaking, in the group defined as 'disorientated and disorganised'. . . We feel that most of these children have been *unable to build a memory of an attachment figure* who is emotionally available to them. (Barrett and Trevitt, 1991, p. 185 my emphasis)

Consider the consequences of a child not 'attaining his full intellectual potential'. This could lead on to feelings of inadequacy. It could result in a general lack of self-confidence. Ultimately it could affect the child's ability to do well in educational examinations. There is also evidence that time and space perception are sometimes affected.

Attaining one's full intellectual potential appears to depend upon factors which in some way form a network or a system, the separate parts or aspects of which are not independent but are, to a greater or lesser degree, interdependent. Many research papers bear out these connections. For example, cognitive (thinking) and affective (emotional) connection has been attested by Gaussen (1984), Rutter (1985) and Murray *et al.* (1993). Depression in mothers has been shown to be associated with impaired cognitive development in the children (Murray *et al.*, 1993). Even psychomotor development appears to be a part of this interdependent network (Henderson, 1987; Roussounis *et al.*, 1987; Johnson *et al.*, 1987; Stiefel, 1997).

Now consider Fahlberg's fifth developmental factor, 'develop a conscience'. If it is true that conscience development and attachment experience are linked then we are on to something of immense importance.

We cannot devote the space in the present volume to a discussion on this proposition, but we can say that conscience and morality development are linked by some theorists to the development of **empathic** understanding and that empathic understanding itself is related to good-enough parenting (Hoffman, 1984).

Judy Dunn also relates the development of altriusm and sensitivity (to other people's feelings) to a childhood providing the care and affection that we are stipulating:

> One recent study of very young children showed particularly clearly that a child's concern for others was most effectively fostered in families in which the mother drew the child's attention clearly and forcibly to the consequences of his unkindness and aggression for the other person, and firmly prohibited such actions, *but in which the mother was also warm and loving* to the child. (Dunn, 1984, p. 108, my emphasis)

We have expanded briefly on only two of the developmental and socializing tasks named in Fahlberg's list above. When we consider how much a good parenting and attachment experience means to a child in terms of feelings and security, confidence, encouragement and trust, it becomes easier to agree that the other items on the list are also likely to be more richly achieved within a satisfactory attachment experience.

Viewpoints Concerning Attachment
We have noted the importance of attachment and it will be helpful to consider some of the theory concerning this subject. However, it must be emphasized that the attachment process (the attachment experience) should not be seen as an entity totally isolated from other developmental and socializing factors.

It is often necessary, in studying an aspect of human development, to separate the various strands of experience and development – to practise a form of reductionism in fact – but the attachment process encapsulates many aspects of personality development which were identified before much thought or study had been given to attachment as a unique factor in human development.

In the lower animals and birds it is possible to identify a more elementary infant-protection process called imprinting. Imprinting probably combines certain basic learning and instinctual mechanisms. The famous naturalist, Konrad Lorenz, did a lot of experimental work on imprinting. He studied 'following' behaviour, i.e. behaviour in newly born (or newly hatched) dependent creatures which results in their following, and maintaining contact with, their parents, with all the protection this affords the infant. Under normal conditions, for example, ducklings and goslings follow their mother soon after hatching, perhaps stimulated by her movements, her vocalizations, or both. However, the same following behaviour may be produced by almost any perceptible object which moves, provided the young creature is deprived of the natural parent and is given the substitute 'parent' within a very short time after hatching or birth. So, in Lorenz's experiments the goslings and ducklings became 'imprinted' to him or to other substitutes, some of them not even live objects. Provided he moved the objects about, the infants would imprint. He demonstrated that a coloured balloon could become the imprint object, so that the young creatures would follow it in lieu of a real mother.

Once a creature is imprinted with a substitute parent, the imprinting cannot be undone. Imprinting is irreversible. A bird imprinted to a human being does not subsequently imprint to its natural mother or to any other bird supplied later.

In the more highly developed animal, and in human beings, the process of parent–child joining is more complicated and influenced to a far greater extent by their complex learning capacity, but it still serves vital psychosocial and psychobiological functions.

Age for Onset of Attachment Development

Professor H.R. Schaffer has studied and compared a broad spectrum of research data concerning attachment and bonding as these factors relate to human beings.

Schaffer points out that in very early infant life the care-takers (parents, etc.) are 'interchangeable' (Schaffer, 1990). At birth, it appears, the child does not 'know' its mother or anyone else, and a process of familiarization has to take place. Familiarization involves learning. But to say that care-takers are interchangeable does not mean that a very young baby has no recognition of particular voices or particular faces. There seems to be adequate evidence for saying that some children as young as eight weeks can recognize the familiar from the strange, and that some may recognize the mother's voice, for instance, much earlier:

> However, being able to recognize the mother by, for instance, smiling at her more readily or being more easily comforted by her touch does not in itself signify that an attachment has been formed to her. Such recognition is only a prerequisite to attachment formation; in all other respects infants remain quite indiscriminate. Thus, they will accept care and attention from anyone, however unfamiliar, and show no sign of upset when separated from the parent or any orientation towards her during her absence. (Schaffer, 1990)

Schaffer is here speaking about infants aged less than six months. He has also indicated that research results show a unanimity in fixing the third quarter of the first year as the age when most infants exhibit vulnerability to separation from a continuous care-giving other. In placing babies for adoption, for example, it would seem unwise to keep them in 'temporary' foster-homes beyond five months, assuming them to have been so placed soon after birth. In practice we may find infants remaining for ten or even eighteen months. The evidence from the research is that such infants can become traumatized by the break in the attachment process.

In one study undertaken to examine the psychological effects of hospitalization in infancy, use was made of the separation situation 'to highlight the extent to which infants of different ages within the first year of life require their mother's presence and refuse to accept attention from other people (Schaffer and Callender, 1959).

This study showed that the behavioural syndromes resulting from separation through hospitalization fell into two categories, each associated with a particular age-range and divided from each other at approximately seven months. Infants above the age of approximately seven months showed the classical (Bowlby) separation syndrome, with depression indicators and negative behaviour towards strangers, disturbed feeding, 'desperate' clinging to the mother during visits, disturbed sleep, etc.

Infants below the age of seven months displayed few of these symptoms, and most were able to make an immediate adjustment to the hospital environment and the people who looked after them. On returning home the older age-group showed far more 'disturbed' behaviour.

Nowadays, in many countries, parents are able to stay in the hospital with their sick infants, but this 1959 study enables us to see the difference in attachment experience and loss experience as they affect infants below or above the age of about six months.

Another useful longitudinal study (rather than cross-sectional as the one reported above) was carried out by Schaffer and Emmerson. This study examined a group of 60 infants every four weeks for the first year of their life and then again at eighteen months of age. Everyday situations were studied, such as everyday separation situations where an infant might be left for a short time alone because the mother had left the room, or being left in the care of a baby-sitter, or put to bed. (Schaffer and Emmerson, 1964)

Separation 'protest' was recorded, and in particular the onset of this protest behaviour. 'For the majority of infants this was at the beginning of the second half-year', the same as in the previous studies discussed here.

L. J. Yarrow (1967) carried out an interesting investigation concerning 100 infants who were placed for adoption. Some of these children were over eight months old. Yarrow found that all the children who were eight months and over showed 'strong overt disturbances to permanent separation from the mother'. The younger the infant when separated, the less (statistically) were the overt signs of disturbance. At three months no infants exhibited disturbance signs; at five months, 20 per cent did so; and at six months 59 per cent showed disturbance signs.

Clearly, those interested in the subject will need to go beyond this brief résumé and compare the research methodologies as well as the conclusions.

Interactional Factors in Attachment Development

Although here and there we have mentioned, in the research projects and the various hypotheses, the importance of the type of parenting to the attachment process, we have not looked closely at the child–adult interaction, which appears to play a central part in the attachment experience. Leading practitioners, many of whom are also researchers, have contributed to our understanding of this aspect of the development of attachment.

Vera Fahlberg, to whom we referred earlier, has been involved in practice, teaching and writing. She has highlighted the ideal inter-actional relationship between child and parent and also shown the effects of various degrees of movement away, not so much from the ideal but from the good-enough relationship. We shall direct the reader's attention now to some of the best relationship attributes that Fahlberg and others mention, because this will help us reflect on the very great shortfall experienced by some children.

Despite all that has been said above concerning the age at which children can be said to have attached, it is refreshing and reassuring to find someone like Fahlberg writing about 'setting the stage for bonding' (Fahlberg, 1991) and looking at important factors in the 'pre-natal period'. She feels that there are many subtle factors and nuances which begin well before a baby's birth, but which affect the quality of the attachment–bonding process.

These would include even the images which parents develop concerning their unborn child. Are they looking forward to having a child, or is this an unexpected nuisance? The relationship between the parents during pregnancy, according to Fahlberg, affects the bonding that will occur with the child.

Fahlberg is also concerned with what she calls the 'bonding at birth'. Most mothers, for example, use their first contact with the child to 'explore him, to count fingers and toes, and just generally to see if he is physically normal'. Are the parents enjoying contact with the child, with the new-born baby? How about body contact?:

> Body Contact between mother and child also contributes to bonding between them. In most societies children are in more frequent body contact with their mothers than they are in western industrial countries. The rhythmic movements that the child experiences as he is carried about by his mother are similar to what he experienced before birth. (Fahlberg, 1979)

It is important to remember that although attachment itself in a recognizable and to some degree measurable state may be said to take place later, the actual psychological development of the child begins to be affected from birth (or earlier) on account of interactional factors.

Reciprocity between adult and infant is well demonstrated in the developmental cycles used by Fahlberg. Before describing the use of these cycles as a means of illustrating two of the important processes involved in attachment and bonding, however, it may be helpful to discuss some of Fahlberg's concepts concerning this process. On the parental side she appreciates two kinds of interaction which greatly affect the quality of the process. These are (a), the speed and intensity with which the parenting figure responds to crying; and (b), the extent to which the parenting figure (or figures) initiates positive interactions with the infant. These criteria are held by Bowlby, whom Fahlberg quotes (Fahlberg, 1991).

Young infants, Fahlberg maintains, normally have a relatively high perceptual threshold, and when, because of external or internal stimuli (hunger for example), tension is high, the infant, to use Fahlberg's expression, discharges tension (or attempts to do so). This can be seen in the behaviour and body changes taking place in the child. The child moves his arms and legs, cries, goes red in the face, and makes squirming movements. As long as the child is in this state his full perception of the outside world is blocked, and the longer it goes on, and the greater the frustration, the more blocked becomes the perception. Many a child, who later becomes the concern of social workers and medics, has experienced continuous tension resulting in heavy blocking of the type described, so that 'As a result, his intellectual development that depends on such perceptions is hampered or blocked' (Fahlberg, 1991, p. 26).

The opposite of displeasure, says Fahlberg, writing of babies, is not pleasure or happiness but quiescence, or contentment. She sees a vital parenting role in returning the frustrated (displeased, needy) infant to a state of quiescence in which she will either sleep or find an interest in her environment.

Figure 7.1 shows the 'arousal–relaxation cycle', an illustration of the process which, it is important to remember, the healthy infant 'pushes round'. He or she does not lie there dormant in the face of unmet needs and internal frustration. The illustration is self-explanatory, but it should be noted (*a*), that successful fulfilling of the repetitive cycle leads towards trust, security and attachment, and (*b*) that the cyclic process continues into adulthood although the needs will differ from those in infancy.

The development of a 'sense of' (or feeling of) trust in infancy is of course a developmental need postulated by Erik Erikson, with a 'sense of' mistrust as its opposite (Erikson, 1963). The frustration and anger generated during the uncycled displeasure/frustration state also relate to Klein's 'splitting' process and her concepts of **'projective identification'**, the 'paranoid schizoid position' and the 'depressive position' in infant development (Mitchell, 1986). They also relate to Miller's 'narcissistic rage':

> We cathect an object narcissistically . . . when we experience it not as the centre of its own activity but as part of ourselves. If the object does not behave as we expect or wish, we may at times be immeasurably disappointed or offended almost as if an arm ceased to obey us or a function that we take for granted . . . lets us down. This sudden loss of control may also lead to an intense narcissistic rage. (Miller, 1986, p. 48)

However, Fahlberg warns against jumping simplistically to the conclusion that in every case of infant frustration, poor parenting is the cause; or erroneously tracing back to infancy a poor-parenting factor in every disturbed child. Some children, perhaps on account of an organic problem, do not respond as they should even to negative stimuli, and there are others who respond negatively to positive stimuli. Some prematurely born infants may respond in these ways and fail to 'push the cycle round'; the same may be said for some children who experienced a difficult birth or where the amniotic fluid was lost too early in the birth process. Some infants, for one reason or another (not always traceable), may be 'impossible' to comfort.

Some infants react with non-comforting behaviour as a result of the parent figure's own physical or psychological illness, e.g. depression, or to a parent figure who is overburdened, perhaps caring for other already disturbed older infants (Politano *et al.*, 1992; Barnett, 1991 *et al.*, 1986; Sandberg *et al.*, 1980). Fahlberg recalls the case of a child referred to her when he was 3 years old, but whose history subsequently revealed that

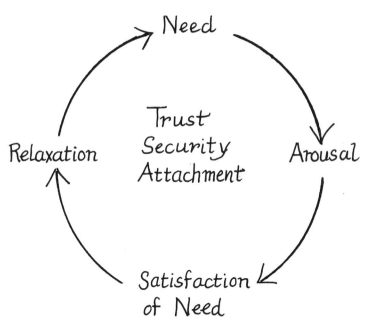

Figure 7.1 *Arousal–relaxation cycle (After Vera Fahlberg)*

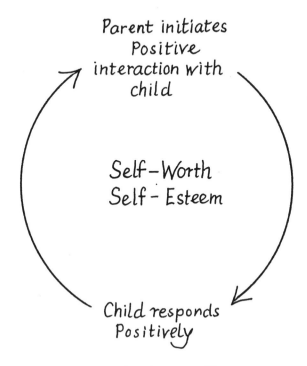

Figure 7.2 *Positive interaction cycle (After Vera Fahlberg)*

from the third day of his life he was prone to seizures of a rare and dangerous type. The mother herself noted that if she touched the infant a lot he tended to have a seizure (touching – the very thing recommended in good-enough nurture!). Consequently the child was deprived of holding, rocking, and various forms of 'play' early in life.

The arousal–relaxation cycle must therefore refer to the normal behaviour (pushing the cycle round, 'demanding' attention and then relaxing) of healthy infants. Psychologists have coined the term 'learned helplessness' for deprived children, some of whom were 'institutionalized' in poor examples of residential care. Such children 'stop trying to exercise control over their environment' (Schaffer, 1989). This, of course, is an alternative description to 'failure to push the cycle round'. Many disturbed children, however, appear to be pushing, i.e. they are 'pushy', but in fact they are static at the arousal phase, and carry resentment and anger.

Fahlberg's other cycle, the 'positive interaction cycle' (see Figure 7.2), should be 'pushed round' by the parent figures. It refers to the active positive intervention by the good-enough parent, who provides stimulation even when the child cannot, in any way, ask for it. In the early months this will include 'simple' gestures and behaviours such as smiling, looking at, 'talking' to, but as the child develops it will include many forms of social support, playing with, teaching, etc.

This cyclic process is concerned with the parental initiative rather than the infant's unconscious (later conscious) pushing the cycle round. Good-enough parent figures may be quite unaware of factors such as 'initiative' or 'pushing', yet they tend intuitively to react in a manner stimulating to the infant. One can see this even in the early cooing or talking to the baby and in the adult smiles, or patting and touching. Much later in childhood the adult may suggest a walk, a game, or initiate some form of learning.

As long ago as 1952 Ainsworth and Boston pointed out as a result of their studies that social interaction, not routine care, is the most important part of mothering, and we would change that to 'parenting' because we believe fathers have a very important role in initiating this positive interaction cycle. If the initiating occurs with good will and results from a genuine feeling of warmth and cherishing, not simply because the parent feels the child should be 'trained', and not done in such a way as to diminish the child, then, as the illustration indicates, feelings of self-worth and positive self-esteem are generated.

Before moving on from this discussion of the Fahlberg cycles let us emphasize that good-enough parenting does not mean removing every challenge or every moment of discomfort, nor even the small experiences of pain which come along in life – don't 'cotton wool' children. Fahlberg, referring to R. Spitz (1965) says that

> it is probably as harmful to deprive an infant of the feeling of discomfort as to deprive him or her of quiescence. If, for some reason the child does not experience any discomfort, it is possible that he or she may lack a degree of 'push' to bring about change. (Fahlberg, 1991, p. 27)

The Effect of Attachment Problems and Poor Nurture on Personality Development

In Chapter 2, where we outlined Donna's case, we were able to report that she was attaching to a family and beginning to take her place in life as a normal, satisfied and stable young woman. However, that is by no means always the case with people who have experienced similar psychosocial experiences. Many are left with psychological, somatic, behavioural or social problems; or indeed with some combination of these factors.

One way in which we can study the effects of poor attachment experience on children's development is to look at what happened when children were deprived of effective parenting. In recent years we have, sadly, had examples in Europe of such neglected children. The 'orphaned' children of Romania, who were discovered after the fall of Communism, are an example.

It may appear callous to call on such examples to prove a point, but ideally the study of such tragic lives will help us ensure that children do receive the care and affection they need in order to develop healthily both physically and mentally.

However, we can go even further back in our search for evidence. John Bowlby, whose name and work are so closely associated with the study of attachment in human infants, produced a monograph as early as 1951 entitled *Maternal Care and Mental Health*. There are some interesting statistics in that work relating to 'institutionalized' children.

At the time Bowlby was attempting to show that adverse developmental reactions could be seen in children who were not cared for in infancy by their natural mothers. He drew therefore on a number of research undertakings which in the main compared children looked after in institutions (and therefore separated from their mothers) with children who were looked after by their mothers. The institution children came off worse. For example, a piece of work undertaken by Gesell and Amatruda (1947) studied the appearance of 'adverse reactions' in institutional infants compared with infants cared for in their own families. 'Adverse reactions' in fact seems to have reflected slow development, lack of drive (my word) and idiosyncratic behaviour. Examples from the research tables are:

- Diminished interest in, and reaction to, surroundings.
- Excessive preoccupation with strange persons.
- Blandness of facial expression.
- Relative retardation in 'language behaviour'.

(Bowlby, 1951, p. 17)

Another piece of work used by Bowlby to illustrate his hypothesis concerned research undertaken by Spitz and Wolf into the effect that institutional care might have on the infant's general 'development', or **developmental quotient** (DQ). They studied four groups of children, one group being the institution group, and the other three groups representing children from three 'classes' of citizen ('professional', 'peasant' and 'delinquent unmarried mothers'). The researchers measured the DQ of all the groups at 4 months old, and then again at 12 months. Their findings indicated that whereas the babies cared for by their mothers had maintained their DQs (they were practically the same at 4 and 12 months), the institutionalized babies (cared for in 'an hygienic institution') showed a catastrophic drop in DQ from 124 at 4 months to 72 at 12 months (figures represent averages).

Another researcher, Goldfarb, compared children who had spent their first three years of life in an institution with 'controls' who had not. He measured 'intelligence', 'ability to conceptualize', 'arithmetic' and social behaviour such as 'ability to keep rules' and 'speech'. Readers interested in pursuing this study will of course find details of tests and results in Bowlby's work. This piece of research again showed the institutionalized children to be at a developmental and social-behaviour disadvantage, with a mean intelligence quotient (IQ) of 72.4 compared with 95.4, and only of 20 per cent of the institutionalized compared with 80 per cent of the family children showing 'ability to keep the rules'.

On the face of it these figures may seem impressive, but in fact they have been much criticized in recent years. Why the criticism? Well, apart from some of the methodology there is the question of just what the research was revealing. Was it really all down to the absence of the natural mother or was it the absence of good-enough nurture and good-enough attachment and bonding? Was it due to 'institutional' care or something that was missing from the care. Could those children have been given good-enough 'parenting' even in an institution? We must remember that the institutions investigated were often places holding several hundred children, with sometimes as few as one member of staff to twenty children. Even in the Spitz (1946) comparison (above) Bowlby himself states 'It is true that these infants were living in conditions especially bad from a psychological point of view as not only was there but one nurse to some seven children but, for reasons of hygiene, the children were kept restricted to cots and cubicles in what amounted to solitary confinement'. So here, presumably, were toddlers (at one stage) confined as described, in cubicles. If mothers had been present but treating the children as described by Bowlby they would still have been deprived children. No wonder their expressions were 'bland'! (Gesell and Amatruda, 1947).

Later on Bowlby himself recognized that 'natural' parents, although desirable, were not essential for a satisfactory attachment and nurturing experience. Of course it may be more difficult and far more expensive to provide parenting of quality in an institutional setting, but remember that such a 'setting' these days could include as few as six children.

Readers who wish to pursue this study, i.e. a critique of Bowlby's work, are directed to Holmes (1993) and Sylva and Lunt (1982). However, there has been substantial literature, ever since the 1950s, to uphold the contention that (despite 'survivors', see later in this chapter) a poor attachment, parenting and nurturing experience in infancy is likely to have extensively detrimental effects on the child's development. Much will depend upon the temperament (effect of genes) of the child and the intensity and length of the deprivation (or privation).

In the course of our clinical work with children who could be described as having been deprived of good-enough parenting during infancy, covering as much as a year or longer before the age of 5, we have registered the effects in four 'developmental functional' modes: emotional, social, cognitive and somatic. Examples of these effects are shown in Table 7.1.

Notice the way that what is called 'affection' takes on different qualities so that we find some children exhibit what has been called 'shallow' affection – they are apparently unattached emotionally. Observe its effect in column 2, 'would easily move to new care-givers'. Then we find 'indiscriminate' affection and 'narrowly discriminate' affection. Narrowly discriminate affection can cause problems when such children are first placed in adoptive or foster-homes. It is important that care-givers should understand that some children are at the stage where they can share affection (deeply) with only one other. Later, they will be able to spread affection further. 'Poor impulse control' causes many problems. Such behaviour is 'normal' in the 2-year-old, but if it is of the same quality when the child is 11 or 12, there are difficulties. We are back to the 'stuck' child we described in Chapter 1.

1. Emotional (affective)	2. Social (interactive)	3. Cognitive (thinking, knowing)	4. Somatic (physical)
Examples:	*Examples, many of which would be 'normal' at one age but not 'normal' at another:*	*At an age when they would normally be beyond these problems:*	*At an age when they would not normally have these problems:*
Shallow 'affection'	Would easily move to new care-givers?!	Problems concerning conceptualization of time, space, shape, number	Motor control and co-ordination may be affected
Indiscriminate affection	'Affectionate' to everyone, not selective	Child cannot understand meaning of 'week', 'month'.	Fine control affected, e.g. use of scissors, tying shoe-laces, doing up buttons
Narrowly discriminate affection	Selects one foster-parent and 'rejects' the other	Cannot tell clock time	Gross control (unable to catch a ball, unable to skip)
Inability to share affection – clinging, jealous	Demands teacher's attention Demands parent's attention Rejects foster siblings	Cause and effect do not belong together	Often seem 'clumsy'
	Temper tantrums Demands immediate gratification, 'I want now' Violent, destructive, aggressive	Logical reasoning (for age) undeveloped	Difficulty getting dressed
Nil or poor impulse control	Swings from over-dependent to too independent		Smaller physique than normal for age and sex
	Little or no 'conscience', no guilt feeling	**Note:** Such children may be quite 'sharp' and accurate over such matters as their pocket money amounts. They are not just 'dull'.	Somatized behaviour such as tics
Little or no empathy			Failure to grow, i.e. 'failure to thrive' where there is no organic failure evident

Affect-lame

Table 7.1 *Developmental functional modes adversely affected by privation and deprivation (abuse, neglect, etc.)*

The reader's attention is drawn to the somatic column in the Table (column 4). Note that motor control and co-ordination may be affected. We have already referred to this condition. Certainly many older children seen by us came with descriptions of 'clumsiness'. But other forms of muscular control may be affected, so that we find a large percentage of referred children suffer from encopresis or enuresis. Another description often occurring in case files relating to infancy is the statement 'failure to thrive', which refers to the child not having put on weight, or to other growth indicators, when hospitalized in infancy or early childhood, despite normal food ingestion. Much of this somatic area can be included under the heading of psychomotor difficulty. However, children showing psychomotor problems should also be checked out medically, and any signs of spasms or 'tingling' feelings should be noticed.

Up to date research is bearing out the clinical observations given above. Stiefel (1997) to whom we shall refer widely in this section, states 'The attachment relationship may function in different ways, having a significant effect on emotional, cognitive, social and motivational development in young children'. She uses an interesting paradigm when she refers to the good-enough care-giver 'scaffolding', i.e. sensitively tuning-in to the child's needs and providing appropriate behavioural support without overwhelming her with demands or intrusiveness. This kind of care-giving, she says, tends to foster 'ego competencies' as described by Matas, Arend and Stroufe (1978). Other researchers have stressed the effect of a secure attachment on the child's conceptualization concerning self, and self in relation to other (for example Greenberg *et al.*, 1993).

In the paper referred to (Stiefel, 1997), the writer is concerned with the link which appears to exist between a 'sub-group' of children with **attention deficit hyperactivity disorder** (ADHD) and a 'lack in sustained parental attention during the first years of the child's life'. She develops a model which makes use of two cycles called (*a*), demand–dissatisfaction and (*b*), demand–satisfaction cycle. These are shown in Figures 7.3 and 7.4. Readers will be interested to compare these diagrams with the earlier developmental cycles of Fahlberg already referred to. What Stiefel does in her model is to push the boundaries of unsatisfactory care outwards to include lack of support for parenting figures – this is very important. What is also interesting from our point of view, as therapists, is Stiefel's hope that 'by delineating the different possible pathways to ADHD' clinicians may be able to offer specific multi-model treatment programmes, which is what we are about in this book.

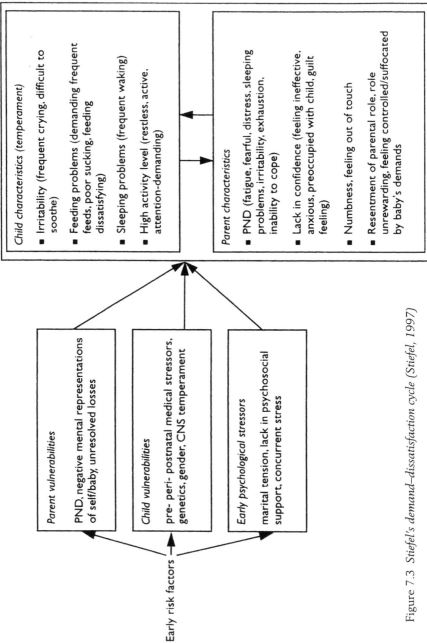

Demand Dissatisfaction Cycle

Child characteristics (temperament)

- Irritability (frequent crying, difficult to soothe)
- Feeding problems (demanding frequent feeds, poor sucking, feeding dissatisfying)
- Sleeping problems (frequent waking)
- High activity level (restless, active, attention-demanding)

Parent characteristics

- PND (fatigue, fearful, distress, sleeping problems, irritability, exhaustion, inability to cope)
- Lack in confidence (feeling ineffective, anxious, preoccupied with child, guilt feeling)
- Numbness, feeling out of touch
- Resentment of parental role, role unrewarding, feeling controlled/suffocated by baby's demands

Parent vulnerabilities

PND, negative mental representations of self/baby, unresolved losses

Child vulnerabilities

pre- peri- postnatal medical stressors, genetics, gender, CNS temperament

Early psychological stressors

marital tension, lack in psychosocial support, concurrent stress

Early risk factors

Figure 7.3 *Stiefel's demand–dissatisfaction cycle (Stiefel, 1997)*

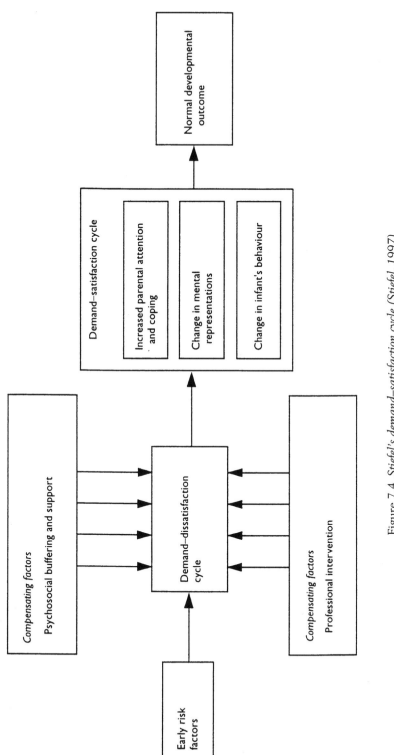

Figure 7.4 Stiefel's demand–satisfaction cycle (Stiefel, 1997)

Classifying Types of Attachment Disorder: Diagnostic Handles

In this penultimate section we shall review the categorization of children into different groups, according to their behaviour and the history of their care and parenting, when diagnosing 'reactive attachment disorder'. We would not wish it to be understood, however, that children can be put neatly into slots, nor that the classification types below are anything more than a guide, albeit a scientific guide and one useful diagnostically. We shall refer to such eminent publications as the *Diagnostic and Statistical Manual of Mental Disorders*, Fourth Edition (DSM-IV), 1994, and to Mary Ainsworth, who has done so much scientific work relating to attachment, but when it comes to therapy, and especially care-therapy with individual children, we shall find both that they don't fit the boxes neatly, and that they require therapists who are able to respond in different but specific ways to children of the same 'category'.

However, it is important that social care workers, psychotherapists and others closely involved in childcare should understand the diagnostic terminology currently in use by child psychiatrists and researchers concerning attachment disorder.

The DSM-IV (1994), which is used by many child psychiatrists, specifies only two 'types': A1, inhibited type; and A2, disinhibited type. The A1 type infant is also very 'ambivalent'. He will sometimes appear to reject or avoid the approaches of the care-givers and others. These children may also be hypervigilant and contradictory. They may even exhibit 'frozen watchfulness'.

It is important to remember, however, that these behaviours are based on a study of mother–child interaction in the first year of life. These experiments were devised by Mary Ainsworth and we shall refer to them again. The question is, however, do these patterns of behaviour survive into later childhood? Subsequent studies of older children confirm that, statistically, they do, which is not to say, however, that individual children will be trapped into unchangeable behaviour patterns. Much will depend upon subsequent experiences and the way they are nurtured.

However, if the parenting continues to be poor, these inhibited type children are likely to turn out at, say, 10 years of age, to exhibit conduct difficulties, struggles with parental authority, argumentativeness and anxiety.

The A2 type infant (an older child under poor conditions) exhibits a lack of in-depth attachment and an inclination to 'attach' to anyone (indiscriminate affection?). They show 'excessive familiarity' with strangers, i.e. 'disinhibited'. These children may also tend to be 'controlling'.

In DSM-IV this attachment type categorization is found under the heading 'Reactive Attachment Disorder of Infancy or Early Childhood'. Children are not diagnosed as such unless, as well as A1 and A2 characteristics (above) predominating, three other criteria B, C and D are also met. These are:

B   The criteria for A1 and A2 are *not* accounted for solely by developmental delay such as mental retardation (organic) or pervasive developmental disorder (See DSM-IV).

C   'Pathogenic' care is evidenced by *at least one* of the following:

C1 persistent disregard of the child's basic emotional needs for comfort, stimulation, and affection;

C2 persistent disregard of the child's basic physical needs;

C3 repeated changes of primary care-giver that prevent the formation of stable attachments, e.g. frequent changes in foster-care.

D   There is a presumption that the care in criterion C is responsible for the disturbed behaviour in the criteria for A1 or A2.

Using two very broad categories may prove somewhat limiting when you come to describe (or attempt to categorize) individual children, and indeed DSM-IV scatters other characteristics of attachment disorder under quite separate 'disorders', so that we find, for example, 'separation anxiety disorder' showing many characteristics associated with attachment problems.

Other Categorizations

Mary Ainsworth used what she called the 'stranger situation' to study the reaction of infants (in the first year of life) to their mother's three-minute 'abandonment' of them, and leaving them with a stranger (Ainsworth *et al.*, 1978). She found a correlation between the type of attachment behaviour in the child (at one year) and the maternal relationship in the preceding twelve months, a finding that has been replicated in other research (Main and Weston, 1982; Sroufe, 1979).

Jeremy Holmes, who is recommended reading on Bowlby, states:

In summary, prospective studies show that mothers of secure one-year-olds are responsive to their babies, mothers of insecure avoidants are unresponsive, and mothers of insecure-ambivalents are inconsistently responsive. (Holmes, 1993)

The reader will note the use of different terminology here when naming categories of children. In fact Ainsworth's work finally produced four major patterns or types, termed A to D, which we give below. For some reason the secure group was given the category letter 'B' (rather than 'A'). Setting these out, therefore, as Holmes (1993) does, we have:

1 Secure attachment ('B') These infants are usually (but not invariably) distressed by the separation. On re-union they greet their parent, receive comfort if required, and then turn to excited or contented play.

2 Insecure-avoidant ('A') These children show few overt signs of distress on separation, and ignore their mother on re-union, especially on the second occasion when presumably the stress is greater. They remain watchful of her and inhibited in their play.

3 Insecure-ambivalent (insecure resistant) ('C') They are highly distressed by separation and cannot easily be pacified on re-union. They seek contact, but then resist by kicking, turning away, squirming or batting away offered toys. They continue to alternate between anger and clinging to the mother, and their exploratory play is inhibited.

4 Insecure-disorganised ('D') This small group has recently been demarcated. They show a diverse range of confused behaviours including 'freezing' or stereotyped movements, when re-united with their parent.

Subsequent studies have been able to add to the characteristics typical of children in these groups. Group A children have been linked with consistent but non-supportive environments, including low parental warmth (Crittenden et al., 1996). Group C children maximize their attachment behaviour by trying to engage the care-givers and others in either an anxious/dependent or a wilful and argumentative way. An undercurrent of ambivalence and anger is often present; the child's play is fragmented; relationships with 'attachment figures' are uneasy; struggles and arguments are frequent.

Long-term childhood risks include anxiety, attentional problems and conduct difficulties.

These group C children seek contact, often in an indirect way, yet they may resist the care-giver's attempt at closeness. This causes problems in foster- and adoptive placements, especially with older children. They are the 'suffering skin' children. They may develop the attention deficiency and hyperactive disorder (ADHD) (see Stiefel, 1997). These children tend also to show lower scores on motivation and competent play, and show difficulty in modulating impulses (poor impulse control), in delaying gratification (must have it, or do it, 'now') and in expressing affect. They may be typically 'affect-lame'. Sometimes they will destructively interrupt the care-giver's attempt to talk to a third party.

Group D children are often associated with greater social adversity, including parental pathology and abuse. Sometimes the parent is perceived as frightening. Children in this group may engage either in parentifying, 'care-giving' behaviour or try to control the parent figure through refusal, derogatory or commanding behaviour. Long-term risk includes, as in C, the possibility of ADHD.

Clearly, these groups are not exclusive so far as behaviour and symptomatology are concerned. In practice, although general patterns may be recognized, many of the behaviours will be spread among the groups.

In this chapter so far we have emphasized the importance of the attachment process. Of course, we are aware that many other elements influence the development of what we call personality. Starting with genetic factors we can add the family and parenting experience, plus peer-group influence and interaction, plus the effect of the cultural and sub-cultural influences, plus group influence (and group pressure), and so on. We feel however, that the early attachment experience is the foundation of all environmental influences (non-physical) and therefore to some extent influences the child's response to other factors.

A cautionary note should be sounded here concerning research and conclusions relating to attachment and the 'strange' (or 'stranger') situation studies. Among developmental specialists there is, at the time of writing, some difference of opinion concerning whether or not the strange situation does highlight personality differences. As Judy Dunn points out 'some researchers have argued, for instance, that the differences in Strange Situation behaviour reflect temperamental differences in response to stress rather than attachment security' (Dunn, 1993). Dunn here, especially Chapter 2 of her book, is recommended further reading.

The Survivors

One of the most interesting developments in research concerning vulnerable children, or rather adults who were vulnerable as children, is the shift from the study of what makes for failure, for neurosis or for delinquency to what makes some vulnerable children ('at risk' children) into survivors? These studies, aptly drawn together by Mark Katz (1997), confirm the view expressed in this book that, as well as the basic temperament, what Katz calls 'inward qualities', the sources of resilience, of being able to change and outgrow the poor start, are seen again and again to depend upon the quality of the life experience.

The quality of the life experience is affected by the 'risk factors', and multiple risk factors may affect a child's social and intellectual development. Risk factors include severe marital discord, low economic status, paternal criminality, maternal psychiatric disorder, and we could add more. Michael Rutter (1979) (Katz states), assessed that a child exposed to four risk factors had a likelihood of developing a psychiatric disorder ten times greater than a child exposed to only one factor. To be 'exposed' here means to have had an experience lasting for months if an infant and for several years if older.

What, then, helped many 'exposed' children to become survivors – adults able to take their place in society – and to be able to cope? The key factors appear to be these:

1 Affectional ties with parent substitutes, such as grandparents or siblings.
2 'External' support from which they gained feelings of being valued and recognized. This could have come from a teacher, a church worker or others, including their peers.
3 Certain 'core beliefs', including –
   • the world to be 'benevolent' (basic trust)
   • the world to be meaningful
   • self-worth high enough to overcome doubts.

Readers will appreciate these as being associated with the good-enough nurturing, parenting and attachment factors we have urged as the basic rights of childhood. When researchers study the factors which help people overcome early disadvantages and even maltreatment, in other words the healing factors, we find these experiences to be pertinent:

1 Help in expressing emotions and in learning to trust.
2 Opportunities to reappraise experiences (insight).
3 Support from carers and caring people.

4 A sense of hope, and a high enough self-image being developed and maintained.

5 A feeling (as the person grows up) of having some influence over one's destiny – having a satisfactory degree of control.

6 The responsibility of helping someone else.

The professional social worker must aim to support and help each child in his care in such a way that these experiences, these 'sources of resilience', become part of the child's experience so that they shall also become part of his adult experience.

We have touched only lightly upon the enormously important role of the childcare worker. No single individual will be able to craft together the needs of a damaged, hurt and vulnerable child. The team must include the residential workers, the foster-parents and adopters, the educationists, health workers, police, therapists and legal experts, as well as others. But the professional role in child social work demands knowledge, skills and a commitment which adds up to care-therapy. The authors of a document published in 1989, *The Care of Children: Principles and Practice in Regulations and Guidance*, were surely right when they wrote:

> Principles are the colours on the social worker painter's palette. The range and quality of colour helps to produce a good painting, but it is the painter's skill which makes or mars the picture. Excessive caseloads or lack of necessary resources can be as disabling to the social worker as lack of paint to the artist, but failure to understand and apply essential principles can spoil even the best resources so that they become damaging to those they were intended to benefit. (Page 9)

In the same document there are some very wise and important words concerning the application of the principles we have mentioned (and others):

> Principles must never be applied blindly but used intelligently with common sense and sensitivity because it can be dangerous to over-emphasize any one principle to the extent that others are ignored or flouted. (Page 6)

Postscript

This book is being published at a time when governments and child welfare organizations across the world are regretting the way children in the care of the state have been bundled from placement to placement. Perhaps in our haste to foster children we lost those facilities which could help them, gently, to recover from the vicissitudes of their lives. In Chapter 2 we pointed out that these children are often faced with the questions, 'Who am I?' 'Who do I belong to?' and 'What is to happen to me?'

Helping children to answer these questions in a way which ensures feelings of security and emotional satisfaction demands understanding, skill, empathy and patience. Adopters, foster parents, social workers and others can be found who have these qualities, but so often they (and the children) have been let down because the training, skills and other resources have not been available.

It is to be hoped that the skills and the philosophy of child counselling and therapy, as well as the basic attachment needs we have written about, will be better met for many children if these pages are able to influence training, caring, and therapy roles. But remember, care and therapy are not and should not be separate entities; that is why we speak of 'care-therapy'.

APPENDIX 1

Parent–child nurture ('good-enough parenting')

Includes:

1 **Environmental physical care.** For example the provision of adequate shelter, food, warmth, clothing, etc., but goes much further.

2 **Appropriate holding and touch contact.** It is natural (and intuitive) for a parent when holding a baby, to actually stroke the baby. This is often done quite instinctively and without thinking about it, so that we may see a mother holding a conversation with a friend and patting or rubbing her own infant's leg or arm.

   Touching (appropriate touching) is an important element in healthy child development. This includes giving and receiving hugs, and romping.

3 **Intellectual stimulation.** This starts, not from school or nursery age, but from day one. Obviously I am not restricting 'intellectual' stimulation here to advanced reasoning or to thinking at all. Babies should be inquisitive. Babies can also 'learn' about sounds, including voice sounds. Even before they have words they can learn through the intonation of a parent's voice. Intonation may even convey ideas about being loved, about feeling safe.

Later when 'talk' is possible there is the opportunity of chatting with children. When putting the child's shoes on we can refer to her red shoes or black shoes. Nursery rhymes and stories later become part of intellectual stimulation, but so do building bricks and old cardboard boxes and any opportunity to discover and explore.

4 **Overt signals of Affection.** Children need to become aware, quite early on, that they are valued (loved, cherished) just for existing, and not only when they do the 'right' thing. H.R. Schaffer refers to a quality (in good-enough parents or care-givers) which he calls 'sensitive responsiveness', i.e. 'the extent to which a parent is aware of the child's signals and communications, interprets them correctly, and responds to them promptly and consistently' (Schaffer, 1985).

5 **Appropriate Interaction.** This includes interest, encouragement, guidance, training, correcting, forgiving and setting role-models. Extremely incorrect role-models are seen where a parent sexually abuses a child, i.e. it sets two wrong models, the parent's role and the child's. This of course would involve inappropriate touching.

6 **Association with the peer group.** The opportunity, especially from adolescence onwards but throughout childhood, to associate with and learn from interaction with one's peer group. We are noting here the importance of 'group' experience in social and personal development.

7 **Appropriate adult/child role-change.** As the child grows up role-changes are appropriate for parents as well as children. Often it is the parent who is unable to change and to adapt to the maturing child and adolescent (by which I do not mean that the parents have to throw out all their own values and beliefs, but there has to be an adjustment).

So, when we talk about a child having experienced poor-quality nurture we are referring to some or all of the areas of interaction listed above.

APPENDIX 2

Check list on preparation for placement

Question (*re* task or condition)	Extension of question	Further comments
Set A READINESS EXPRESSED BY OR OBSERVED IN THE CHILD		
1. Has the child been able, with help, to adjust satisfactorily to the loss of old parenting ties? Or do you have sufficient evidence to feel that the child is dealing with this loss and will be able to continue to cope with emotional adjustment to such loss? To 'adjust' does not mean to forget. It implies that the child will be able to 'survive' and move into new relationships.	This can be extended to loss of other ties such as siblings. 'Loss' refers to a state in which matters are 'inevitable', such as the death or long-term imprisonment of the attachment figure, or where such a person has abandoned the child. It does not refer to situations where the child can be in touch, and wishes to be in touch, with a previous attachment figure.	It need not be that the child has resolved the loss completely. This may take several years. But the worker must know that the child has had an opportunity to come to terms with such loss, and is likely to be able to deal with the new relationships pending, without unresolved problems of this nature inhibiting the relationship unduly.
2. Is the child able to accept a new parenting relationship?		The question is obviously a pair question with the one above. However, the answer to this question will only emerge as a result of a process of assessment, not a one-off interview. The question will only be answered adequately as a result of counselling and considering the child's history and his experiences in previous placements.
3. Is the child able to accept a new, or a first-ever sibling relationship?		By which we mean adoptive or foster-siblings.
4. Does the child show a satisfactory degree of being able, intellectually and emotionally, to accept the facts about the practical possibility or impossibility of returning to previous care-givers?		This also pairs with question 1, but we have in mind here the sort of situation in which the child needs help in understanding and accepting some administrative factor causing separation, e.g. both parents on a 'life' sentence. Again we cannot expect emotional problems to disappear. We are more concerned here with the child's ability, with help, to have coped adequately with the facts.

5. Has the child expressed sufficiently strongly and without pressure a wish to be placed in the type of placement in mind?	Does the child want to be fostered, or adopted? Does he like the idea of going to live with his or her 'uncle' and 'aunt'? What criteria have you used to establish your answer?	Obviously the answers must to some extent relate to the age and ability of the child. Some children have first-hand knowledge of fostering. Some could not be expected to understand, but a young child will talk about going to live with people who will look after him.
6. With older children, in the case of a plan for adoption, has the child been explicit enough in showing a wish for this?	Does the child understand sufficiently what is meant by legal adoption?	The age of the child must count here, as well as intellectual development. It is up to the worker and the potential adopters to be intellectually honest if they know the child is able to understand.

Set B TASKS IN DIRECT WORK WITH THE CHILD

7. Have the questions in column 2 been dealt with sufficiently with the child?	Most of the children need answers to these questions: 'Who am I?' 'To whom do I belong?' 'What is going to happen to me?' How will people who already know me be able to keep in touch with me?' 'Suppose I am unhappy in the place I'm going to?' 'Will I be able to meet the people who will care for me, before I move in?'	
8. Has the child had sufficient opportunity to review his own history?	And has he used it to make adjustments or to gain new perceptions?	The 'opportunities' will include flow charts, life-storybooks, photographs, visits, birth certificates, etc., and discussions or counselling using these objects.
9. Have the child's feelings concerning people and events in his history been brought out and coped with?		This is a delicate area and skill and understanding are required so as not to probe just for the sake of probing.

Question (*re* task or condition)	Extension of question	Further comments
10. Has work been undertaken with the child to establish any emotional 'blockage' or symptoms of denial?	Has it been possible to help the child (to unblock?) sufficiently for placement to proceed?	Again, provided the emotional blocks will not adversely affect the placement, it is far better (and more likely) for the healing to take place within a developing attachment/bonding matrix. But we must have confidence, as a result of work so far undertaken, that the child is making progress and will most likely continue to do so. Do not place a child blindly, hoping for blockages to disappear. Problems often re-emerge years after the start of a placement.
11. Has work been undertaken with the child to establish the level of emotional development?	This question concerns the emotional/social development. Consider, for example, Tables 7.1. Some older children may function 'intellectually' at an IQ level of 'normal' or well above, but respond emotionally as 2- or 3-year-old children.	Development will take place within a satisfactory attachment/bonding matrix, but it is essential that care-givers know at what level the child is functioning when he first joins them, and how to relate to him.
12. Has the child been helped to mourn the loss of any attachment figure?		

Set C ASSESSMENT AND INFORMATION OBTAINED FROM DOCUMENTATION, OTHER PROFESSIONALS, FAMILY, ETC.

13. Has an assessment of the child's development and the stages he is functioning at been made?	Includes: emotional, social, physical, and educational or academic development. Also moral understanding, 'conscience' development and empathy development.	This information should be obtained early and before beginning any in-depth direct working with the child.
14. Has the worker obtained a true-as-possible and detailed-as-possible history of the child?	This will be obtained from various sources (official and otherwise) but it must not be overlooked that the child may often be the only one holding factual information.	It is advisable for the worker to make a detailed administrative flow chart of the child's history before commencing direct work (see Chapter 6). We are not referring here to a flow chart done with the child.

15. Has a study been made concerning the child's present and previous attachment figures?	Who were/are they? Are they still interested in the child? Is their interest a healthy interest and one which should be encouraged? If attachment has really taken place, what help will be given or has been given to the child if such attachment figures do not figure in the prospective placement?	Unless the worker is aware of such people in the child's life it is possible that other questions set above will not be sufficiently covered.
16. Has an assessment been made concerning the extent to which the child's self-image (self-identity) or ego may have been adversely affected by previous events?		The degree to which this aspect is assessed or investigated will depend on a number of factors. Many children will not require a full assessment made by a psychologist or other therapist; others will.
17. Has an assessment been made to establish if there are important areas of missing life experiences?		These may be the seemingly 'small' things in life like never having seen the sea! Or, much more important self-identity areas such as the child who has missed 'being a child' because they hard to 'take charge' of things from a very tender age.
18. Has an assessment been made to establish any areas of misperception of an ontological nature?		Some children who have 'missed out' or been unable to relate in a normal way find it hard to understand aspects of time, space, sound, etc.

Set D TASKS WHICH THE CARE AGENCY MUST ENSURE HAVE BEEN UNDERTAKEN

19. Has the preparation work taken account of the views of other workers and people in touch with the child?	This includes specialists such as psychiatrists, psychologists, psychotherapists. Also field and residential social workers, teachers, medical people, members of the child's family and others who are or should be involved.	Of course, if other specialists are involved the whole process should be a team undertaking, and an early decision has to be taken concerning 'key' workers and who will undertake the direct work with the child.
20. Has a profile of the child's behavioural adaptations been made?	This involves aggressive behaviour, withdrawn behaviour, 'telling lies', stealing, sexual behaviour, etc., as well as helpful behaviour, empathy, kindness to younger children and/or animals, socializing abilities or tendency to be a loner.	Some interpretation of the psychosocial goal, and also the aetiology and onset will be helpful. This information helps the worker to deal with other tasks referred to above.

Glossary

aetiology that part of medical science dealing with the causes of disease.

affective (adj.) and **affect** (n.) a feeling, emotion or desire, especially as leading to action.

affect-lame this term implies that the child is dysfunctional in one or more expressions of affect (see above).

analytic psychology specifically, the psychology appertaining to Jung's form of psychoanalysis and theory of mind, personality, etc. For example, Jung has three levels (against Freud's two) of mind: conscious, personal-unconscious and collective-unconscious. Also used loosely to refer to psychological theories which break the mind (or psyche) into 'parts' or components.

Attention Deficiency and Hyperactive Disorder (ADHD) an essential feature is a persistent pattern of inattention and/or hyperactivity-impulsivity.

behaviourism/behavioural a theoretical approach in psychology emphasizing an objective study of actual responses, and purporting to change behaviour by use of 'reward' and 'punishment' procedures.

behaviourist one who practises therapeutic treatment using a behavioural approach (see above).

catharsis the release of tension or anxiety as a result of some counselling or psychotherapeutic process.

cathexis/to cathect in psychoanalytic theory, the investing of libidinal (mental, psychic, sometimes sexual) energy in an activity, an object or a person.

cognitive a general term covering all modes of knowing: perceiving, reasoning, judging, remembering, etc.

cognitive-behavioural a theoretical approach in psychotherapy which draws upon both the cognitive and behavioural aspects, as defined in this glossary.

collective unconscious Jung's term for that aspect of the unconscious shared by all people. In Jung's hypothesis the collective unconscious consists of the residue of the evolution of mankind (Reber, 1985).

denial a 'defence mechanism' by which the person simply disavows thoughts, feelings, wishes, etc., which cause anxiety.

depressive position refers to Melanie Klein's theory of anxiety, especially in babies. There is a stage at which the infant, although angry with the mother, feels guilt and anxiety for the damage it has done, i.e. the baby is in the 'depressive position'.

Developmental Quotient (DQ) although calculated in a way similar to the Intelligence Quotient, is concerned with general physical and mental development, of which intelligence is only a part. A DQ of 90–110 represents average development.

direct work refers to forms of counselling involving the social worker, therapist or other, working directly with the child (as distinct from an advisory role) and using various art and other media as part of the counselling process.

disclosure work the process (involving police, medics and social workers) of the child disclosing to the authorities, often leading to court appearances, the details of a sexual abuse or other form of attack.

ecological from 'ecology', the study of the interaction of people with their environment.

empathy/empathic a vicarious affective response to the emotional experiences of another person that mirrors or mimics that emotion (Reber, 1985).

existential counsellor from existential psychology and existentialism. Existentialism emphasizes subjectivity and individuality. Existential therapy focuses on free will and individual choice and action.

family therapy a form of group counselling which analyses and attempts to utilize the dynamic processes within the family group.

frozen awareness a psychological state seen in young children when, due to shock, extreme grief, trauma or loss of an 'attached' person, the child withdraws socially to a state resembling a trance, or has lost all drive and activity. (See also 'Frozen Watchfulness', DSM, 1995).

genogram a pictorial style 'map' or diagram showing relationships between individuals within a family or any other group.

Gestalt (therapist) from **Gestalt psychology** which argues that psychological phenomena can only be understood if they are considered, viewed, as organized structured wholes (or Gestalten, the German word). Gestalt therapy is a form of psychotherapy drawing on this theory. It attempts to broaden the person's awareness of the self by drawing on past experiences, bodily states, dreams, etc., and helping the person to form a meaningful configuration of self, past and present.

holistic approach the treating of the whole person, including mental and social aspects, and including environmental as well as subjective factors.

insight (1) any self-awareness or apprehension or new knowledge; and (2) a changed awareness about one's mental condition which has previously escaped awareness.

Jungian analyst a therapist (psychiatrist, psychotherapist) who practises a form of psychotherapy which draws upon analytic psychology (see above).

Kleinian (terms), pertaining to or drawn from the works of the post-Freudian, Melanie Klein. (See, for example, 'projective identification', below.)

narcissistic/narcissism the love of self that results from a withdrawing of libido (mental, psychic and sometimes sexual energy) from objects and persons, and investing it in oneself.

ontology/ontological a branch of metaphysics dealing with the nature of being, of existing.

personality typology refers to a rather complex hypothesis from which Jung identifies certain basic type distinctions in human personality. The two popularized distinctions are extraversion and introversion, but these are collateral with several other type distinctions.

preconscious knowledge, emotions, images, etc., not momentarily in consciousness, but which are easily accessible (Reber, 1985).

projective identification refers to Melanie Klein's theory of anxiety in babies, which may involve a process of mentally 'splitting off' parts of the self and projecting them onto another person. This process can also be seen at any age.

psyche the mind, but in some psychologies the concept of 'soul' or 'spirit' is included. The very (mental) essence of the person.

psychoanalytical/psychoanalytic specifically, to do with psychoanalysis. Generally, refers to any psychodynamic theory of psychology.

psychodynamic (adj.) concerning psychological systems and theories which postulate internal 'drives' and internally driven motivational factors as central to the system.

psychomotor pertaining to mental events which affect the movement of muscles, or vice versa.

psychosynthesis (counsellor) a theoretical and practical approach in psychotherapy which aims to foster the development of a well-integrated personality and which acknowledges the 'spiritual' aspect of being as well as the physical and social aspects. The essence of psychosynthesis is that each of us has a purpose in life.

rationalization a 'defence mechanism' by which the person produces, and believes, a 'good' or 'logical' reason for his behaviour, motivation, likes and dislikes, but which is in fact spurious.

recovered memories refers specifically to memories, usually from childhood, which are recovered as a result of a therapy process such as hypnosis and which were previously obliterated from memory. A disputed area of psychology and psychotherapy.

Reinforcer (a debatable psychology term); one definition is, 'any set of circumstances which the person finds pleasing or leading to satisfaction, and which reinforces a particular type of behaviour'.

role-play/role-playing performing particular parts or roles in mini-plays or open-ended acting-out games.

somatic of or relating to the body, especially as distinct from the mind.

somatization (see somatic) the apparent or real bodily symptoms which are linked to mental states such as anxiety or depression. May be pain, organic dysfunction or behaviour such as twitches or tics.

testing out refers to behaviour which is directed, consciously or unconsciously, at seeing how far the child can push behaviour aimed at discovering attitudes and/or intentions held by others.

third objects any object, game, artistic medium or activity used in a one-to-one counselling situation, the 'first' and 'second' objects being client and therapist.

transference the displacement onto the therapist of attitudes, behaviour, prejudices, etc., usually held towards other persons, e.g. parents, siblings.

References

Abraham, K. (1924) 'A short study of the development of the libido, viewed in the light of mental disorders' in *Selected papers of Karl Abraham* (1927). London: Hogarth Press.

Ainsworth, M., Blehar, M., Waters, E. and Wall, S. (1978) *Patterns of Attachment Assessed in the Strange Situation and at Home*. Hillsdale, NJ: Erlbaum Associates.

Ainsworth, M.D. and Boston, M. (1952) 'Psychodiagnostic assessment of a child after prolonged separation in early childhood', *British Journal of Medical Psychology*, **25**, 169–201.

—— (1998) 'Children looked after by local authorities'. House of Commons, Health Committee. London: HMSO.

Bakeman, R. and Adamson, L.R. (1984) 'Co-ordinating attention to people and objects in mother–infant interaction', *Child Development*, **55**, 1278–89.

Barclay, P.M. (1982) *Social Workers, their Role and Tasks*. London: Bedford Square Press.

Barnett, B. and Parker, G.(1986) 'Possible determinants, correlates and consequences of high levels of anxiety in primiparous mothers', *Psychological Medicine*, **16**, 177–85.

Barnett, B., *et al.*, (1991) 'Maternal anxiety: a 5-year review of an intervention study' *Journal of Child Psychology and Psychiatry*, **32** (3)

Barrett, M. and Trevitt, J. (1991) *Attachment Behaviour and the School Child*. London, New York and Canada: Routledge.

Bawkin, H. (1949) *Journal of Paediatrics*, **35**, 512.

Bettelheim, B. (1987) *A Good Enough Parent*. London: Thames and Hudson.

Bowlby, J. (1951) *Maternal Care and Mental Health*. Geneva: World Health Organization.

—— (1979) *The Making and Breaking of Affectional Bonds*. London: Tavistock. London: British Agencies For Adoption & Fostering.

—— (1989a) *Attachment*. Vol. 1. Pelican.: First published by Hogarth Press, 1969.

—— (1989a) *Care of Children: Principles and Practice in Regulation and Guidance.* London: HMSO.

CCETSW (1991) *The Teaching of Child Care in the Diploma in Social Work.*

Clarkson, P. (1989) *Gestalt Counselling in Action.* London, California and New Delhi: Sage.

Cousens, P. and Nunn, K.P. (1997) 'Is "self-regulation" a more helpful construct than "attention"', *Clinical Child Psychology and Psychiatry,* **2**(1), 27–43.

Crittenden, P. and Claussen, A.H. (1996) 'Comparison of two systems for assessing quality of attachment in the pre-school years'. Symposia presented at the WAIMH, 6th World Congress, Finland.

Curtis, P. (1983) 'Involving children in the placement process', *Adoption and Fostering (Journal)* **7**(1), 45–7.

—— (1994) *Diagnostic & Statistical Manual of Mental Disorders* (4th edn) (DSM-IV). American Psychiatric Association.

Deurzen-Smith, E. (1988) *Existential Counselling in Practice.* London, California and New Delhi: Sage.

Dockar-Drysdale, B. (1990) *The Provision of Primary Experience.* London: Free Association Books.

Doise, W. and Mugny, G. (1984) *The Social Development of the Intellect.* Oxford: Pergamon Press.

Donaldson, M. (1978) *Children's Minds.* London: Fontana.

Dunn, J. (1984) *Sisters and Brothers.* London: Fontana.

Dunn, J. (1993) *Young Children's Close Relationships: Beyond Attachment:* Sage.

Erikson, E.H. (1963) *Childhood and Society.* Penguin Books, Hogarth Press.

Fahlberg, V. (1979) *Attachment and Separation.* London: British Agencies for Adoption and Fostering.

—— (1991) *A Child's Journey through Placement.* London: British Agencies for adoption and Fostering.

Field, T. *et al.* (1982) 'Non-nutritive sucking during tube-feedings: effects on preterm neonates in an intensive care unit', *Pediatrics,* **70**, 381–4.

—— *et al.* (1986) 'Tactile/kinesthetic stimulation effects on preterm neonates', *Pediatrics,* **77**, 654–8.

Fraiberg, S. (1959) *The Magic Years:* Methuen.

Franz, M.L. (1964) in *Man and His Symbols.* (ed.) C. Jung: Pan Books (Picador).

Freud, A. and Burlingham, D. (1942) *Young Children in War-Time London:* Allen & Unwin.

Freud, S. (1900) *The Interpretation of Dreams.* London: Hogarth Press.

—— (1923) *The Ego and the Id.* London: Hogarth Press.

Gaussen, T. (1984) 'Developmental milestones or conceptual millstones: some practical and theoretical limitations in infant assessment procedure', *Child Care, Health and Development,* **10** (2), 99–115.

Geldard, K. and D. (1997) *Counselling Children: a Practical Introduction.* London: Sage.

Gesell, A. and Amatruda, C. (1947) 'Developmental diagnosis: normal and abnormal child development'. Clinical methods and pediatric applications (2nd edn). New York.

Goleman, D. (1996) *Emotional Intelligence.* London: Bloomsbury Publishing Plc.

Goodensky, A. (1997) *Mum's The World.* London: Cassell.

Greenberg, Mark, T. *et al.* (1993) 'The role of attachment in the early development of disruptive behaviour problems', *Development and psychopathology,* **5**, (4), 191–213.

Greenfield, S. (1997) *The Human Brain: A Guided Tour.* London: Weidenfield & Nicolson.

Hakimi-Manesh, Y. *et al.* (1984) 'Short communication: effects of environmental enrichment in the mental and psychomotor development of orphanage children', *Journal of Child Psychology and Psychiatry*, 25(4), 643–50.

Harlow, H. and Zimmerman, R. (1959) 'Affectional responses in the infant monkey', *Science*, 130, 421–32.

Hay, D.F. (1994) 'Prosocial development', *Journal of Child Psychology and Psychiatry*, Annual Research Review, January; 29–71.

Henderson, S.E. (1987) 'Assessment of "clumsy children", old and new approaches', *Journal of Child Psychology and Psychiatry*, 28(4), 511–25.

Hoffman, M.L. (1984) 'Moral development' in M.H. Bornstein and M.E. Lamb (eds) *Developmental Psychology: An Advanced Textbook*. New Jersey: L. Erlbaum Association, pp. 279–324.

Holmes, J. (1993–97) *John Bowlby and Attachment Theory*. London:Routledge.

Hsu, L.K.G. (1990) *Eating Disorders*. New York: Guilford.

Johnston, O. *et al.* (1987) 'Poorly co-ordinated children: a survey of 95 cases', *Child Care, Health and Development*, 13 (6), 361–76.

Kagan, J. (1972) 'Do infants think?' *Scientific American*, 226, 74–82.

Katz, M. (1997) *On Playing a Poor Hand Well*. London: W. Norton.

Klein, M. (1969) *The Psycho-Analysis of Children*. London: Hogarth Press.

Kraemer, G.W. (1992) 'A psychobiological theory of attachment', *Behavioral and Brain Sciences*, 15, 493–541.

Lago, C. and Thompson, J. (1997) 'Counselling and race', in S. Palmer and G. McMahon (eds) *Handbook of Counselling*, (2nd edn). London: Routledge.

Lamb, M.E. and Sherrod, L.R. (eds) (1981) *Infant Social Cognition*. Hillsdale, NJ: Earlbaum.

Lask, B. and Bryant-Waugh, R. (1992) 'Early-onset of anorexia nervosa and related eating disorders', *Journal of Child Psychology and Psychiatry*, 33(1).

Laungani, P. (1999) 'Client centred or culture centred counselling?' in *Counselling In a Multicultural Society*. S. Palmer and P. Laungani (eds). London: Sage.

Lowenfeld, M. (1979) *The World Technique*. London: Allen & Unwin.

Lush, D. *et al.* (1998) 'Psychoanalytic psychotherapy with disturbed adopted and foster children: a single case follow-up study', *Clinical Child Psychology and Psychiatry*, 3(1).

Maccoby, E.E. and Martin, J.A. (1983) 'Socialization in the context of the family: parent-child interaction' in E.M. Hetherington (ed.) *Handbook of Child Psychology, Vol. IV: Socialization, Personality and Social Interaction*. New York: Wiley.

Main, M. and Weston, D. (1982) 'Avoidance of the attachment figure in infancy', in C.M. Parkes *et al.* (eds) *The Place of Attachment in Human Behaviour*. London: Tavistock.

Maslin-Cole, C. and Spieker, S. (1990) 'Attachment as a basis for independent motivation' in M.T. Greenberg *et al.* (eds) *Attachment in the Preschool Years*. Chicago, IL: University of Chicago Press, pp. 245–72.

Matas, L.A.R. and Sroufe, L.A. (1978) 'Continuity of adaptation in the second year: the relationship between quality of attachment and later competence', *Child Development*, 49, 547–56.

McGuire, J. and Earls, E. (1991) 'Prevention of psychiatric disorders in early childhood', *Journal of Child Psychology and Psychiatry*, 32(1), 129–53.

Miller, A. (1986) *The Drama of Being a Child*. London: Virago Press.

Millman, H. and Shaefer, C.E. (1997) *Therapies for Children*. San Francisco: Jossey-Bass.

Mitchell, J. (ed.) (1986) *The Selected Melanie Klein*. London: Penguin Books.

Montagu, A. (1978) *Touching: The Human Significance of the Skin* (2nd edn). London: Harper and Row.

Oaklander, V. (1978) *Windows to our Children*. Moab, Utah: Real People Press.

Palmer, S. (1999) 'In search of effective counselling across cultures', in S. Palmer and P. Laungani (eds) *Counselling in a Multicultural Society*. London: Sage.

Papousek, H. (1969) 'Individual variability in learned responses in human infants', in R.J. Robinson (ed.) *Brain and Early Behaviour*. London: Academic Press.

Phillips, A. (1988) *Winnicott*. London: Fontana Press.

Politano, P.M. *et al.* (1992) 'Differences between children of depressed and non-depressed mothers', *Journal of Child Psychology and Psychiatry*, $33(2)$, 451–5.

Rawson, D. *et al.* (1999) 'The challenges of counselling in a multicultural society', in S. Palmer and P. Laungani (eds) *Counselling in a Multi-Cultural Society*. London: Sage.

Reber, A.S. (1985) *Dictionary of Psychology*. London: Penguin Books.

Redgrave, K. (1987) *Child's Play: 'Direct Work' with the Deprived Child*. Cheadle: Boys' and Girls' Welfare Society.

—— (1991) *If Only Someone Had Told Me*. Cheadle: Boys' and Girls' Welfare Society.

Roussounis, S.H. *et al.* (1987) 'A 2-year follow-up study of children with motor co-ordination problems identified at school entry age', *Child Care, Health and Development*, $13(6)$.

Rowan, J. (1990) *Subpersonalities: The People Inside Us*. London and New York: Routledge.

Roy, R. (1999) 'Culturally sensitive therapy: accents, approaches and tools', in J. Campbell *et al.* (eds) *Art Therapy, Race and Culture*. London: Jessica Kingsley.

Roy, S. (1997) 'Dirt, noise, traffic: contemporary Indian dance in the western city', in H. Thomas (ed.) *Dance in the City*. London: Macmillan.

Russell, Isabella A., and Belsky, Jay (1991) 'Interactional synchrony and the origin of infant-mother attachment: a replication study', *Child Development*, 62, 373–84.

Rutter, M. (1979) 'Protective factors in children's responses to stress and disadvantage', *Primary Prevention of Psychopathology* (Vol. 3 pp. 49–74). Hanover, NH: University Press of New England.

Rutter, M. (1985) 'Family and school influences on cognitive development', *Journal of Child Psychology and Psychiatry*, 26 (5), 683–704.

Ryce-Menuhin, J. (1992) *Jungian Sandplay: The Wonderful Therapy*. London: Routledge.

Sandberg, S. T. *et al.* (1980) 'Hyperkinetic and conduct problem children in a primary school population: some epidemiological considerations', *Journal of Child Psychology and Psychiatry*, $21(4)$.

Schaffer, D.R. (1989) *Developmental Psychology – Childhood and Adolescence* (2nd edn). California: Books/Cole Pub. Co.

Schaffer, H.R. (1990) *Making Decisions about Children: Psychological Questions and Answers*. Oxford: Blackwell.

Schaffer, H.R. and Callender, W.M. (1959) 'The psychological effects of hospitalization in infancy'. *Paediatrics*, 24, 528–39.

Schaffer, H.R. and Emmerson, P.E. (1964) *The Development of Social Attachments in Infancy*. Monograph of the Society for Research in Child Development, 29, (3) (Serial No. 94).

Schanberg, S.M., and Field, T. (1987) 'Sensory deprivation, stress and supplemental stimulation in the rat pup and preterm human neonate', *Child Development*, 58, 1431–47.

Sharp, S. and Cowie, H. (1998) *Counselling and Supporting Children in Distress*. Sharp.

Sluckin, A. (1998) 'Bonding Failure: "I don't know this baby, she's nothing to do with me"', *Clinical Child Psychology and Child Psychiatry*, 3 (1), 11–24.

Spitz, R.A. (with Wolf, K.M.) (1945) 'Hospitalism: an inquiry into the genesis of psychiatric conditions in early childhood (1) in *The Psychoanalytic Study of the Child*, **1**, 53.

Spitz, R.A. and Wolf, K.M. (1946) 'Anaclitic depression: an inquiry into the genesis of psychiatric conditions in early childhood' (2), *The Psychoanalytic Study of the Child*, **2**, 313–20.

Spitz, R.A. (1965) *The First Year of Life*. New York: International Universities Press.

—— (1999) 'Working together to safeguard children: a guide to inter-agency working to safeguard and promote the welfare of children'. Dept of Health. London: HMSO.

Sroufe, A. (1979) 'The coherence of individual development', *American Psychologist*, **34**, 834–41.

Stein, M. (1995) *Jungian Analysis*. Open Court Press.

Stevens, R. (1983) *Freud and Psychoanalysis: An Exposition and Appraisal*. Buckingham: Open University Press.

Stiefel, I. (1997) 'Can disturbance in attachment contribute to attention deficit hyperactivity disorder? A case discussion', *Clinical Child Psychology and Psychiatry*, **2**(1), 45–64.

Sylva, K. and Lunt, I. (1982) *Child Development: A First Course*. Oxford: Blackwell.

Triseliotis, J., Sellick, C. and Short, R. (1995) *Foster Care: Theory and Practice*. London: Batsford.

Utting, W. (1998) *Children Looked After by Local Authorities*. House of Commons Health Committee Report. London: Stationery Office.

Vygotsky, L.S. (1978) *Mind in Society*. Cambridge, MA: MIT Press.

Weinrib, E. (1983) *Images of The Self*. Boston, MA: Sigo Press.

Wertsch, J.V. *et al.* (1980) 'The adult-child dyad as a problem solving system', *Child Development*, **51**, 1215–21.

White, R. *et al.* (1990) *A Guide to the Children Act, 1989*. London: Butterworths.

Whitmore, D. (1991) *Psychosynthesis Counselling In Action*. London: Sage.

Williams, D. (1994) An audiotape recording by Audio Literature, PO Box 7123, Berkeley, CA.

Winnicott, D.W. (1964) *The Child, The Family, and the Outside World*. London: Penguin.

Wolff, S. (1989) *Childhood and Human Nature: the Development of Personality*. London and New York: Routledge.

Yarrow, L.J. (1967) 'The development of focused relationships' in H. J. Seatle (ed.) *Exceptional Infants: The Normal Infant*, Vol. 1, Washington: Special Child Publications.

Further Reading

BOOKS

Attachment

John Bowlby and Attachment Theory. Holmes, J. London: Routledge, 1993.

Attachment Across the Life Cycle. Parkes, C.M. *et al*. London and New York: Routledge, 1991.

Attachment and Loss (Vols 1 to 3). Bowlby, J.: Penguin Books, 1978–80. These volumes represent 'deeper' reading and are 'heavier'.

A Child's Journey Through Placement. (Details under General reading.) Not specifically about attachment: Will be helpful but not exhaustive or highly technical.

Counselling and psychotherapy using third objects

Counselling Children: A Practical Introduction. Geldard, K. and Geldard, D. London, California and New Delhi: Sage, 1997/98.

Foster Care: Theory and Practice. (Details under Parenting and care-giving.)

Windows to Our Children: A Gestalt Approach to Children and Adolescents. Oaklander, V. Moab, Utah: Real People Press, 1978.

Parenting and care-giving

First Steps in Parenting the Child who Hurts: Tiddlers and Toddlers. Archer, C. London: Jessica Kingsley, 1998.

First Steps in Parenting the Child who Hurts: Tykes and Teens. Archer, C. London: Jessica Kingsley, 1998.

Foster Care: Theory and Practice. Triseliotis, J., Sellick, C. and Short, R. London: Batsford, in association with British Agencies for Adoption and Fostering, 1995.

Mothering (Developing Child series, Bruner, Cole, Lloyd (eds)) Schaffer, R. London: Fontana, 1985.

A Good Enough Parent. Bettelheim, B. London: Thames and Hudson, 1987. This can be described as 'heavier' reading.

General reading and child development

A Child's Journey Through Placement. Fahlberg, V.: British Agencies for Adoption and Fostering. This is a very thorough book which covers the attachment theory and elements of child development as well as placing children for fostering and adoption.

Making Decisions about Children: Psychological Questions and Answers. Schaffer, H.R. Oxford: Basil Blackwell, 1990.

The Ethical Use of Touch in Psychotherapy. Huntrer, M. and Struve, J. London: Sage, 1998.

Listening to Children: A Guide to Practice. Birgit, C. and Milner, P. London: Sage, 1998.

Child Development: A First Course. Sylva, K. and Lunt, I. Oxford: Basil Blackwell, 1989.

On Playing A Poor Hand Well. Katz, M. London: W. Norton, 1997. Insights from the lives of those who have overcome childhood risks and adversities.

Counselling and Supporting Children In Distress. Sharp, S. and Cowie, H. London, Thousand Oaks and New Delhi: Sage, 1998.

Multicultural and cross-cultural factors

Anti-Discriminatory Practice: A Guide for Workers in Childcare and Education. Millam, R. London: Cassell, 1996.

Art Therapy, Race and Culture. Campbell, J. *et al.* (eds) London and Philadelphia: Jessica Kingsley, 1999.

Counselling in a Multicultural Society. Palmer, S. and Laungani, P. (eds). London, Thousand Oaks and New Delhi: Sage, 1999.

Sand-tray work

Images of the Self. Weinrib, E. Sigo Press, 1983.

The World Technique. Lowenfeld, M.: Allen & Unwin, 1979.

The Lowenfeld World Technique. Bowyer, R. Pergamon paperback, 1970.

Sandplay. Kalff, D.: Sigo Press, 1980.

Jungian Sandplay: The Wonderful Therapy. Ryce-Menuhin, J.: London: Routledge, 1992.

Sandplay: Silent Workshops of the Psyche. Bradway, K. and McCoad, B.: London: Routledge, 1998.

REPORTS AND GUIDELINE DOCUMENTS

(These can be found in the reference departments of central libraries)

Children Looked After by Local Authorities. House of Commons Health Committee, 2nd Report, vol. 1. London: Stationery Office, 1998.

Someone Else's Children: Inspection of Planning and Decision Making for Children Looked After, and The Safety of Children Looked After. Department of Health Social Care Group. London: Department of Health, 1998.

On the Move Again. Jackson, S. and Thomas, N. Ilford: Barnardos, 1999.

Working Together to Safeguard Children. A guide to inter-agency working to safeguard and promote the welfare of children. Department of Health. London: The Stationery Office, 1999.

Index

adoption 65,196
adoptive (child) 65
adoptive parent (adopter) 76, 89, 221
affect lame: table 1 64, 219
affection 36, 64, 157, 158
affective (mode, aspects) 3, 5, 13, 14, 49, 189, 199; *see also* glossary
aggression/aggressiveness 5, 189
agoraphobia 117
ambivalent/ambivalence 64, 114, 185
analytic psychology 12; *see also* glossary
anger/angry 7, 11, 14, 30, 32, 33, 38, 75, 101, 132
animal(s) 71, 96, 121, 126, 157, 158
anorexic (anorectic) 122, 133, 148
anxiety(ies) 65, 102, 107, 182
anxiety reducer 116
archetypal/archetypes (Jungian) 8, 124, 149
aromatherapist 150
aromatic oils 145
arousal relaxation cycle 206, 208
art-therapy (-work) 2, 18, 52, 136, 139, 153
assess/assessment/assessing 19, 159, 172, 193, 194
assessment principles 174

attachment 5, 6, 9, 44, 135, 198, 206; *see also* Chapter 7
disorders (types) 216
process 2, 20, 198
Attention Deficit, Hyperactivity Disorder (ADHD) 213, 219
attitudes 13, 18, 133
audition (hearing) 15
autistic/autism 147
aware-experience 10, 11, 12, 13, 14, 20, 24, 26, 29, 30, 35, 36, 54, 58, 77, 106

baby/babies 139, 141, 147, 205
beetle(s) (game) 102, 183
befriender(s) 24, 43
behaviour
age-appropriate 42
anger 7, 11, 14, 30, 32, 33, 38, 75, 101
denial 12; *see also* glossary
dysfunctional 7
fixated 6, 8
frozen awareness 5, 216
rationalization 12
repressed 7
rocking 23

behaviour therapy 10
behavioural
    of action 69
    mode 5
    psychology 49, 197; *see also* glossary
behaviourist (methods) 9; *see also*
    glossary
beliefs 18, 19, 24, 37, 54, 92, 133
birds' nests 104
birth-box 84
blame 29, 110
'bombardment' (game) 154
bond/bonding 139, 188, 198
box-file 89
brain 17, 137, 147
Brazelton scale 17
bridge(s) 65, 130, 132, 162, 163
bridging 24, 43, 68, 158-71
brief therapy 112, 172

candles 95
care-givers (carers) 41, 84
Care Order 23
care-therapy 1, 2, 3, 6, 8, 9, 10, 13, 19,
    47, 57, 61, 63, 68, 75, 86, 112
case conference(s) 42
catchment area needs 195
catharsis 30; *see also* glossary
Central Council for Education and
    Training in Social Work 1
change 112, 169, 179, 185, 186, 187,
    189
Children in Need 173
children's home(s) 23, 86, 92, 157, 192
choice 123
clarification 12, 24, 35, 75, 91, 134
'clash boxes' 134
clay 15, 34, 68, 135, 148, 149
clumsy 213
cognition 15
cognitive (behavioural) 5, 8, 62, 117,
    187; *see also* glossary
cognitive (development) 5, 199, 213
cognitive (methods) 12
cognitive (mode) (aspects) 12, 14
collective-unconscious 124; *see also*
    glossary
communicate/communication 18, 41,
    172, 195
computer 146
conceptual/conceptualize 210, 213
conduct disorder 1, 15
confidential/confidentiality 56

conflict(s) 19, 30, 32, 76, 86, 92, 102,
    135, 168
conscious 63, 69, 97, 127, 178, 200,
    208
consistent 191
contact-indicator 47, 165, 187
continuity 159
'continuo' 56
contribute/contributing 57, 157
control
    of environment 71, 221
    impulse 9
    inner 3, 9, 139
co-ordination of treatment aspects 3
corporate parenting 191-7, 194
creative stimulation 2, 153
cross-cultural (factors) 18, 133, 136
cultural 19, 194, 195
curiosity 18
cycles (developmental) 205

dance 154
decision, decision-making 113
defence 29
demands 7, 10
demand–dissatisfaction cycle 213
demand–satisfaction cycle 213
denial 12; *see also* glossary
depression 112, 206
depressive position 206; *see also*
    glossary
deprivation/deprived 211
de-stressing (managers) 58
development
    behavioural 138
    cognitive 5
    infantile behaviour 5
    learning disablement 6, 138
    mental 5, 137, 138
    physical 5, 50, 137
    psycho motor 50, 200, 213
    psycho-social 5
    quotient 210; *see also* glossary
    understanding 14
developmental modes 5, 205, 211
direct expression of feelings (direct
    discussion) 101–16, 103
direct work 41, 44, 86; *see also* glossary
    insight Ch 3,4
    sensory Ch 5
directing/directive 123, 155, 172
disclosure (work) 25, 30; *see also*
    glossary
'discussion rosette' 123

disinhibited type (attachment) 216
doctrine 9
doctrinaire 9
dolls' houses 95, 153
Donna (case study) 21
doors 117, 187
double consciousness 133
double-list (options) 113
drama (play-acting) 154, 157, 183
drawing *see* media 8
drift 174, 194, 197
drum(s) 152
dysfunctional behaviour 7
dyssemia/dissemic 185

eclectic (approach) 8, 10
ecology/ecological 174; *see also* glossary
ego 30, 62, 213
elevator 162
emergent (effects) 189, 190
emotionally disturbed 1
empathy, empathetic 4, 64, 200; *see also*
       glossary
emotional/emotions 5, 13, 14, 50, 213
encopresis 213
enlightenment 169
enuresis 213
environment (manipulation of) 16
ethnic factors 195
ethnic groups 19
ethnic minority 18
ethnicity 19
existentialist (groups) 3; *see also*
       glossary
explore/exploration 139

face (cards) 119, 181
fairy stories 156
family-less (children) 82
family-therapy 73, 75, 160, 174; *see also*
       glossary
fantasy/fantasies 71
fantasizing 127
fear 11, 14, 26, 110, 160
feeding bottle 15, 150
feeling(s)
       affective states 13, 63, 68, 101, 116,
           151, 181
       aspects 69
       attitudes 13, 18, 133
       becoming aware of 24, 33, 59, 91,
           181
       Donna 26, 27
       important 13, 32, 91

in touch with 11, 14, 33, 59, 91, 96,
       107, 139
non-verbal 132
polarized 44
pots 32
prejudices 133
thermometer 30, 32
feeling cards 181
feeling drawings (paintings) 14, 26, 32,
       107, 110, 183
feeling pots 32
feeling–caring (activities) 14, 157
feeling(s) 54, 133, 157
feely-bag 149
finger painting 26
fixated (behaviour) 6, 8
flow-chart *see* life flow-chart 84
focused therapy 123
foot-painting 34, 147
foot-washing 34
foster (child, children) 196
foster (home) 157, 196
foster (parent) 76, 86, 89, 135, 221
free association 49
free choice 62, 117
Freud/Freudians 9
frozen awareness (watchfulness) 5, 216;
       see also glossary

genetic (factors) 17
genogram 18; *see also* glossary
gestalt
       approach 34
       gestaltist(s) 7, 17, 141, 157; *see also*
           glossary
       schools 8
       therapist 7, 12
grief 182, 189
groups (sibling etc.) 160
guilt 5, 11, 29, 32
gustation (taste) 15

happy/happiness 101, 110
healed/healing 3, 9, 20, 37, 38, 49, 52,
       97, 98, 127, 137, 220
healing–mending approach 3, 127, 137
hate (self) 11
hearing 15
hearing–guessing game 151
height/weight 84
holistic approach 2, 9, 14; *see also*
       glossary
hope 110

ice-breakers 55
imagination/imagery 4, 16, 18, 54, 77, 96, 112, 119, 127, 154, 155
imprint/imprinting 201, 202
impulses *see* control 3, 211, 219
incorporated treatment concepts 10
indirect (reactions) 178
indiscriminate affection 211, 217
infant nurture program 10, 24, 40, 41, 42, 148, 150
infants (work with) 110
infantile (behaviour level etc.) 5, 6, 23
inhibited type (attachment) 216
insight 10, 11, 13, 29, 58, 62, 75, 76, 77, 106, 134, 169, 178, 220; *see also* glossary
instability (i.e. insecure placement) 159
institution/institutionalized 209
intelligence 210
interactive factors 4, 186, 204, 208
introspective 184
Iranian orphanage children 50

jealous(y) 101, 107
jigsaw puzzle 169, 186, 187
joy, joyful 16, 79
Jungian analysis 12, 124; *see also* glossary

kaleidoscope 146
key worker 2
Kleinian 135; *see also* glossary

learned helplessness 208
learning 138
'left out' feeling 101, 102
libidinal (energy) 64
life flow-charts ('flow charts') 75
life-story (book) 85, 86, 184
lonely 101
loss (sense of) 189
loving steps 44, 162, 180
loving water 36, 37, 180, 186

making (things) *see* creativity 153
maltreat/maltreated 190
manages 195
manipulation (of environment) 16
masturbation (Donna) 42
media
    drawing ⎫ 4, 8, 17, 19, 34, 35, 52, 58,
    music ⎬ 105, 117, 135, 136, 151,
    painting ⎭ 152, 153, 157, 176, 177

memory/memories 15, 25, 77, 138, 139, 145, 151, 183, 189
memory-seeing (a 'game') 146
mental development *see* development 138
micro-cultural 19
motivation/motives 75, 219
motivational development 213
motor (body activity) 140, 213
movement 130
Mulberry Bush School 9
music 35, 151, 152, 153; *see also* media
music-therapy 151, 153
'My Tree' 178, 183
'My World' 120, 158, 178, 183
mythological (material) 8

narcissistic 3, 189, 206; *see also* glossary
narrow-lens assessment 175
needs 10
neonates 17
neurotic/neurosis 65, 127, 132, 140, 220
'nibblers and squeezers' 58
non-directive 123
non-verbal 185
nurture (child-nurture) 5

objects 95, 125
obsessional 107
off-side rule 57
olfaction (smell) 15
oligohydramnios 126
ontological 91, 184; *see also* glossary
'options' 113, 114
organistic (qualities) 5
overdose(d) 71

pacifiers 17
paint/painting 34, 35, 105, 117; *see also* media
panic attack 122, 182
paranoid schizoid position 206
parenting 5
peep-show 146
people houses 63
people tree 58, 178
percussion 152
photographic record 126
physical development 138; *see also* development
physical retardation 5
picture contacts 165
place of safety 23

plasticine 58, 148
play-acting 156; *see also* 'drama'
play technique 49
poetry 155
positive interaction cycle 208
Post-Freudians 9
potted plants 157
preconscious 177, 178; *see also* glossary
prejudice 18, 19, 134, 135
preparation 160
projective identification 206
protective (mechanism) 23
protective feeling 110
psychoanalysis, psychoanalytical,
    psychodynamic 3, 30, 49, 62, 63,
    172; *see also* glossary
psycho-imagery 14, 24, 29
psychological development 127, 135,
    147, 159, 199
    stability 49
psychology 140, 147
    aspects 65, 135, 206
psychomotor 50, 200, 213; *see also*
    glossary
psychopathology 7, 174, 182
psycho-social 40, 76, 159, 184
psychosynthesis counsellor 11, 49; *see*
    also glossary
psychotherapeutic (approach) 8
psyche 3, 124; *see also* glossary

racial/racism 18, 133, 196
rationalization 12; *see also* glossary
reactive attachment disorder 216, 217
reception centres 158
recovered memories 25
regress/regression/regressive 9, 35, 42,
    150, 188, 189
reinforcer 65
relationship(s) 64
repression/repressed 7
residential (social) worker(s) 76, 157,
    221
resolve/resolving (problems) 91
respite (placement) 82
risk (factors) 220
rocking (behaviour) 23
role-change 160, 161, 185, 186
role-play 4; *see also* 'drama'; glossary

sand-tray therapy (sand-therapy, sand-
    world therapy) 8, 42, 62, 63,
    122, 124, 125, 136, 184

school refusal (phobia) 132, 135
school(s) 42, 188
self 54, 91, 98, 110, 183, 189, 213
self-confidence 200
self-esteem 208
self-image 221
semantic criticism 3
sensitive (development periods) 17
senses (i.e. the five senses) 15, 141
sensory
    abuse 15
    deprivation 211
    experience 14, 16, 20, 26, 35, 40,
        49, 54, 77, 137, 139, 140, 143
    stimulation 2, 10
    work 26, 33, 41
separation anxiety (disorder) 132, 134,
    217
sexually abused 1
shallow (affection) 211
share/sharing 25, 77, 91, 92
shields 68, 69, 184
shock 117
siblings 5, 91, 160, 166, 191
sight (experiences) 15, 145, 146
sight (sense of) 15, 145
signals 179
skin 16
smell, smelling 15, 35, 144
social adaptation 44
social development 42, 213
social reality factors 9
social psychology 133
social worker(s) 56, 76, 89, 160, 174
sociological aspects 133
somatic (mode) 5, 49, 213; *see also*
    glossary
sound (sense of) 151–3
sound-memory game 151, 152
sounds (outside) 152
specific tasks 117
spectrum
    bridging, attachment and bonding
        188
    change focus 186
    differentiation of feelings 180
    expressing feelings 182
    getting in touch with self 183
    outward expression 177
    reflecting upon interactive behaviour
        185
    sensory 176
    understanding events 179

spectrum of experiential and therapy objectives 173, 175
split/splitting (off) 140, 206
squeezy bottle (paints) 106
stereotype/-typing 19
stranger situation 217
stuck (children) 5, 6, 7, 8, 23, 211
'suffering skin' 38, 186, 219
surprise 189
survivors 220
suspicion 189
symbolic fantasies 8, 121, 127
symbolism, symbolize 8, 36, 37, 38, 49, 52, 54, 58, 65, 68, 69, 95, 97, 121, 124, 127, 148
synthesis (approach) 8
systematic approach 2, 41, 47
systematic psycho-social approach 2
systemic (view) 122

talking therapies 4, 62
taste 15, 15
taste-tray 15, 34, 142, 183
teachers 42, 135, 188
team
    approach 10, 24, 41, 42, 56
    concept 10, 41, 221
temper tantrum 6
temperamental (qualities) 5
testing out 190; *see also* glossary
therapeutic (approach) 42, 84, 86, 140
therapeutic forgetting 190
therapist (variables) 5, 18, 43

theory
    (incorporated) 4
    (symbolism in) 8
thermometer (feelings) 30, 32
touch/touching 15, 16, 26, 35, 41, 138, 146–50
    materials 15, 26, 34, 148
    third objects 2, 4, 13, 20, 54, 58, 61, 69, 77, 84, 97, 112, 118, 133, 147
training 160, 174, 185, 195
training guidelines 1, 160, 174
transcultural (therapy) 10
transference 9, 30, 123 *see also* glossary
trauma/traumatized (child) 8, 117, 134, 203
trauma (of birth) 126
treatment, tree 10, 97; *see also* 'my tree'
trust 47, 165, 206, 220

umbilical cord 165
unconscious, the 8, 12, 18, 30, 69, 97, 177, 178, 208
unfinished business 157, 179

violence 126, 127, 130, 148
vision 15
vulnerable (children) 173

wall-building 44, 161, 186
water ('play' etc.) 36, 149, 150
weight (gain) 17, 84
'wide-lens' assessment 175
womb 127
word list 101, 102
worker 5, 133